CREATIVE ARTS THERAPIES
AND THE LGBTQ COMMUNITY

D1380803

CREATIVE ARTS
THERAPIES *and the*
LGBTQ COMMUNITY

THEORY AND PRACTICE

EDITED BY BRIANA MACWILLIAM, BRIAN T. HARRIS,
DANA GEORGE TROTTIER, AND KRISTIN LONG

Jessica Kingsley *Publishers*
London and Philadelphia

First published in 2019
by Jessica Kingsley Publishers
73 Collier Street
London N1 9BE, UK
and
400 Market Street, Suite 400
Philadelphia, PA 19106, USA

www.jkp.com

Library of Congress Cataloging in Publication Data
A CIP catalog record for this book is available from the Library of Congress

British Library Cataloguing in Publication Data
A CIP catalogue record for this book is available from the British Library

ISBN 978 1 78592 796 6
eISBN 978 1 78450 802 9

Printed and bound in the United States

Contents

Acknowledgments

We would like to extend deep and heartfelt thanks to our contributors and our peer reviewers. Without their soulfully brave and honest contributions, this text would not have come together. Our deepest gratitude for all of your hard work and for putting your faith in us, to help carry your voice into the creative arts therapies community, and beyond. We would also like to acknowledge our gratitude to the LGBTQ community and the members of the community whose rich lives have been integral to the knowledge and wisdom in this book.

Introduction

DANA GEORGE TROTTIER, KRISTIN LONG,
BRIANA MACWILLIAM, AND BRIAN T. HARRIS

Within the field of creative arts therapy, research has demonstrated that creative arts therapists often identify as affirming and open to working with the LGBTQ community. Yet the vast majority of creative arts therapists report a lack of training in delivering therapy to the LGBTQ community and feel unprepared to work with this population. In a survey conducted with 409 music therapists, more than 50% reported that they did not receive any training in LGBTQ issues and 60% reported feeling under-prepared to work with this community (Whitehead-Pleaux *et al.*, 2013). Similarly, among 136 North American drama therapists, more than half reported feeling unprepared to serve LGBTQI and GNC (gender non-conforming) individuals (Beauregard *et al.*, 2016). Most recently, in a survey among dance/movement therapists 33% reported receiving no training in LGBTQI/GNC issues, and of those who did receive training only 36% reported that the training sufficiently prepared them to work with LGBTQ individuals (Kawano, Cruz, & Tan, 2018). Across the research, it was revealed that despite high reports of insufficient training and feelings of unpreparedness, very few creative arts therapists actually seek supervision, consultation, or continuing education to expand their practice, knowledge, and understanding of LGBTQ issues and community.

Overall, there seems to be a lack of awareness around diverse sexual orientation and gender identity, unfamiliarity with language and terminology such as heteronormativity and cisnormativity, and limited understanding of legal, social, or political issues impacting the LGBTQ community aside from marriage. What is more, there seems to be a limited use of each modality's artistic inclination to explore and understand the issues that impact the LGBTQ community as well as lack of training in the use of specific creative arts therapy interventions to address their clinical needs. To that end, this book aims to fill the current gap in literature, education, and training to build best practices in working through creative arts therapy with the LGBTQ community.

The Editorial Process...

Essential to our overall purpose for this text is an understanding of the importance of process. We begin by offering insight into our process in compiling this book, and our collaboration as an editing team with the contributors to this volume. We hope that whatever may be stimulated for the reader will function as an open invitation to dialogue with the material, without slipping into feelings of shame, criticism, or judgment.

The idea for this book came about in the way that most ideas do, and that is through the cumulative layering of one experience upon the next. At the inception of this project, as an ally and as a teacher of personality development at the graduate level, Briana was keenly aware of her access to resources that could make a difference in filling in some of the gaps mentioned above, including exercising her connections, creating a frame, offering feedback on the writing itself, and managing the administrative aspects of assembling a contributed volume. Ultimately, this project unfolded in a way that was very different to previous editing projects Briana had completed. In talking with the contributors, there was a desire for more of a group process around the assemblage of each chapter. This led to opening up the project to co-editors, and here Dana, Kristin, and Brian transitioned from the roles of contributors to the roles of co-editors. We would come to reflect on expanding the project to an editing collaborative as one of the best things that could have happened to this book, as it added a rich texture to the process and to the product.

Editing a book is not easy; editing a book that holds a mirror up to the lived experience of some of the editors and contributors is even harder. An underlying desire exists for the book to be perfect, because the LGBTQ community deserves it. We resolved ourselves to the fact that it would not be perfect, but it certainly could be good enough, especially given the careful eyes and lived experiences attached to the book, as editors and contributors. In writing this introduction, we reflected on our own personal journeys and experience of the process, which it felt important to include.

Beyond filling in the gaps in the literature, Briana felt that her motivations for initially pursuing this project stemmed from revelations of identity among her closest friends, extending back to adolescence. Additionally, in her own professional, clinical experiences, she has had well-intentioned yet ignorant missteps, which bore a certain weight and compelled her, as well. Throughout the process, she experienced anxieties around feelings of shame and belongingness, given that there is an innate challenge for her, as she does not identify as queer. Briana shares: "I felt our process as co-editors reflected a wonderful flexibility and capacity for truly being able to create our own realities, through dialogue. What evolved in the transitional space became so much more than just the sum of its parts, and I am delighted and privileged to have participated in it."

Kristin and the other editors expressed some feelings of protectiveness for the contributors and for their words, paralleling the protectiveness felt for the queer community at large. This was a challenge when offering suggestions from a place of care and curiosity, and not feeling sure if they would land in the spirit with which they were given. It also made it uncomfortable at times to be firm with editorial changes that needed to be made. The roles of therapist and editor don't always hang out together easily!

Brian wished to emphasize an openness to play and humility. He expressed excitement when encountering new questions around identities and concerns within the LGBTQ community, and exploring our reasons for the labels we choose. He recognized the serious nature of the material covered in this book, but also recognized the importance of playing with our own knowledge; using the tools we possess as creative arts therapists in approaching the topics. Brian shares: "Information related to LGBTQ communities is rapidly changing... When we view knowledge as fixed and certain, we hinder the ability to grow and transform."

Dana noted falling into a slump while writing, and experienced a significant resistance to finishing his contributions to the book and the overall manuscript. He turned to expressive writing to find an understanding of where this uncommon resistance was coming from, and found feelings of anger and hopelessness, as well as his humor and resiliency. As a queer person, Dana realized that from the time he started researching his community, in an effort to educate himself more and guide those who are less familiar, there have been several assaults, insults, and invalidations that have occurred against the LGBTQ community on a large scale. He raises questions: "How can I feel safe when the President's Justice Department says anti-gay discrimination is legal? How can I cement LGBTQ narratives in a book knowing that systems of oppression continue to control, interrupt, and silence our stories?"

As Dana traveled through the empirical research about and personal narratives from the LGBTQ community, he felt relatively content with some of the progress that has been made from within his community, but still struggles with the heteronormative and cisnormative society he finds himself living and breathing in, each day. As if a call to action, Dana shares: "So, I will cry, and probably continue to cry. I will get angry and challenge the normative ways of thinking… And with each step regain my hope, my queer resiliency, and reignite my light. After all, I want to be flaming when they come for me."

Laying the Foundation…

The process of editing this book brought about several different perspectives, sometimes ones that were at odds with each other. At times, some of the editors were challenged by certain contributions and certain language use. As we have come to know, language and labeling within the LGBTQ community grows, expands, and changes often in an effort to keep up with the evolving spectrum of sexual orientation and gender identity, and even more so to maintain a level of inclusive visibility for each.

One surprise was the tendency to group together "LGBTQ" as an umbrella term, even when only discussing one of these groups; this came up a few times in several chapters. It became obvious that in an effort to be inclusive by using the term *LGBTQ* to speak to the community as a whole, aspects of identity and challenges were being ascribed in a way that felt more like overgeneralization and overidentification. This was an important reminder that the experiences of some within the LGBTQ community are not the experiences of the entire community. The beauty of the LGBTQ community lies in their differences: differences from the gender and sexual majority, as well as the difference among the minority community. Writers acknowledged their own unawareness in certain areas and challenged themselves to grow and learn.

As editors, we understand the heart that contributors put into their chapters and, as writers ourselves, we understand the vulnerability that comes with having one's work constructively critiqued. Our conversation with contributors became one that felt like an important mutual lesson in cultural humility and the collaborative flexibility required for working with marginalized communities. These lessons are applicable to LGBTQ-identifying therapists as well as therapists who identify with the majority. As a result, we discovered that co-editing could feel playful and creative, as well as challenging. The act of working together on this has held a sense of creativity that we hope threads through the book.

Within our professional, clinical experiences, we have all had many well-intentioned yet ignorant missteps, which bore a certain weight and compelled us to complete this project. In order to move through it, humility was needed, both personal and cultural. Collaboration became necessary, which should not have surprised us as much as it did, given our work as creative arts therapists and some of our connections to queer community. These two communities thrive on collaboration. Lack of collaboration breeds isolation and silence, which feels like a shared parallel shame dynamic between the creative arts therapy community and the LGBTQ community. As creative arts therapists, we fell back into a place of playfulness, and this led us to complete the book in front of you today. While we acknowledge the serious nature of the material covered in this volume, we also recognize the importance of maintaining a playful stance with our knowledge. When we view knowledge as fixed and certain, we hinder our ability to grow and transform.

Throughout the editing process, contributors and editors collaborated in conversations through telecommunication, in-person meetings, and email correspondences. Early in our process, the question that often came up was, "Why has this book not existed prior to this?"

One potential reason was the fear of re-pathologizing the queer community. Although the depathologizing of queer identities was celebrated by some, it also revealed the external "isms and obias" that exists within the social world at large. When speaking to the mental health concerns of the LGBTQ community, it is important to remember that mental health challenges do not originate from holding a minority identity, but rather come from the lived experience of being a marginalized individual in a social and political world that prioritizes the majority and privileges normativity. Understanding the experience of being othered, dismissed, and cast aside sheds more light on the origins of some of the mental health concerns of the LGBTQ community.

Limitations...

Information related to LGBTQ communities is rapidly changing. In this book we will be presenting current perspectives that may shift within the coming years. We anticipate this book will require updating within ten years. We've outlined several reasons for this below.

- The language and vocabulary will most likely evolve with increasing awareness of stigmatization and the way language shapes our realities.

- The acronym LGBTQ, in the title, excludes intersex, asexual, questioning, pansexual, and two-spirit individuals, among others. Although some of the chapters may mention and discuss these populations, we have excluded the acronyms from the title to limit the scope of the book at this time. We acknowledge that some populations not explicitly included in the acronym may identify with "queer"; however, it was necessary to draw a line somewhere, in order to fully cover those populations we have included in depth.

- We acknowledge that while the contributors of this volume are from a variety of backgrounds and identity demographics, they are all primarily practicing on the East Coast of the United States. Additionally, all four editors live and practice in New York City. We acknowledge this may have had an impact on the overall "voice" of the text.

- While we attempted to recruit authors across a variety of disciplines, and we believe that many of the chapters apply across specific modalities (e.g. dance/movement therapy, drama therapy, art therapy, music therapy, and play therapy), we acknowledge there are some modalities that may appear underrepresented, and hope their voice will be offered in future editions.

Given the current limitations and potential future limitations, we invite an interaction with the chapters that raises questions and points of discussion rather than commands certainty and mastery. In this vein, we also invite humility. Whether the information in this book is new to you or you are using it as a teaching tool, we invite you to engage with the material with curiosity and openness, knowing that missteps are part of the work as clinicians, and this is where humbleness can come into play and support both therapist and client in the therapy space.

Why This Book, Why Now?

The LGBTQ community continues to face stigmatization and discrimination and experience minority stress, which can lead to emotional distress, substance use, ostracism, mental health challenges, and suicide, among other issues, as you will read in this volume. Any of these may be addressed through the practice of creative arts therapies, and this is why this book is so needed. It offers creative arts therapists, other clinicians, and educators a review of theoretical approaches relevant to engaging in therapeutic work with the LGBTQ community. While there are a multitude of books and research articles on the topic of clinical issues in working with LGBTQ populations, there are few that offer direction for approaching treatment in the field of creative arts therapies. As a result, this book expands the body of knowledge through qualitative, quantitative, and arts-based research. It offers practical interventions in the form of illustrative material, including self-studies, case studies, and clinical narratives as well as protocols or curriculum for replication. *Please note that names and some case details have been altered to protect and maintain confidentiality. Artwork is presented with permission from the artists.*

There are several important elements that set this book apart:

- It includes a comprehensive review of currently popular and evolving theoretical models.

- It considers the impact of intersectionality and systems of oppression.

- It provides self-studies, clinical case material, and practical curricula, lending itself to manual use.

- It provides clinical narratives from and practical approaches to working across the lifespan.

- It is focused on creative arts therapies interventions with offerings from perspectives in drama therapy, art therapy, music therapy, and dance/movement therapy.

- It provides some perspectives from contributors as well as editors who identify as LGBTQ, highlighting voices from the community who provide creative arts therapy for the LGBTQ community, shifting the long-standing cultural history of the privileged majority speaking for the marginalized minority.

- It provides LGBTQ-identifying therapists, and non-LGBTQ therapists for that matter, with practical guides or schools of thought for navigating therapeutic relationships with straight, cisgender, and queer clients. It was important to provide ways to care for the therapist as well as the client in an effort to expand capacity and explore the nuances that play out during therapeutic relationships.

An Invitation...

In the spirit of invitation and compassionate exploration, we have shared with you a bit of our process in editing this text. We hope to leave you with more questions rather than answers. A new perspective to be inquisitive and curious about the topic. An increased sense of humility but a decreased sense of shame in relation to the material. There are charged and challenging topics that may provoke some discomfort in the reader. This discomfort is useful as it relates to growth potential. Given our process we would like to invite the readers of this book to engage with curiosity and openness rather than rigidity. Regardless of your identities, we hope you will find new ideas and points of inquisition.

References

Beauregard, M., Stone, M., Trytan, N., & Sajnani, N. (2016) 'Drama therapists' attitudes and actions regarding LGBTQI and gender nonconforming communities.' *Drama Therapy Review 2*, 1, 41–63.

Kawano, T., Cruz, R. F., & Tan, X. (2018) 'Dance/movement therapists' attitudes and actions regarding LGBTQI and gender nonconforming communities.' *American Journal of Dance Therapy 40*. https://doi.org/10.1007/s10465-018-9283-7.

Whitehead-Pleaux, A., Donnenwerth, A., Robinson, B., Hardy, S., *et al.* (2013) 'Lesbian, gay, bisexual, transgender, and questioning: Best practices in music therapy.' *Music Therapy Perspectives 30*, 2, 158–166.

1

Exploring Social Justice and Dismantling Dominant Narratives through Creative Arts Peer Supervision

DANA GEORGE TROTTIER AND BRITTON WILLIAMS

Our Context, Our Lenses

As we considered writing this chapter, we (Dana and Britton) thought a great deal about what lenses we bring to this chapter given our own identity categories. Our shared identities are mostly professional in nature. We are both licensed creative arts therapists in New York and registered drama therapists for the North American Drama Therapy Association, and, at the time of writing this chapter, both work in hospital settings and private practice. Additionally, we both have an affinity towards the work of social justice, equity, equality, human rights, and dignity. We find healthy differences in and across our individual intersecting identities. In order for you (the reader) to know the lenses through which we view the world and wrote this chapter, it feels necessary to share with you those identifiers that inform and color the choices made for this chapter.

Dana

I identify as queer, which I view as an encompassing term for the intersections of my sexual orientation, gender expression, and political views. Mostly, I pass as cisgender, although I play with gender expression and performance through ear piercings, long hair, clothing, and the playful interchange of gender pronouns he and she in my social interactions with friends. I have white, male privilege that I recognize as being both a source of comfort and agita given my cultural history. Mostly, I have moved through life with very few, yet some workable moments of, negative reactions towards my sexual minority identity. Having grown up in a heteronormative society, however, I am aware of the effects of oppression and have felt the fear that accompanies this awareness. I am a member of and ally within the LGBTQ community.

Britton

I am a heterosexual, cisgender, black woman. I am aware that I have hetero and cisprivilege and am mindful of the many ways in which those privileges manifest in and around my life and within the larger world. The intersections of my race, gender, sexual orientation, gender expression, and education arise in my life as a fluid and ever-changing experience of being both marginalized and privileged. I am an ally to the LGBTQ community and committed to challenging oppressive hetero and cisnormative structures.

An integral part of our work, continued growth, and practice as clinicians is ongoing peer supervisions where we explore and discuss the ways in which identity, power, privilege and oppression impact our clients' lives, our experiences, and the therapeutic process and encounter. This chapter will offer current research and literature on systems of oppression and social justice in the creative arts therapies. Furthermore, it provides a frame for engaging in dialogue with colleagues about power, privilege and oppression in clinical practice by providing an excerpt of our (Dana and Britton) peer supervision.

Creative Arts Therapy and Social Justice

Basic human rights for marginalized groups are currently being challenged, restricted, and violated through laws, social tensions, violence, and other forms of unrest. To ignore these conditions and their impact is to be complicit with the marginalization of groups and individuals; furthermore, to not push against these structures is to comply with the perpetuation of oppression. It is well established that microaggressions and oppressive systems cause mental and physical distress (Sue, 2010; Nadal, 2013). Living under frequent and/or constant strain of oppression contributes to an increase in mental health issues, suicidality, interpersonal disruptions, and other issues. For marginalized communities and individuals this can be a chronic and persistent experience.

An open awareness of dominant narratives, privilege, and marginalized populations are the foundation of a social justice framework in counseling (Ratts, 2009; Fouad, Gerstein, & Toporek, 2006). Being mindful of how factors such as microaggressions and oppressive systems impact clients' emotional, cognitive, and behavioral functioning is important when working with marginalized clients. According to Sajnani, Marxen, and Zarate (2017):

> [D]ominant narratives function as a form of social control. The implication here is that, in addition to contending with a person's personal history, it is important to consider how social, economic, and/ or political violence in the form of racism, homophobia, or poverty for example, contributes to expressions of distress in the form of anxiety or otherwise. (p.34)

While for many it is considered socially unacceptable and/or taboo to be openly and outwardly discriminatory, LGBTQ people continue to experience blatant forms of prejudice.

The constructs that perpetuate the systemic oppression of LGBTQ individuals and culture are heterosexism and heteronormativity (Smith, Shin, & Officer, 2012), and genderism, cissexism, and cisnormativity (Serano, 2016). Acknowledging and challenging these and other oppressive societal structures that impact LGBTQ individuals is a necessary aspect of our work as clinicians. In fact, working solely with groups or individuals who are marginalized without addressing the oppressive constructs within their social and cultural environments can have a detrimental impact (Ratts, 2009; Vera & Speight, 2003). Without actively denouncing oppressive constructs, the work shifts from challenging and changing these hostile systems to the client's response and ability to cope (Ratts, 2009; Vera & Speight, 2003; Smith et al., 2012). This way of working complies with oppressive systems and furthermore perpetuates social injustice (Albee, 2000).

While awareness of power, privilege, and oppression is important, action through activism, advocacy, and/or other forms of challenging discriminatory practices is also necessary. As clinicians, if we truly wish to treat our patients effectively, we must not only tend to groups and individuals when they are in the room, but also address oppressive conditions and environments that cause them distress. A social justice approach to counseling integrates social advocacy and activism to address inequality across social, political, and economic conditions that impede the development of individuals and communities (Ratts, 2009). In other words, social advocacy is necessary to mitigate the oppressive structures that impede the growth and development of those marginalized in and by society. To create a more just society for sexual and gender minorities, activism needs to take place at the community, institutional, and structural level (Smith *et al.*, 2012). In fact, there are many ways in which clinicians can contribute to social justice practices.

Many within the creative arts therapy field have explored and implemented a social justice framework within educational curricula and clinical practice. Clinical educators have underscored the importance of acknowledging and exploring personal identity, bias, and relationship to power and privilege (McMullian & Burch, 2017; Powell, 2016; Williams, 2016) in addition to social justice and anti-violence discourse in the curricula (Gipson, 2015; Sajnani *et al.*, 2017). At the foundation of these curricula is the belief that clinicians must attend to their own relationship to power, privilege, marginalization, isms, and phobias, and explore the subsequent influence and impact on the therapeutic encounter (Hays, 2008; McMullian & Burch, 2017; Powell, 2016; Williams, 2017). When we identify, explore, and challenge our own biases as clinicians, we contribute to creating a more just world. The awareness that can be gained from such a practice is not restricted to one's clinical practice; rather, it refocuses the lens through which one views the world. It is only after acknowledging where we are situated in relation to power and privilege and what biases we have downloaded that we can engage in open discourse with others, including our clients.

As the arts are often at the forefront of social and political change, there is an opportunity as well as a need for the creative arts therapies to actively take part in social action initiatives. Baines (2013) proposed that an Anti-Oppressive Practice in Music Therapy would include clinicians "recognizing that the power imbalances in our society affect us all" and holding in mind the impact of the social and political climate on the client (p.4). Although they noted that anti-oppressive music therapy was still in the process of development, Bain, Grzanka, & Crowe (2016) considered how music therapy could contribute to social justice through being mindful of how its practices can be both helpful and harmful. On the one hand, they noted music's ability to foster healthy interpersonal interaction and facilitate supportive connections among marginalized groups and, on the other hand, they highlight the importance of being aware of the ways in which music can serve to further oppress.

The creative arts therapies have the ability to access creative ways of bringing voice to issues of equity and justice in the work and also in the world. Wright and Wright (2017) proffered that art therapy is aligned with "critical social justice feminisms" through seeking to serve and support those who are underserved, marginalized, and/or distressed. They go on to say that practicing art psychotherapy entails embodying "the principles and values of anti-oppressive practice that aim to enable empowerment" of the aforementioned populations (p.8). Gipson (2015) supports a critical consciousness framework within clinical practice and asserted "that a meaningful social justice framework in art therapy will take seriously the questions now being posed by contemporary activists" (p.145). There is no doubt that we are in a tumultuous time where we need to grapple with difficult questions and take action towards creating just practices and communities.

Ally Development

Given that LGBTQ individuals experience greater levels of psychological distress than heterosexual and cisgender clients (Nadal, 2013; Meyer, 2015) it is important for therapists to be educated and prepared to provide professional, allied support for sexual and gender minority clients. Therapists are in ideal positions to serve as allies (Rivers & Swank, 2017). The Human Rights Campaign Foundation, the largest national LGBTQ political organization, defined ally as "someone who is supportive of LGBT people," including "straight allies as well as those within the LGBT community who support each other" (2014, p.16). For example, a self-identifying queer man can be an ally for a transgender woman and vice versa. In the context of therapeutic work, an ally is "a counselor or a client who provides therapeutic or personal support respectively" to an individual or group who self-identify as LGBTQ (ALGBTIC LGBQQIA Competencies Taskforce, 2013, p.38). The role and work of an ally can be held by a family member, friend, coworker, mentor, teacher, therapist, partner, spouse, to name a few. Finnerty *et al.* (2014) wrote:

> Ally work is by its very nature a third-order change process, to assist people in dismantling ways of thinking, long-held biases and beliefs,

and ways of being within the world. People become agents in the change process and leaders in guiding new ways of integrating with and meeting others in their universe. (p.329)

In other words, the role of an ally is not only to support, but to challenge paradigms, promote critical consciousness, and make change by transforming and developing culture.

PFLAG National, an LGBTQ advocacy organization, published two ally-friendly guides that are equal parts accessible, fun, and comprehensive: *Guide to Being a Straight Ally* (Navetta, 2011) and *Guide to Being a Trans Ally* (Navetta, 2014). PFLAG National developed a Straight for Equality Ally Spectrum, which provides the ally or potential ally with the opportunity to identify where they are in their ally development. Identifying where you fall on the spectrum assists the ally in identifying their role and offers information and resources on the current developmental stage; it could be said that the ally spectrum allows the ally to identify where they are on their own journey of coming out, towards becoming fully realized as an ally. The playful spectrum includes the following types of allies chronologically: the "I'm not really an ally...but I'll listen" ally; the "I'm starting to get it" ally; the "I really said it!" ally; the "I'm focusing my time on learning" ally; the "I'm talking about LGBT equality" ally; and the "I'm Super Ally! Let's change some laws" ally. This spectrum is useful in that it serves as a reminder that although allies come in different forms, they are allies nonetheless, and allows allies to find themselves rather than be defined by others.

The LGBTQ community deserves competent allies who are also therapists. The ALGBTIC LGBQQIA Competencies Taskforce (2013), established by the American Counseling Association (ACA), henceforth referred to as the Taskforce, outlined several competencies for therapists who are allies. It is expected that therapists who are allies educate themselves on current issues and challenges impacting the LGBTQ community through engaging with individuals in the community, reading about the community (personal narrative, history), and attending continuing education focused on the LGBTQ community. Additionally, allied therapists must understand how LGBTQ people experience their intersecting identities as well as understand how institutional practices affect the community. An allied therapist works to create and maintain a supportive environment that demonstrates community support by creating an office space that represents diverse perspectives; they furthermore use inclusive and supportive language including on intake forms and clinical documentation.

When a client is on or about to begin their coming-out process, an allied therapist will be a very important support for the LGBTQ client to have. In terms of supporting the coming-out decision and process of LGBTQ individuals, the Taskforce (2013) stress that counselors should be mindful and acknowledge that the choice and extent of coming out is the decision of the individual. The allied counselor can support through validation of the challenges with navigating the process, allowing the client to define and name their own process. Moreover, the competent ally will work to "counter statements regarding affectional orientation or gender identities that are not relevant to decisions or evaluations concerning" LGBTQ individuals (p.23). All the while, the competent ally needs to seek support and consultation from an experienced supervisor and continue to develop their own best practices to make adjustments as they continue to serve the LGBTQ community.

When it comes to experiences with healthcare, among a sample of 6450 TGNC (transgender and gender non-conforming) individuals, 50% of TGNC individuals reported having to teach their physicians how to care for them, 28% reported experiencing verbal harassment in a medical setting, and 19% were refused treatment (Grant *et al.*, 2011). Although a full examination of these nuances is beyond the scope of this chapter, we did want to provide the reader with some best practices around transition-related decisions as well. TGNC-affirmative care is not about pushing a client towards making a decision to transition or not, but rather about providing a space to explore gender identity and expression. Most trans individuals seek some sort of transition-related care, and most often counseling and hormone therapy are utilized (Grant *et al.*, 2011). It is important to remember that for some, medical transition may not be part of their personal journey towards affirmation; for example, a gender non-binary individual may not seek hormone replacement therapy (HRT) as they may be most comfortable in their non-binary expression of gender and are not interested in surgical treatment. For others, the financial cost of medical transition may be prohibitive and an unrealistic option for affirmation.

Some medical providers continue to require a letter from a qualified counselor stating that an individual is ready for transition-related medical care, which at times places therapists in the role of gatekeeper to trans individuals seeking to medically affirm their gender. TGNC individuals may seek out therapy specifically for this reason. More recently, trans activists have been advocating for an informed consent approach, where TGNC individuals are offered the necessary education and advisement, and the decision is left to the patient alone. Organizations like Planned Parenthood currently practice the informed consent treatment model for access to HRT. Often, therapists will focus on the social and emotional aspects of transitioning. The World Professional Association for Transgender Health (WPATH) (2011) provides a comprehensive standard of care for working with trans adults and children and assisting them in finding comfort with their gendered selves. This assistance may include primary care, medical care, reproductive options, voice and communication therapy, mental health services, and hormonal and surgical treatments. Ultimately, the standard calls for collaboration among healthcare professionals in an effort to provide optimal care for health and well-being.

Allied therapists may be tasked with ally development as well as counseling allies; the allied client is one that self-assumes the role of ally and may seek support in their ally development. Within this unique relationship, the allied therapist working with the allied client needs to validate the importance of their support to the LGBTQ community, while helping the ally understand their own sexual orientation, gender, intersecting identities, privileges, and oppressions. The allied therapist will assist the client in identifying and processing microaggressions, prejudice, discrimination, genderism, and heterosexism as well as "empower allies to minimize the internalization of those messages and to use their voice in speaking out against such acts as determined appropriate by the individuals involved" (ALGBTIC LGBQQIA Competencies Taskforce, 2013, p.25). After all, research demonstrates that "understanding oneself as an ally must evolve towards an incorporation of understanding and confronting social injustices" (Rivers & Swank, 2017, p.29). The therapist may also support the ally in processing their own prejudice and discrimination they may experience from identifying as an ally. Additionally, therapists may work with allies who are also LGBTQ and should support these specific allies in supporting the community, while also balancing supporting themselves. For additional information on ally competencies and best practices, please see the ALGBTIC LGBQQIA Competencies Taskforce full report (2013) as well as the WPATH Standards of Care.

Social Justice Model of Supervision

Although literature and research on the use of a social justice model of supervision is lacking in the field of creative arts therapy, we can borrow from our psychotherapy counterparts to begin to create our own supportive model. It seems only natural that as we integrate social justice aspects into our creative arts therapy, we incorporate a similar model into clinical supervision and training. In the introduction to this book, we have already shared the limitations of the state of the current education of the creative arts therapist. We believe that by integrating social justice advocacy into our clinical supervision we can address some of the limitations that exist in our current educational systems. Ultimately, we hope to propel other creative arts therapists to practice with a commitment to social justice.

A social justice model of supervision then assists creative arts therapists in acknowledging systemic and social inequities and locating every client within these oppressive systems, while also addressing the health, wellness, and development of each client. This model of supervision functions from a culturally responsive place that assumes that we cannot separate the therapeutic relationship from the larger socio-political world, but need to situate and contextualize the client, the therapist, and the therapeutic relationship within the social world the client inhabits, acknowledging that the world of the client may, in fact, be different from the world of the therapist.

Peer Supervision: An Excerpt

The previous sections speak to the impact of systems of oppressions on the LGBTQ community as well as the role of ally and advocate to mitigate said systems. It also serves as a call to action for therapists to continue to pursue that path of social justice and allyship to reduce the potential for continued perpetuation of these detrimental systems of oppression and begin to work to dismantle dominant narratives: transphobia, heterosexism, genderism, cisnormativity, and heteronormativity. We now present to you an excerpt from our own peer supervision. This excerpt provides a sample of conversation, rather than a specific guideline of how-to. It is our hope that our conversation can be utilized to spark other conversations in an effort to continue to move the conversation forward and dismantle systems of oppression.

Our peer supervision is rooted in a social justice framework and recognizes that systems of oppression are downloaded into our ways of thinking, behaving, and relating. Throughout our supervision, we call each other into a discussion that is, at times, difficult, given that recognizing, challenging, and fighting against oppressive systems is demanding, and necessary. We place high importance on increasing our capacity to acknowledge and speak to our own complicity and perpetuation of oppression. All the while, we hold compassion towards ourselves and each other.

To explore the use of a social justice model in creative arts therapy supervision, we recorded a conversation in the context of a peer supervision on these topics, exploring in particular questions such as:

- What does it mean to be an ally for the LGBTQ community?

- What are you willing to sacrifice?

- Where does the role of ally intersect with the role of therapist, and in what capacity do we see ourselves playing the role of ally within our practices?

- What practices and/or tools are you implementing to militate against being complicit with and/or perpetuating systems of oppression?

- How are you using creative arts interventions to explore these issues?

- What does cultural competence mean to you?

- How do you challenge the oppressive nature of normative thinking in your practice?

- How do you navigate questions from clients about your own identifiers?

- What does it mean to have a therapist that shares identity categories with their clients?

- What do you do to continue to work on yourself?

Several themes emerged from this conversation, including risk taking in allyship; intersections of therapy and advocacy; attunement; conscious and unconscious belief systems; discomfort as empathy building;

intersections of power and perpetration; political as personal; systems of oppression; cultural humility; fatigue and perseverance; and self-reflective processing. Below, we examine excerpts from the dialogue and illuminate the evolution of these themes. Ideally, this will offer other clinicians a framework for a social justice model of supervision to explore ally development and dismantling dominant narratives in clinical practice.

EXPLORATION OF THE RISKS AND BENEFITS OF ALLYSHIP IN CLINICAL PRACTICE

Britton: For me, this idea of allyship is aligning myself with a fight, and a resistance against oppressive structures with a willingness to sacrifice my own safety and comfort. When I hear things that are said, even if there is something I stand to lose in pushing against what is being said, or what I see being done, that I still address it anyway. As an ally, I position myself not as someone who supports only when it's comfortable, but I am someone who says, "I am in this alongside you and I am willing to do what it takes to push against the oppressive structures that I see arise." That's both outside of myself, but also in the places where I see it in myself, so that also means challenging myself when I see "isms and obias" rise up in me that I am not expecting. Am I willing to sacrifice my desire to always be a "good person" to recognize that I too am fallible? Will I recognize places where I have been steeped in a belief system without even realizing it, and be willing to own that? Not just in the privacy of my own home, but also openly in dialogue and discussion, whether it's that someone else calls me out or I say something or do something and then call myself out for it.

Dana: I am thinking about what it means to be an ally within the community. For me, this has been a shortcoming of mine. It can be easy to lump everyone within the LGBTQ community into one collaboration where everyone supports each other. It was not until recently when we heard the news about the government rolling back the rights of trans individuals in the military, or the even more recent move to establish an Office of Civil Rights within Health and Human Services with the sole purpose to restrict LGBTQ rights to healthcare, that I started to think about what it means to be an ally within the community. And even within that, being able to call out my queer cohort members and even call out myself for missteps, and overstepping and for over-identifying—thinking that everyone is going to feel the same way within the community about a certain action.

In this moment, we are speaking to the fact that being an ally is more than just emotionally supporting and standing by a member of the LGBTQ community. An ally commits to challenging the normative thinking that occurs in society and actively works against oppressive ideas, regardless of what the ally stands to lose as a result (Finnerty *et al.*, 2014). This also illuminated the idea that an ally is not immune to missteps or perpetrating, despite their commitment to their role. The ally lives and moves within the world with cultural humility acknowledging when they misstep and open to being called out for behavior that does not align with allyship. As we found ourselves further exploring the role of the ally, Dana became stimulated by the idea of the potential connection between risk taking as an ally and the queer experience:

Dana: I can connect this to when we were speaking about risk taking and how being an ally you may sometimes be the only ally in a room. This may result in you having an inherently queer experience, which is being alone, and isolated, and fighting against the majority. Even as we sit here talking about this idea, it even raises up for me in my stomach and into my heart, "Oh, I know this, the embodied performance of risk taking." But for me, it is also something that typically indicates for me that I am doing something I believe in and doing something that is right.

EXPLORATION OF INTERSECTION OF THERAPY AND ADVOCACY

Dana: I remember us speaking a lot in our training about the differences between being a therapist and being an advocate, and how sometimes being a therapist you may have to align with treatment planning, or the system, who perhaps holds a different view than yours. Now, we are leaning more towards being social justice advocates. I am wondering where the line comes that we feel like we are also allies within our practice.

Britton: I think some people say, "Oh, well, my role as a therapist is not to be a social justice advocate." And for me, because of who I am personally and professionally, I feel like when I see injustice within the mental health system, and justice to me is a nonnegotiable, I see it directly impacting clients, like when colleagues do not make use of a client's pronouns. We need to be mindful of that. It is witnessing disappointing conversations among colleagues and coworkers and being able to say, "Hey, this conversation does not sit right and this is why." And truly standing behind the idea that if I see what I know to be an injustice being done and I don't speak up to it, then I am actually part of the injustice.

I also want my clients, whether we have a connection of identity or not, to know that whether they are there in person in my office or not, that I have them in mind. Just the way I want to believe that my own therapist, supervisor, or medical doctor that is caring for me has my experience in mind. Not just Britton, but Britton and all that I am in all my multiple intersecting identities. I want to move in a way that I have my clients in mind, so, therefore, in treatment, even if it's my own practice I am calling out things that are unjust. As Maya Angelou would tell us, "When you know better, you do better." So, I hope that when I recognize things that don't make sense I know better and do better.

We begin to see the intersection of allyship and therapy, of advocacy and therapy, in the conversation. Dana recalls that in his education and training he was initially instructed to separate the role of advocate and therapist, whereas now he finds himself leaning into this role with the implementation of a social justice paradigm (Ratts, 2009; Fouad *et al.*, 2006). For Britton, the intersection of the roles is necessary and to not marry the two roles would be an injustice and continued perpetration of the oppressive systems we seek to dismantle. To remain silent in the face of injustice is to be complicit with an oppressive system. In a social justice model of supervision, the creative arts therapist should work towards an integration of the role of therapist and the role of advocate and ally.

Exploration of Attunement as a Tool to Respond to Microaggressions

Dana: I am thinking about a story of when I took a risk as an ally in my practice. I was working in acute care in a hospital. The patient who was scheduled to come in next for treatment planning was a gay-identifying, cisgender male. In the pretreatment meeting, I was sharing some of the things the patient had divulged in individual sessions about medications resulting in impotence and feeling like he was not able to perform fully as a man. Information he had not shared with the heterosexual, cisgender female psychiatrist. So, the patient came in and the psychiatrist was facilitating a conversation around the patient's auditory hallucinations that are persecutory about his sexual orientation. She then brings into conversation the patient's family and his experienced rejection and disownment. The psychiatrist then talks about the side effects, and grills the patient in a way that felt very uncomfortable and in a way that I had never heard her speak to straight-identifying clients about their sexual side effects before in a public forum. And it kept going and I said, "I think it's time for this meeting to be over, given our time." Because I could see visibly that the patient was being shamed and reaching out to me in that identifying and shared space.

I ended the meeting and afterwards I spoke with everyone about it. If I had spoke to it in the presence of the client, I feel it would have created a different problem, or greater challenge in terms of splitting and all those components, not to mention my fear around how it may turn back towards the patient. I said to the psychiatrist, "I feel like I have never heard you speak to a straight male client about their sexual side effects with the intensity you were speaking to this gay patient. I feel like you were connecting aspects of his identity to his symptomatology and side effects." It was met by the psychiatrist with "Don't you realize I have been treating gay people forever? I had a practice in the West Village."

Britton: "My best friend is gay."

Dana: Exactly. So, here we have this doctor who does not think she is doing anything wrong and perhaps unconsciously or even consciously does not believe she is doing something wrong, and that is a problem. I got so upset and I just kept saying, "We need to be mindful about this because you are treading the line of pathologizing sexuality." I felt a real ally role come in, and it is unfortunate that it took me recognizing shame in my client before I said something. I know I have shared this story with you before, but even today my body responds viscerally to it, and maybe part of that is my shame, or embarrassment, too. It was an all too familiar felt experience.

In this story, Dana recalls a moment that is multilayered. Reflecting on it still today, his somatic memory indicates an embodied understanding of the client's experience—an experience that is both the client's, his own, and their shared experience. In this moment, the dominant narrative is at play attempting to establish control by inducing shame in the marginalized (Sajnani *et al.*, 2017). He also recalls his own shame in not putting a stop to the behavior sooner, a shame that also feels connected to the patient's experience. Dana's attunement to the patient's body language and facial expressions is ultimately what led to the choice to react to the microaggressive behavior. This attunement feels mutual in that the patient was seeing a shared identity in Dana and making an effort to seek safety in the likeness.

Exploration of Dissonance between Conscious and Unconscious Belief Systems

Britton: One of my places of frustration, and, therefore, interest in bias, is around this idea that "I don't mean anything by this." There is this assumption that can become dangerous, when people think consciously, "I am a good person and I mean no harm to anyone," that does not mean an unconscious mechanism is not at work that could be harmful to patients. I certainly have had similar experiences of seeing patients pathologized because of how they identify or how they are asking to be received, because it makes someone else uncomfortable and defense mechanisms come up. It reminds me of a situation where a cisgender male colleague was really struggling with a particular patient and pathologizing this client's experience around gender identity. This was a teenage genderqueer client and my colleague was dismissing their experience, like it was something the client was "just going through"—a phase.

Dana: Like they will grow out of it.

Britton: Exactly. And I became frustrated, especially when my colleague responded with "Look at how much time we are spending on this. It makes me so uncomfortable to have to think about this all the time, and I feel like I am going to do the wrong thing, or say the wrong thing." And I think these are the moments I get frustrated and I want to believe that there is always an entry point to have someone see something in a different way.

At this point in the conversation, Britton hypothesizes that her frustration with bias also fuels her interest in researching the topics of conscious and unconscious beliefs. Through this processing, Britton speaks to the notion that despite an individual's best effort to be consciously inclusive, they can also unconsciously perpetrate, creating a dissonant experience for the individual (Williams, 2017). As a result of this dissonant experience, the superego of the individual may come to play in the form of defense mechanisms in an effort to reduce the discomfort of dissonance. We believe that rather than responding from a defended place in the face of dissonance, the therapist could utilize this embodied reaction or embodied verification to better understand the patient experience—a useful tool for processing within a social justice model of supervision.

EXPLORATION OF DISCOMFORT AS EMPATHY BUILDING
Directly connecting to the aforementioned theme, the use of discomfort as a tool for empathy is explored:

Britton: What if we actually used the discomfort we feel sometimes to try to understand what it might feel like for someone to feel uncomfortable every single moment of every single day? We might say something that is offensive to a client and if our fear of this and discomfort with engaging with a client can help us understand that this is something that the client perhaps experiences on a daily consistent and persistent basis that might actually allow us a portal to...

Dana and Britton: Empathy.

Britton: It could be an opportunity to consider: What would it feel like to walk around feeling that all the time? And then add onto that, "I am not safe." And what is upsetting, in the example that you're using and I am using, is that we are talking about people who treat people, who have a direct impact on their lives, a direct impact on what goes into the chart, a direct impact on the stories that get told about our clients, and a direct impact on what our clients take in of the experience of sitting across from someone who on some level refuses to take them in as they wish to be seen and received. And that is an injustice, to be denied the right to be seen and received as you want to be seen and received.

Using discomfort as a bridge to empathic understanding, the therapist may be able to speak more directly to the patient's experience. To not attempt to connect these experiences is to potentially collude with the forces of social injustice (Albee, 2000). A social justice model of supervision allows the therapist to process their own discomfort, while the supervisor or colleague assists the therapist in connecting their felt experience to the lived experience of the client.

Exploration of the Intersection of Power and Perpetration

Britton introduced the ramifications of systemic oppression in mental and medical health care settings, which led Dana to speak about the Pulse nightclub shooting not being labeled a hate crime:

Dana: It was easy on that day for people to talk about it as a shooting, but hard to talk about it as a hate crime, so much so that I don't think it is even considered a hate crime on the books. And what is that, that straight-washing, that cis-washing, we are doing with our history. It is easier to talk about gun violence, but it's harder to talk about this assault rooted in hate that occurred in a queer space—a queer space on Latin night—that was supposed to be safe. I mean it's a hate crime, and it's an assault that it's not labeled as such.

Britton: This speaks to a grand denial that happens societally. There is a real tendency to not own how deeply prejudiced we are as a country. This sits at the underbelly of our country's birth story. We are so—and by *we* I mean society and culturally—resistant to owning it, which I think makes it really difficult to heal and move through. I think there is also a real resistance to speak to the fact that there is a large body of hate. To see the underbelly actually raise itself, and to deny it is a perpetuation of oppression. To deny things that are real, visible, and have been widely publicized…for there to be a denial that the Pulse shooting was a hate crime… I think about erasure: the number of trans women of color who are killed—I don't see them or hear their names except in the bubble of the community I have sought out, that have the intentions to share these stories. There is the denial and then the erasure, which makes space for these atrocities to continue.

Britton demonstrates how the dominant culture executes power over the marginalized by fueling a narrative rooted in denial of the lived experience of the marginalized. We point to erasure as a tool that demonstrates the potential harm that exists at the intersection of power and perpetration. The covert and subtle nature of this form of oppression enters into our lives daily. Through a social justice model of supervision, clinicians need to locate themselves, speak to the dominant narratives they have internalized, and move towards open discourse with other clinicians and their clients.

EXPLORATION OF POLITICAL IS NOW
PERSONAL: A PARALLEL PROCESS

Here, Dana attempts to pull from queer theory and speak to the idea of the political as personal and explore how political moments manifest in affective responses in the therapeutic encounter:

Dana: As I am listening to what you're saying, I am thinking about our clients who are coming in and for who there is a real fear that is rooted in the reality being proposed to us and how that is increasing levels of fear and anxiety. I have worked in acute care for many years now and when changes like this happen, broad-stroke changes like the ban on transgender people in the military, or tragedies happen like the Pulse nightclub shooting, these impact our clients in real ways. Sometimes it plays out in ways that are able to be recognized and conscious, and sometimes in unconscious ways performing as anger or aggression on the unit. And people don't know what to do with all this information, or who to talk to, or who is safe company.

Britton: When I think about that question: Who is safe to speak to, who can I talk to about these things? For any group that has been marginalized, who knows what it is to be oppressed on a daily and persistent basis, needs to know that when showing up to your therapist, this is a place that I can talk about what is upsetting to me and to know that the therapist is upset too. Speaking for myself, I would want to know walking into my therapist's office that their experience of what is happening politically across many sectors is upsetting and troubling to them. If I didn't know that, I don't think I would be able to go, sit across from them, and feel safe because I am directly and indirectly impacted by what is happening politically right now.

Together, we begin to speak to the relationship between the political and social world and the fear and anxiety that plays out in the therapeutic encounter during times of social and political unrest. Dana connects this even more closely to himself given that he identifies as a member of the LGBTQ community and hypothesizes that for the therapist with a marginalized identifier these prejudiced events may have a deeply felt impact on the therapist and the patient. As story begets story, we are reminded of moments in practice in the days after the Pulse nightclub shooting and how these may perform in the queer-identifying therapist and the allied therapist:

Dana: I remember the morning after the Pulse nightclub shooting, I did not hear about the massacre until my train ride into work. It was a Sunday morning; I guess technically the same day. When I got to the unit, I stopped in the day room to watch the news with my clients, and the client closest to me looked at me and just said, "I am so sorry this happened." It was clear they were saying "I am sorry" to me as they were associating me with that community, I believe. That's what it felt like. It meant a lot. We did not necessarily speak more to it, and in that moment it felt like enough. And you may bring these topics up in a group setting, and sometimes they will want to speak about it and sometimes they won't. This daily rigmarole of changes to policies and freedoms, and tragedies that are happening, is getting closer and closer to home, things are just going to spike up even more.

Britton: Sadly.

Dana: Sadly, right.

Britton: A couple days after Pulse nightclub when I was seeing clients, there was this shared understanding that something devastating happened. I allowed myself to share with my clients, "Yes, this is devastating. I am upset by this." For some people it was a direct conversation and dialogue, and for some we held silent space in recognition.

Self-awareness and social justice seem to walk hand in hand. To understand oneself as an ally and advocate, the therapist must also extend themselves to understand and resist social injustices (Rivers & Swank, 2017). In a social justice model of supervision, the therapist's self-reflection is beneficial for the therapeutic relationship as well as the growth and expansion of the therapist.

EXPLORATION OF CREATIVE ARTS THERAPY
TO PROCESS SYSTEMS OF OPPRESSION

Dana: I think this is where our creative arts approach comes in because we can couch or frame these larger travesties or these challenges we are working through in metaphor. We can approach them from a place of distance that allows us to move in and lean into them, to then hopefully lead to the more direct conversation.

In this moment, Dana begins to propose how creative arts can be utilized to process these experiences. He begins to speak to the use of distance and how distance itself can facilitate these conversations. He is then reminded of a recent clinical encounter where he was able to bring in his own misstep around misgendering. He goes on to speak about his recent recognition of cisnormativity in his style of play in drama therapy:

Dana: I think a place where I am becoming more aware of it about myself, especially around heteronormative and cisnormative roles and automatic thoughts around gendering to categorize, is in my play. Today, I was facilitating a group and I brought in the outline of a body that is nondescript and I asked the group to think about who this character might be. And today the group decided that this character was Bigfoot and I automatically started referring to the character as "he." I stopped and reflected to myself, even my play can be dominated by normativity. I wonder if that goes back to the way I was socialized and in my early childhood when I was mostly playing with cis and heteronormative roles, and perhaps it's also my assumption that the members of my group typically identify with the cisheteromajority. But in this moment, this is Bigfoot. So I identified it to the group saying, "I keep calling Bigfoot he, but I haven't given Bigfoot the chance to tell us how Bigfoot identifies." I continued to refer to Bigfoot as Bigfoot and switched the pronoun to they. Even in our play we have to be mindful of how we are perpetuating dominant narratives, and with that what stories are being erased, left out, or left behind.

This sharing of personal story leads Britton to suggest a metaphor for us to utilize to further explore this topic. Britton introduces into the conversation the metaphor of children on a playground in an effort to explore the origins of normative and oppressive thinking and acting:

Britton: If we watch children on the playground, all they want to know is who's going to play well in the sandbox… They are not looking for: Who do you like? What's that color on your skin? Who do you pray to or not? This is not how children decide who comes into the sandbox.

Dana: I mean the image that comes up for me is a playground full of segregated sandboxes. And how every child would be alone in their own box.

Britton: As soon as we find out we pray to the same person, but your skin is "not right," and who you like is "not right."

Dana: It's a playground free of intersectionality. It's just a sad reality.

Britton: It would be horribly sad. I think using this image that we all start in the same sandbox and that we begin to segregate ourselves in some instances and capacities, due to these messages that get internalized, there is something really sad about that.

Dana: And it puts up a wall. That's when it gets ingrained, and we put up a wall that doesn't allow us to reach across to make relationship or create possibility of dialogue or even existing in the same place. I mean, free the sandbox.

Britton: I mean right, free the sandbox. If you can't be free in the sandbox, we have a problem. Even in this riff that we just had, what we are speaking to is one way we can mitigate these things which is by having a diverse group of people around you. When I think about my practice and the way I move within my work, I think what helps me is I have a very diverse group of friends. Now, am I suggesting that I have the most diverse group of friends one could have? Of course not, because there is a depth and breadth to diversity.

EXPLORATION OF CULTURAL HUMILITY

As the conversation continues, Britton speaks to her own experiences with a recent misstep in her private practice and her way of responding to this moment from a place of humility:

Britton: I have a strong ability to call myself out. This was not always the case. I developed this practice through consistently engaging in conversations such as this one. It doesn't mean that I like to see what emerges, but I have a really good group of people that I communicate with. These conversations are a daily part of my life and my self-awareness as a person and as a professional. I continue to do my work and research on all the ways "isms and obias" impact life experiences, the work that we do as therapists, and my own practice; I have to check it and recognize it. I recently started using a new service for my practice paperwork and there is a form that I can't even send out because it does not represent a wide experience of identity with only male, female, other…

Dana: Other?

Britton: …which feels wildly dismissive and dichotomous. I emailed them and asked them to update the system with some ideas on how. It's recognizing that I have to have that process: Am I looking through my materials? I noticed these things and realized I can't send them out. There was another piece of material that I had that only said his/her all throughout and I had given that out to people before I even realized. The point is, on the one hand, it is something I am aware of and, on the other hand, something slipped by me. I have to be aware of that, I have to recognize it. Do I love that it slipped through? No, and in that way I was complicit in binary and normative thinking. Just because I have these conversations, just because I am trying to be wildly mindful, it does not exempt me from perpetuating systems of oppression. It does not exempt me from having hetero and cisnormative tendencies seep into my language and into the materials I am using. It is imperative that I own and recognize the inevitability that I will microaggress; I will make an assumption about someone that is incorrect because I am human. I don't say this because I am proud of it; I say it because I am aware of it. It has to be an ongoing process of awareness of checks and balances on myself.

In this moment, Britton is speaking from a place of cultural humility. As therapists, we will make mistakes. Checks and balance is a call to action that encourages the therapist to not just witness and embrace their fallibility, but to make change, and that is social justice in philosophy and practice. Witnessing is passive in a social justice framework; this is not to deny the role of witness, but to speak to the need of making change for ourselves, our clients, and for the community. By owning fallibility, the therapist is able to respond authentically in the moment and make an active choice to do better and fight against systems of oppression.

The conversation continues to explore the resistance that can occur when faced with the choice to challenge these systems:

Britton: And I think in some of the places where I recognize resistance and reluctance to push against oppressive structures, what I hear in that narrative is "I haven't allowed myself to reach across the table and meet a person that I don't share identity with." I think it is sad when we do not allow ourselves to do that.

Dana: I agree. And why don't people do that? Why don't people allow themselves to reach across? What stops them? And that's more rhetorical right now for this conversation, because we can't answer that question fully. It is worth asking, though. But perhaps it's a self-reflective question.

Britton: Absolutely. Especially in our field.

Dana: Oh, for sure.

Britton: Because here's the thing: if I am not reaching across the table in my life, how can I reach across the table in my practice? And that's why it's an important question.

Dana: There are clinicians who say I can reach across the table in my practice, I can work with anyone, but I am not reaching across the table in my life.

Britton: I don't know if that is possible. Do you have to sit at a table with someone from every culture and corner of the world? No. But if there is a group of people that you struggle to understand, or you are not making an attempt to diversify your group of colleagues and friends, I do challenge how you are able to meet a diverse group of clients and experience them in a way that is open and aware to your perceptions and assumptions of others.

Exploration of Fatigue and Perseverance within Social Justice

Dana: You know we are really tying allyship and social justice together in a nice way, but I am also thinking about how tiring and exhausting it is. You can have the same conversation over and over again. I know for sure I have not corrected something, or called myself on a misstep. And I know I have misstepped. I just know the fatigue that comes with it especially when it is a community I feel connected to and that I am a part of. I mean, what do you say to someone who feels so fatigued by it?

Britton: I say, I know that fatigue.

Dana: Is that empathy?

Britton: There it is, empathy. There is a mountainous component to this work. There is a narrative that says look how far we have come as a country, but I would say yes and look at how far we have not come as country, when we have so many disparities. This is mountainous, what we are speaking to. Resisting these oppressive structures will always be a part of who I am. I will resist and fight until I am not here. Where I sit right here, right now today, I believe that I will not see the world in the way I wish to fully see it. But I also know ripples become waves, and that I will always work to be part of the ripple that will create the wave, whether I get to see the wave or not. But especially right now, it can be hard to see the other side of the mountain, but I know the other side of the mountain is there. You know?

Dana: Yes, and I appreciate the metaphor of the ripple on the wave. What I love is just how powerful and strong waves can be. As I was thinking about putting this book together and even this chapter, the stories and narrative and future movement of the LGBTQ community is being challenged every single day. I write a new word on paper and the fear is that by the time it gets published something is going to have changed—and by changed I don't mean a forward movement, but a push back. And I know that is part of the wave, but it contributes to my own reluctance or low readiness to be able to, at times, contribute to the ripple. But I am trying, and certain days are better than others. Although I am tired, I am going to keep going.

The responsibility and work of the therapist committed to social justice is exhausting and self-care is imperative. The fatigue we speak to comes from the fight for equity and justice; it is exhausting to be in a social justice movement because people are losing their lives, and the same conversations are being held with little change. We believe that anyone who has a social justice practice will know this fatigue, which is a consistent cry without fully being heard. We acknowledge the presence of this in our lives and our work. It can be difficult to keep up with a movement especially as it continues to be pushed back, and Dana connects this directly towards writing contributions for this book. Britton attunes to this exhaustion and offers a useful metaphor to understand the collaborative nature of this work:

Britton: One of the ways we keep going is unplugging sometimes. I consider that part of my activism—the unplug. I am thinking about our good friend and colleague, a drama therapist, Alexis Powell, who once said to me, "It is like a choir, that when one section takes a breath, the other section continues." We take a break knowing the other section will continue, and then when that section needs a break, this section continues. And I do consider that an important part of this work. This is the other piece that makes the ripple so powerful: I am not the only one contributing to the ripple. So the wave will happen because even when I take a moment for myself to recharge, someone else is adding to that ripple. In that way, we create the collective wave.

Dana: That's beautiful.

Britton: I do have to take that breath and trust that the sound will continue. And to know that we take that breath because we know there is a lot of song left to sing. This is the piece. If we think about the fact that it started before we were here, and it will continue long after we are gone.

EXPLORATION OF CREATIVE ARTS METHODS
IN SELF-REFLECTIVE PROCESSING

Britton: How are you using creative arts interventions to explore these issues, both with clients and for ourselves?

Dana: For me, I am a playwright and a play that I wrote a few years back was called *Interrupting Mary*, which explored queering the heteronormative idea of women having babies and men not. It asked the audience to imagine a gay man is pregnant sitting next to a woman who is also pregnant in a doctor's office. It is titled *Interrupting Mary* because it asks the audience to think queerly, imagining that Joseph was pregnant and Mary was not in the most famous birth story. This play was so useful for me to explore some of my own challenges of not being able to give birth and to explore how I can queer through my art.

Britton: I am a poet and poetry is a way for self-supervision and also a way to internalize and grapple with the world around me and the injustices that I see happening. So I use it both in my practice and also in my own understanding of all the things I see happening. I use my poetry to understand and ingest the world. My poetry feels very personal to me.

Dana: Yes, and this is where the personal becomes political. We are using these for ourselves and our own exploration, but these could also be used as a form of social justice moving forward.

Britton: Which is why I grapple with putting them out.

Dana: Why do you grapple with that?

Britton: Two things, it is so political, and this is also how I release while still holding. Part of how I keep my energy going is writing my poetry. It is also how I try to contribute to these stories living in some way, in my own mind and in the world because every day we are inundated. I think we are in a particular time where we are seeing a rise in violence. [According to the National Coalition of Anti-Violence Programs (NCAVP) (2017), there was an 86% increase in LGBTQ hate homicides from 2016 to 2017.] There was a time where I could list the names of those who have been slain, but it is harder to hold them in mind in the same way because there are now so many names. So for me, my poetry is one way I try to hold these stories. And yet, in creating these pieces, I am speaking to a story that exists, but also speaking to my perception and understanding of the story, so I am revealing of myself. It is almost like this meeting in the middle, if that makes sense.

As artists, we have at our disposal a wealth of creative possibility to explore the work we do. Together, we explore the role this art making may play in continued advocacy. We echo the ideas of many in our field, that art making can contribute to creating a more just world, enable empowerment, and support critical consciousness (Baines, 2013; Gipson, 2015; Wright & Wright, 2017). By grounding our process and advocacy in art making, we hope to put creative arts therapy on the cutting edge and offer a contemporary approach to activism. We expand on the inherent potential of creative methods to support the efforts of the therapist as social justice advocate and serve as surrogate holder.

Dana: Art making is a surrogate holding because you are allowing it to move through you, and out of you, and into the frame of poetry, of theater, of play. It is not just your body that is holding it, but that actually there is something else containing it, which is a release in itself. I would venture to say it may help to combat some of the fatigue and annoyance and frustration we spoke to earlier.

Britton: I like this idea of the surrogate. It does become overwhelming to hold. These stories are, of course, inside, but there has to be a place, which comes back to the benefits of creative arts therapies and the use of our own art. When it is outside of me in this piece of poetry, I know it is there and it does not feel as heavy. I can close the book and know it is in the book and travels with me, but I don't have to hold it by myself. And that is a parallel of therapy, I can hold this and know that it travels with me, but someone else is walking with me and holding.

Dana: Maybe sharing our art without fear of repercussion can be a form of social justice. Because I know the intention behind our artwork and the ethics behind that intention will certainly carry our stories.

Musing through the metaphor of a surrogate, and in some respects queering our conversation, we speak to the containment of art making in assisting the therapist in creating space and building capacity. A social justice model in supervision offers the therapist a space to make art that contains and holds some of their experiences to be able to create a necessary distance for self-reflection. Creative arts, in all their modalities, work to organize and contain affective experiences that results in creating potential space for movement and playability, which allows for forward movement, rather than becoming stuck in rigid patterns. Although the intention of the art making in this case is not for product, we hope sharing of this art can further militate against systems of oppression and establish creative arts therapy as a tool for contemporary activism.

Conclusion

We do believe there is a "wrong" side of oppression. Our intention is to illuminate that the oppressor has indeed been consciously and unconsciously held, loved, and nurtured on a macro level which trickles down to the individual level. In this chapter, which is grounded in a social justice framework, we ask, "Who will love those that have been killed, denied care, those that walk out of their house in fear every single day?" We are not looking to uplift the oppressor in this piece. We are asking ourselves and each other to uplift the oppressed. Social justice exists because people have not been loved by larger systems and within the relational context.

We (Dana and Britton) are both people who know in similar and different ways what it is to be on the side of a targeted group. We know the joy of being in those identities and the pain, fear, rejection, and lack of love that also comes with it. It is time to shift the narrative. The oppressor has led the narrative for too long. In this chapter, we are speaking to something that is uncomfortable, and as therapists we must love as well as hold the heavy and the difficult. We speak truth in the darkest of spaces knowing that light will not come without walking through the dark. We are saying let's sit together in discomfort in service of our growth and just practices. Inherent in social justice is the idea that something is in fact broken. We can't fix it if we do not speak to the broken pieces.

Overall, this chapter is meant to provide an example of one way this conversation might look; it is our hope that it has sparked in the reader the desire to further explore and apply these topics to their own practice and experiences. Through experimentation with our own peer supervision, we attempted to distill critical themes while building a framework for a social justice model of supervision for creative arts therapists. As a field, we stand at an important moment in time, where we are being asked and are hopefully asking ourselves, "Am I ready to contribute to change?"

References

Albee, G.W. (2000) 'The Boulder model's fatal flaw.' *American Psychologist 55*, 2, 247–248.

ALGBTIC LGBQQIA Competencies Taskforce (2013) 'Association for Lesbian, Gay, Bisexual, and Transgender Issues in Counseling: Competencies for counseling with lesbian, gay, bisexual, queer, questioning, intersex, and ally individuals.' *Journal of LGBT Issues in Counseling 7*, 1, 2–43.

Bain, C.L., Grzanka, P.R., & Crowe, B.J. (2016) 'Toward a queer music therapy: The implications of queer theory for radically inclusive music therapy.' *The Arts in Psychotherapy 50*, 22–33.

Baines, S. (2013) 'Music therapy as an anti-oppressive practice.' *The Arts in Psychotherapy 40*, 1, 1–5.

Finnerty, P., Goodrich, K.M., Brace, A., & Pope, A. (2014) 'Charting the course of ally development.' *Journal of LGBT Issues in Counseling 8*, 4, 326–330.

Fouad, N.A., Gerstein, L.H., & Toporek, R.L. (2006) 'Social Justice and Counseling Psychology in Context.' In R.L. Toporek, L.H. Gerstein, N.A. Fouad, G. Roysircar, & T. Israel (eds) *Handbook for Social Justice in Counseling Psychology: Leadership, Vision, and Action.* Thousand Oaks, CA: SAGE.

Gipson, L.R. (2015) 'Is cultural competence enough? Deepening social justice pedagogy in art therapy.' *Art Therapy 32,* 3, 142–145.

Grant, J.M., Mottet, L.A., Tanis, J., Harrison, J., Herman, J.L., & Keisling, M. (2011*) Injustice at Every Turn: A Report of the National Transgender Discrimination Survey.* Washington, DC: National Center for Transgender Equality and National Gay and Lesbian Task Force,

Hays, P.A. (2008) *Addressing Cultural Complexities in Practice: Assessment, Diagnosis, and Therapy.* Washington, DC: American Psychological Association.

McMullian, S. & Burch, D. (2017) '"I am more than my disease": An embodied approach to understanding clinical populations using Landy's Taxonomy of Roles in concert with the DSM-5.' *Drama Therapy Review 3,* 1, 29–43.

Meyer, I. H. (2015) 'Resilience in the study of minority stress and health of sexual and gender minorities.' *Psychology and Sexual Orientation and Gender Diversity 2,* 3, 209–213.

Nadal, K.L. (2013) *That's So Gay: Microaggressions and the Lesbian, Gay, Bisexual, and Transgender Community.* Washington, DC: American Psychological Association.

National Coalition of Anti-Violence Programs (NCAVP) (2017) *A Crisis of Hate: A Mid-Year Report on Lesbian, Gay, Bisexual, Transgender and Queer Hate Violence Homicides.* Authors: Emily Waters, Sue Yacka-Bible. New York, NY: New York City Anti-Violence Project.

Navetta, J.M. (2011) *Guide to Being a Straight Ally.* Washington, DC: PFLAG National.

Navetta, J.M. (2014) *Guide to Being a Trans Ally.* Washington, DC: PFLAG National.

Powell, A. (2016) 'Embodied multicultural assessment: An interdisciplinary training model.' *Drama Therapy Review 2,* 1, 111–122.

Ratts, M.J. (2009) 'Social justice counseling: Toward the development of a fifth force among counseling paradigms.' *Journal of Humanistic Counseling, Education and Development 48,* 2, 160–172. doi:10.1002/j.2161-1939.2009.tb00076.x

Rivers, B. & Swank, J.M. (2017) 'LGBT ally training and counselor competency: A mixed-method study.' *Journal of LGBT Issues in Counseling 11,* 1, 18–35.

Sajnani, N., Marxen, E., & Zarate, R. (2017) 'Critical perspectives in the arts therapies: Response/ability across a continuum of practice.' *The Arts in Psychotherapy 54,* 28–37.

Serano, J. (2016) *Outspoken: A Decade of Transgender Activism and Trans Feminism.* Oakland, CA: Switch Hitter Press.

Smith, L.C., Shin, R.Q., & Officer, L.M. (2012) 'Moving counseling forward on LGB and transgender issues.' *The Counseling Psychologist 40,* 3, 385–408.

Sue, D.W. (2010) *Microaggressions in Everyday Life: Race, Gender, and Sexual Orientation.* Hoboken, NJ: Wiley.

Vera, E.M. & Speight, S.L. (2003) 'Multicultural competence, social justice, and counseling psychology: Expanding our roles.' *The Counseling Psychologist 31*, 3, 253–272.

Williams, B.M. (2016) 'Minding our own biases: Using drama therapeutic tools to identify and challenge assumptions, biases and stereotypes.' *Drama Therapy Review 2*, 1, 9–23.

Williams, B.M. (2017) 'Role power: Using Role Theory in support of ethical practice.' *Drama Therapy Review 3*, 1, 131–48.

World Professional Association for Transgender Health (WPATH) (2011) *Standards of Care for the Health of Transsexual, Transgender, and Gender Nonconforming People, Version 7.* Accessed on 11/8/2018 at www.wpath.org/publications/soc.

Wright, T. & Wright, K. (2017) 'Exploring the benefits of intersectional feminist social justice approaches in art psychotherapy.' *The Arts in Psychotherapy 54*, 7–14.

2

Queering the Conversation

Facilitating Dialogues on LGBTQ Microaggressions and Systems of Oppression

BRITTON WILLIAMS AND DANA GEORGE TROTTIER

As we were making the choice to title this chapter, we (Britton and Dana) did not think very hard about using the term *queer*. Despite its sordid history, queer, for some, has become reclaimed from being a pejorative taunt on the playground to a theoretical understanding to a political stance to a reappropriated and reclaimed identifier. We use queer as an inclusive term, while also recognizing that there are individuals who will have a differing opinion. For us, the term *queer* speaks of those who reject the narrow definition of what is straight and/or normative. What is more, we use queer as a verb. What does it mean to queer something? We use the verb queering to direct the reader's focus towards moving through the normative and beginning to see what lies adjacent to it. Queering moves us away from the binary, and into a space of possibility. With queering, we follow the guidance of queer theorists such as Eve Kosofsky Sedgwick and Judith Butler, who have been asking us, each in their own way, to queer these conversations since the 1980s. Through queering, we ask you to question normative categories that shape the world, challenge systems that are designed to oppress, and begin to see the world from a non-heteronormative and a non-cisnormative perspective.

In order to have this conversation, we first acknowledge the fact that things will be missed, and that we do not have the space or complete knowledge to fully explain and explore all of the ideas in question. We recognize that we have privileged certain stories over others, despite our best efforts to be inclusive and to share a variety of narratives. We acknowledge this as a privilege as we made specific choices, certainly influenced by our own identities and the temperature of the current social climate, of what to include in this chapter. What we hope we have offered is a *good-enough* presentation of information that will spark curiosity in the reader to seek out additional information, dialogue, and continuing education, all the while challenging your own assumptions, biases, power, and privileges. We finish by providing the reader with a guide to support clinicians and/or supervisors in facilitating these conversations with other clinicians.

Oppression and Privilege

Oppression sits at the center of America's birth story and is deeply rooted within our past and our present. To this day, oppressive systems impact everyone and influence every encounter. Oppression is cruelty, violence, erasure, abuse, and unjust treatment in action. Oppression can be both subtle and blatant. Privilege affords benefit to some, whether intended or not, from the very system(s) that oppresses others and signifies "advantages one holds as a result of membership in a dominant group" (Hays, 2008, p.6). Privilege can cloud our ability to acknowledge and/or even recognize the insidious nature of oppression. The fluid nature of oppression means a person may in one moment be the victim of marginalization and in the next a victimizer; consequently, the complexity of oppression means a person can in the very same moment be both the victim and the perpetrator.

Oppressive belief systems weave their way into the fabric of social and cultural customs. It works in such a way that abhorrent comments and actions become normalized. Sue (2010) said, "When biases and prejudices become institutionalized and systemized into the norms, values and beliefs of a society, they are passed on to generations of its citizens via socialization and cultural conditioning" (p.112). According to Beauregard *et al.* (2016), "It is clear that discrimination and stigma persists in social institutions such as families, schools and businesses as a result of hetero and cisgender normative culture. This creates numerous stressors and impacts the mental health of individuals who identify as LGBTQI and GNC [gender non-conforming]" (p.45). LGBTQ people encounter oppressive communications from various sources and social settings, which can have a compounded impact on a person's experience with oppressive stressors.

Power and Privilege

Dominant voices and narratives within a society can often control how groups labeled as *other* are seen and perceived. Nadal (2013) defined dominant groups as "people in a society with greater power and privilege due to their majority status or historical authority" (p.79). Historically, white cisgender, heterosexual, Christian men have held majority status in the United States. Browne, Mickiewicz, and Firestone (1994) opined that "[m]ajority cultural domination often carries with it the power to stereotype. It is in itself a way to maintain power in fact, because it underlines the ability of those holding power to determine how to portray those who do not" (p.8). Biased messages and stereotypes are perpetuated by dominant groups through various outlets, including political, media, educational, and professional institutions; these messages are communicated through images, narratives, erasure, and other mechanisms. As a society becomes steeped in these biased communications, it can consciously and unconsciously define the ways in which certain groups are viewed and treated by institutions and individuals within the society.

Power is the ability to affect and control the outcome(s) in the lives of individuals or groups. Moreover, it is "the ability to define reality and to convince other people that it is their definition as well" (Nadal, 2013, p.79). A sinister aspect that can emerge within exclusive dominant groups is impeding, restricting, and denying human rights of certain groups while protecting and ensuring them for others. A person does not have to subscribe to the oppressive beliefs and actions of dominant culture to benefit from it. Privilege is "a right, favor, advantage, or immunity specifically granted to one individual or group and withheld from another" (Nadal, 2013, p.79). According to Hays (2008), privilege can isolate individuals in dominant groups from those in marginalized populations and likewise "limit a person's knowledge of and experience with nonprivileged groups, even when a person belongs to a minority group in one cultural domain and a dominant group in another" (p.6).

Under the hetero- and cisnormative culture, there are a plethora of oppressive narratives and actions within political, legal, and social arenas. Political and social institutions have accused same-sex marriage of being a threat to the institution of marriage. Furthermore, LGBTQ persons' rights to serve openly, if at all, in the military have been challenged; in fact, at the time of writing this chapter, Donald Trump, the current president of the United States, published a tweet stating transgender people would no longer be able to serve in the military because the military "cannot be burdened with the tremendous medical costs and disruption that transgender in the military would entail." At the time of editing, this tweet has become policy that will impact any future transgender service members. In some states, businesses can legally discriminate against people based on their sexual orientation and the current secretary of education, Betsy DeVos, has at least twice declined to denounce discriminatory actions in the nation's schools. These and other prejudiced beliefs, actions, and laws are the result of long-held bias against LGBTQ persons and the perpetuation of hetero and cisgender normativity.

Intersectionality

It is important to note that every individual within a group has a unique identity constellation and experience. It cannot be assumed that all members of a particular group have the same set of circumstances within it and/or that they subscribe to the same practices or beliefs. In fact, Crenshaw (1993) notes that "ignoring difference *within* groups contributes to tension *among* groups" (p.1242). Recognizing that every individual is comprised of multiple and intersecting identities (Powell, 2016) helps to account for the fullness and uniqueness of each person's experience.

As a result of individuals' intersecting identities, a person's relationship to power and privilege is not fixed or firmly established. Rather, a person can simultaneously be marginalized and privileged. Therefore, a person can experience extreme stigma in one identity category and benefit from power and privilege in another. Nadal (2013) noted that LGBTQ persons can be marginalized and hold less privilege in the face of heterosexism, cissexism, and genderism and at the same time experience power and privilege in other capacities, offering the following example:

LGBT people who are able-bodied, cisgender, gay, male, and White American are often viewed as having the most power and privilege in the community. The higher the number of these descriptions someone identifies with, the more power and privilege she or he will have. When someone identifies with few or none of these descriptions, the less power and privilege she or he will have. (p.111)

Interestingly, experiencing marginalization in one identity category sometimes challenges a person's ability to acknowledge and/or recognize their privilege and power within another identity category. It is for this reason that self-awareness and mindful attention to one's multiple and intersecting identities are imperative if one is to be truly cognizant of one's own power and privilege.

A person's intersections of identity can also compound their experience of marginalization. McNair (2017) maintained that "[t]here is a cumulative risk to health of multiple, intersecting minority identities, creating interlocking and mutually constituting disadvantages" (p.445); he cites several studies which have shown that LGB individuals who are older or racial minorities experience increased emotional, physical, and mental health stresses. Shaun Lockhart (2012) was an honor roll student who was well liked by his teachers although he struggled with his peers. As a young black boy, he did not feel accepted by the other black children. He recalls an incident in the seventh grade where a popular fellow classmate said to him in front of his peers:

> You don't have to be a bulging, masculine guy. But you—you are very effeminate. I have never met such a weak man. You need to start hanging around more black males. Honey, you are a sissy white boy trapped in a black boy. (p.19)

In this microassaultive attack, Lockhart's gender expression, masculinity, and racial identity were challenged, ridiculed, and questioned. The messages and societal attitudes towards LGBTQ and other marginalized people make microaggressive comments and circumstances a chronic and persistent experience for some.

Internalization of Oppression

No one escapes biased societal messages. The very people who are targeted by oppressive narratives and belief systems may download and internalize them as true. When an individual internalizes stigma, it becomes integrated into their value system (Nadal, 2013). Perez (2005) noted that the marginalization of LGBT people is more accepted than discrimination towards other marginalized groups and underscored that legal, social, and cultural systems perpetuate and support this oppression. As a result of chronic and persistent stigmatization, LGBT people may unconsciously adopt and internalize these oppressive beliefs. The effect of internalized oppression has various manifestations, including denial of sexual orientation and/or gender identity, engaging in risky behaviors, and endorsing and/or perpetuating negative stereotypes (Nadal, 2013; Perez, 2005).

Microaggressions

Microaggressions are implicit and explicit verbal and nonverbal messages that communicate prejudiced beliefs. Perpetrators are often unaware of the harm their words and/or actions cause for the recipient (Sue, 2010). Regardless of the microaggressor's intent, these moments can be upsetting, hurtful, and/or re/traumatizing. Research has demonstrated that LGBTQ people encounter microaggressions of all forms on a daily basis (Beauregard *et al.*, 2016; Lamda Legal, 2010; Nadal, 2013). Microaggressions can take many forms and can be expressed through verbal and nonverbal communications and behaviors.

Types of Microaggressions

Sue (2010) identifies three types of microaggressions which range in the offender's conscious intent. (1) *Microassaults* are intentional and meant to hurt the targeted individual or group and are blatant verbal or nonverbal attacks. These microaggressions might take place in the form of derogatory remarks or actions, such as the use of the slur "faggot." (2) *Microinsults* take form as subtler comments that may sit outside of the perpetrator's purview. These comments often implicitly or explicitly privilege dominant narratives and undermine marginalized individuals or groups. These microaggressions may take place in the form of a supposed compliment, such as saying to someone, "You don't act gay," "I completely believed you were straight until you told me that you are gay," or "You don't sound gay." The implicit insults suggest that identifying as gay has a particular and identifiable performance/presentation and being perceived as heterosexual is a strength. (3) *Microinvalidations* are verbal and/or nonverbal communications that deny, erase, or invalidate the thoughts, experiences, feelings, or perceptions of marginalized individuals or groups. For example, statements such as "You're being too sensitive," when someone expresses an experience of discrimination.

LGBTQ Experiences of Microaggressions

Nadal (2013) identified a need to expand upon previously published categories of microaggressions that only minimally included the experiences of LGBTQ individuals. He collaborated with several peers to offer eight themes regarding sexual orientation and gender identity microaggressions which included: use of heterosexist terminology or transphobic terminology; endorsement of heteronormative or gender normative culture and behaviors; assumption of universal LGBT experience; exoticization; discomfort with/disapproval of LGBT experience; denial of the reality of heterosexism or transphobia; assumption of sexual pathology/abnormality; denial of individual heterosexism (p.46).

In their qualitative focus group study, Nadal *et al.* (2011) sought to categorize microaggressions experienced by LGB people. One participant shared his experience, and recalled:

> One day I had asked my friend, 'cause he was on the football team, and he was the most popular, and I said, you know, "I want to try out for football." He just stood there and kind of laughed at me. I felt, you know, "What are you laughing at?" He was like, "Come on, you're gay! You can't play football!" (p.245)

In this example, an assumption of universal experience was made by the declaration that gay men "can't play football." Generalizations and erasure of individual experience(s) such as this are a common experience for LGBTQ persons and can be deeply hurtful and/or harmful.

Attending to the gap in literature that specifically addressed the microaggressions that transgender and gender non-conforming (GNC) people experience, Nadal, Skolnik, and Wong (2012) conducted a study which resulted in the proposal of 12 categories. The first seven categories were in alignment with previous findings outlined above. Additional themes from the study included (1) physical threat or harassment, (2) denial of individual transphobia, (3) denial of bodily privacy, (4) familial microaggressions, and (5) systemic and environmental microaggressions (p.64).

Chang and Chung (2015) point to the need for more exploration and research into the diverse experiences of transgender and GNC persons. They illustrate that the current research and literature does not encompass the diverse range of identity and experiences among transgender and GNC people. They suggest that "in the future, it may be helpful to identify a microaggression measure that differentiates the experiences of the various individuals within the gender identity minority spectrum. A valid and reliable measure may provide a tool to gather more quantitative data on the experiences of transgender persons" (p.229).

Intersectional Microaggressions

Historical narratives, traumatic personal experiences, and witnessing the discrimination of others may amplify the detrimental impact of microaggressions (Evans-Campbell, 2008; Sterzing *et al.*, 2017). As people are comprised of multiple and intersecting identities, their experiences of bias and discrimination may be compounded. Intersectional microaggressions are "those microaggressions that are encountered as a result of one's intersectional or multiple identities" (Nadal, 2013, p.110); thus, the impact of microaggressions may be "a profoundly more complex issue when experienced by people with intersecting, marginalized identities" (Sterzing *et al.*, 2017, pp.81–82). The research on intersectional microaggressions is currently limited, although there have been some studies that address the issue (Balsam *et al.*, 2011; Nadal *et al.*, 2012).

Indie Harper (2012) remembered, as a young Asian boy, dreaming of a fantastic community of other gay people that would warmly accept him. When the time came for him to meet his community, the welcome he had dreamed of did not come. He recalled approaching a group of men who simply stared at him and walked away. One of the men, he said, even rolled his eyes. The moment was a disappointment and his additional experiences continued to be so even ten years later. As Harper shares his story, he lets the reader in on a back-and-forth conversation with his black friend, who is also gay, where they debate who is least accepted within the gay community, black or Asian people. He said the message of exclusion "gets pounded into your bones, tattooed on your skin" (pp.133–134).

Microaggressions in Clinical Practice

LGBTQ people often delay or decline to seek mental health services for fear of discrimination (Sharman, 2016). There is considerable research on the impact of microaggressions on the therapeutic relationship and client experience. From responses to a focus group of 16 self-identifying LGBQ people in psychotherapy, Shelton and Delgado-Romero (2011) analyzed and distilled seven ways microaggressions occur in the therapeutic space: assumption that sexual orientation is the cause of all presenting problems; avoidance/minimization of sexual orientation; over-identifying; making stereotypical assumptions; expressions of heteronormative bias; assumption that sexual minorities need psychotherapeutic treatment; and warnings about the dangers of identifying as LGBQ (p.215).

Margaret Robinson (2016) is bisexual and has been out for over 20 years with family, friends and coworkers. She chooses, however, not to disclose her sexual orientation to healthcare providers due to several microaggressive experiences. She recounted:

> I've had a therapist ask voyeuristic questions and imply that my bisexuality was the root of my stress, and I've had clinic staff assume that my bisexual identity means I have sex with multiple partners and am at high risk for sexually transmitted infections. These experiences left me feeling powerless and angry, and they did nothing to reduce my stress. (p.176)

As Margaret notes, her experiences are not uncommon. For example, a 2015 study of 2500 LGB people found that bisexual people are less comfortable than gay men and lesbian women speaking to healthcare providers about their sexual identity (Smalley, Warren, & Barefoot, 2015).

Therapists can negatively impact the client's experience and/or progress through microaggressive comments and actions. Spengler, Miller, and Spengler (2016, p.361) offer an example of a potential client named Charlie, a gay man, who was seeking a sexual minority (SM) affirmative therapist. He found someone who advertised that she was interested in issues of diversity. When he called the therapist, he noted difficulties in his relationship as a result of increased anxiety. The therapist responded by asking, 'Okay, we can certainly talk about that. Is your girlfriend or wife planning to attend sessions with you?' Charlie responded by saying, "Oh...well, actually...it's my boyfriend. I'm gay. And actually I was wondering, it's kind of important to me... do you happen to be gay yourself?" The therapist responded reluctantly, noting that she did not usually disclose this information and expressed discomfort with offering a reply. The therapist offered that she and Charlie could continue the discussion in her office and Charlie agreed.

Once at his appointment, Charlie was aware that the brochures and magazines in the therapist's office had images of hetersosexual couples, there were no informationals related to SM issues, and the intake form did not acknowledge or make space for clients with SM identities. Charlie experienced a barrage of microaggressions from the therapist including her comments, assumptions, discomfort, and unwillingness to engage in open conversation as well as an invalidating environment.

Clinicians must be mindful of their default assumptions, and conscious and unconscious biases, and challenge rigid narratives (Williams, 2016). Awareness of the clinician's internalized hetero and gender normative beliefs and how they inform therapeutic interactions and assessments is a necessary component of ethical care. Left unchecked, a clinician's hetero and gender biases can result in harm in the form of microaggressive words and/or actions, potentially causing or contributing to discriminatory stress.

Minority Stress

Prejudice and discrimination can occur relatively unexpectedly. LGBTQ people work to adjust to living in a prejudiced, cisnormative, heterosexist social world. As a result of attempting to fit in, sexual and gender minorities experience significant and debilitating stress. It was once believed that adverse mental health outcomes of LGBTQ people were directly related to their sexual and gender identities. With decriminalization and the removal of homosexuality and gender identity disorder as mental disorders, it is better understood that the mental health challenges experienced by the LGBTQ community are strongly rooted in the adverse social conditions of living with a stigmatized identity within a heteronormative and cisnormative society; we do acknowledge that we still have a way to go, given the current nature of certain diagnostic manuals. Recent research, however, has shown that LGBTQ individuals have a greater risk of mental and physical health challenges or psychological distress than their heterosexual and cisgender counterparts, and this greater prevalence is directly related to stressors that occur as a result of their sexual and/or gender minority status (Meyer, 2003; Velez et al., 2017).

In his seminal research study, "Minority stress and mental health in gay men," Ilan Meyer (1995) offered the term *minority stress*, derived from minority status, to refer to the chronic stress gay people experience as a result of living in a heteronormative society. Like members of other minority groups, LGB people experience stress related to stigmatization, which compounds the general stress all members of society experience. Gay men who experience high levels of minority stress are two to three times more likely to experience high levels of distress (Meyer, 1995). Minority stress is noted, then, to be unique, chronic, and socially based (Meyer, 2003).

The minority stress model has become a widely accepted framework to understand the mental health outcomes of sexual and gender minorities. Meyer (2003) proposed four processes of minority stress relevant to LGB individuals:

> From the distal to the proximal they are (a) external, objective stressful events and conditions (chronic and acute), (b) expectations of such events and the vigilance this expectation requires, and (c) the internalization of negative societal attitudes...[d] concealment of one's sexual orientation. (p.678)

Put simply, the four forms of minority stress, respectively, for sexual minorities are prejudice events (sexual prejudice), expectation of stigmatization, internalized heterosexism (internalized homophobia), and identity concealment (passing or covering).

Although Meyer's research predominantly focused on sexual orientation, the minority stress model is applicable to transgender and gender non-conforming (TGNC) individuals as well. A growing body of research has been exploring the minority stress model to account for the psychological distress and adverse mental health outcomes for TGNC individuals. Bockting *et al.* (2013) demonstrated that TGNC individuals report high rates of depression, anxiety, somatization, and psychological distress compared with their gender normative counterparts and this distress is associated with enacted and felt stigma. In comparison with nontrans LGB individuals, TGNC individuals are more likely to report discrimination, symptoms of depression, and attempted suicides (Su *et al.*, 2016). Gender minority stress, similar to sexual minority stress, ranges from distal to proximal stressors.

Utilizing the Virginia Transgender Health Initiative Survey (THIS) of transgender people, Testa and colleagues (2012) found that both trans men and trans women who have experienced distal stressors such as physical or sexual violence reported higher incidents of suicide, multiple suicide attempts, and/or substance abuse than individuals who had not endured violence. Out of the 350 transgender individuals surveyed almost half reported a history of victimization and out of those physically victimized 97.7% reported that their gender identity and expression was the reason for the victimization.

The National Transgender Discrimination Survey (NTDS), the largest ever study of the experiences of TGNC people, was conducted in 2011 with 6450 TGNC Americans participating. The results of the survey indicated that 63% of participants experienced serious acts of discrimination, defined as events that would have a significant impact on quality of life, and 23% reported catastrophic levels of discrimination, defined by experiencing at least three significant forms of discrimination. These events may have included: loss of job or eviction due to bias; bullying or harassment in school or workplace; physical or sexual assault due to bias; homelessness; rejection in relationship; denial of medical services; and incarceration (Grant, Mottet, & Tanis, 2011). It seems every week in the news we are hearing more and more accounts of trans individuals being murdered, raped, or beaten, especially trans women of color; despite the frequency of news reports, these violent incidents go under-reported, which may be due to TGNC individuals' experiences and fear of being further discriminated against and challenges with proximal stressors.

Despite most previous research having focused on the impact of distal minority stress, recent research contends that proximal or internal stressors may be just as detrimental to the health and well-being of TGNC individuals. Hendricks and Testa (2012) adapted the model to speak to the adverse experiences of TGNC individuals, demonstrating that gender minorities experience proximal stressors such as expectations of future victimization or rejection and internalized transphobia. More recently, Rood and colleagues' (2016) qualitative research explored TGNC individuals' experiences with expecting rejection, which is a specific proximal stressor identified in Meyer's original conceptualization of the minority stress model. Their research demonstrated that the experience of expecting rejection is a common one for TGNC individuals and that these experiences of felt stigma were intense and life-threatening, ultimately internalized as being an expected part of their lived experience of being a gender minority. The occurrence of internalization and normalization needs to be understood and addressed from a clinical and public health perspective in order to support TGNC clients and mitigate systemic oppression.

The aforementioned research focused predominantly on adults, but it is important to understand the implications for LGBTQ youth. Applying the minority stress model to LGBTQ young people, Kelleher (2009) further demonstrated support for the application of this model. The results of her study on LGBTQ youth aged 16–24 demonstrated that minority stressors significantly predicted negative mental health outcomes among the youth studied. Heterosexism was the strongest predictor of adverse psychological outcomes. Additionally, the greater the expectation of LGBTQ-based rejection, the more likely youth reported symptoms of anxiety, depression, and suicidal ideation. It is clear that psychological distress among LGBTQ youth can be causally linked to the cultural ideologies upheld by a heteronormative and cisnormative society—a society that views LGBTQ youth as not heterosexual, not gender normative, and, therefore, other.

Sexual and Gender Minority Stress and LGBTQ People of Color

Research about holding multiple minority statuses is relatively new and results are mixed with regard to whether or not multiple minority identities exacerbates minority stress. Some research indicates that holding more than one minority identity increases minority stress and, therefore, exacerbates adverse health outcomes (Alessi, 2014). According to Meyer, Schwartz and Frost (2008) black and Latinx LGB individuals are more likely to experience stressful events compared with their white LGB counterparts. However, Velez *et al.* (2017) found that there was no significant difference between racial and ethnic minority (REM) sexual minorities and white sexual minorities with regard to level of heterosexist discrimination, proximal minority stressors, or mental health outcomes.

McNair (2017) maintained that intersecting minority identities may result in cumulative risk to health given the compounding disadvantages that come with holding multiple minority roles. The messages and societal attitudes towards LGBTQ and other marginalized people makes microaggressive comments and circumstances a chronic and persistent experience for some. Moreover, the experience of dual minority status of identifying as TGNC and a person of color can compound the stress around expecting rejection. Rood and colleagues (2016) demonstrated that TGNC people of color report being prepared to experience gender-related rejection based on their lived experience of discrimination as a result of their race or ethnicity. TGNC people of color, compared with their white counterparts, experience rejection more frequently, whereas white TGNC individuals have a level of privilege that perhaps reduces the expectation of rejection. Given that some gender minorities may also identify as sexual minorities, future research should explore the intersections of these two identity categories that make up the LGBTQ community and the ways in which those with this specific intersection may experience compounded stress and adverse mental health outcomes.

During a 2013 event, Laverne Cox, a trans actress of color, described an incident that happened which highlights an intersectional microaggressive experience. She explained:

> It was the Fourth of July, and I was wearing a red, white and blue dress. I was feeling very patriotic, and it was really tight. And I passed these two men. One appeared to be Latino, and the other appeared to be black. The Latin guy says, "Yo, mama, can I holla at you?" And the black guy said, "Yo dude, that's an n-word." And then the Latin guy says, "No, man, that's a bitch." The black guy said, "No, that's an n-word." (Keppler Speakers, 2013)

Cox noted that this went back and forth for a bit as she anxiously awaited the light to turn, until at one point one of the men turned to her and said, "You ain't an n-word, are you?" When the men realized she was trans, she said, "It became something else...it turned into something else." Cox noted that this is a common experience for trans women and highlighted the danger that can accompany these experiences. She spoke to the frequency of trans women being harassed, catcalled, and killed when pursuers realize they are trans and said, "Our lives are often in danger simply for being who we are when we are trans women." She highlighted the complexity within the intersections of identity and marginalization that emerge in moments such as this, and noted that in her experience "it was a moment where misogyny was intersecting with transphobia was intersecting with some racist stuff." Cox further underscores how internalized racism might have impacted the way the two men approached her that evening and she roots this point in historical context. Yet what is also illuminated in this incident is the experiencing of proximal stress. The danger that Cox speaks to and the anxiety that she names is at once personal and collective. Standing at this red light, Cox was holding both her lived experience in the moment and also that which she had internalized from knowing and seeing the harm that so many trans women of color have experienced.

Additional research is needed to better understand the compounded experience of multiple minority identities on stress and adverse mental health outcomes. Clinicians must not assume that multiple minority identities are the sole and root causes of a client's stress.

Clinical Implications

It is important to remind our reader that sexual orientation and gender identity are not signs of pathology and should not be treated as such. It is clear, however, that LGBTQ individuals experience significant stress as a result of their sexual and/or gender minority status, as they live in a cis- and heteronormative society which others them, and that this stress, both distal and proximal, lead to adverse mental health outcomes. LGBTQ people are at a higher risk for suicidal behavior, psychological disorders, and substance use than heterosexual and cisgender people (Goldblum *et al.*, 2012; King *et al.*, 2008; Meyer, 2003; Testa *et al.*, 2012). Perceived discrimination is predictive of depressive symptoms among sexual and gender minorities (McCarthy *et al.*, 2014). There is also an indication that minority stress in the form of a prejudice event "can be more damaging to physical health than general stressful life events that do not involve prejudice" (Frost, Lehavot, & Meyer, 2015, p.7).

The minority stress model conceptualizes both distal and proximal causes; therefore, ways of responding, coping, and other interventions need to occur at personal, or individual, levels as well as social, or structural, levels. With distal causes of distress, the focus needs to be on eliminating the sources of stress within the social environment. Additionally, public policy and public health need to create and implement interventions to mitigate prejudice and discrimination, and reduce anti-gay and anti-trans violence, in an effort to create more supportive social environments for LGBTQ individuals (Meyer, 2007). With proximal causes of distress, individual interventions need to be utilized, such as prevention programs, as well as clinical interventions that focus on helping LGBTQ clients deal with issues related to internalized heterosexism, transphobia, rejection, and discrimination. Individual interventions should also take into account, yet not rely upon, the LGBTQ client's resiliency. Additionally, social support should be incorporated into coping with minority stress. It is important to remember that sexual and gender minority identity can serve as a source of support as LGBTQ people find connection within their own community.

Meyer (2007) offers us "minority coping," which is a community-based resource related to the LGBTQ community's "ability to mount self-enhancing structures to counteract stigma" by adopting "some of the group's self-enhancing attitudes, values, and structures rather than the degree to which individuals vary in their personal coping abilities" (p.257). In other words, LGBTQ people may cope with minority stress by maintaining connections to and within their community. By maintaining this connection, minority group members can evaluate themselves and their capabilities based on those who are similar to them (Alessi, 2014). As a result, the LGBTQ community offers a re-evaluation that may ultimately improve mental health (Meyer, 2003).

Like Meyer's original research, current research has been exploring coping strategies and the role of resilience in combating gender minority stress. Rood et al. (2016) explored adaptive responses to expecting rejection, including situational avoidance, environmental assessment of perceived and real threats, rehearsing responses and reaction to identified threats, and moving through potentially threatening environments with friends to increase a sense of safety. Identification with and support from other TGNC individuals has been shown to mitigate the detrimental impact of minority stress through the development of resiliency (Bockting et al., 2013; Testa et al., 2012). Additionally, higher levels of self-acceptance of TGNC identity reduce the potential of depressive symptoms (Su et al., 2016). Moreover, trans men and trans women who had prior awareness of other trans individuals at the time of their coming out were less likely to report feelings of suicidality; the same, however, was not true for non-binary trans people within the community—an important reminder to not assume and apply global experiences to the TGNC community.

Although the minority stress model calls for minority coping and in-group support, it is also important to note the possibility of inter-group conflict within the LGBTQ community, among sexual minorities, among gender minorities, and between LGB and TGNC individuals. Historically, at the early stages of the LGBTQ rights movement, conflict existed between sexual minorities and gender minorities. There was a point where the TGNC community was isolated by their LGB counterparts, as they began fighting and advocating with different priorities in mind. Although the LGBTQ community and their acronym came back together in formation in the 1990s, these historical conflicts may still preside consciously and unconsciously within the community.

Although societally considered a strong community, the LGBTQ community is not free from bias and prejudices against each other. Transphobia, biphobia, and genderism are present within the community as well. Within the TGNC community, you will find differing opinions around medical transition, with some finding this an affirming opportunity, whereas for others it may be less so, especially those who are trans non-binary. Narrative erasure has been present within the community as well. The LGBTQ rights movement can be traced back to starting with two activists who were also trans women of color, Marsha P. Johnson and Sylvia Rivera. Their stories, however, have only recently been given credit and there are those in the movement who continue to refuse to credit gender non-conforming individuals for starting the modern movement, seeking to share a more "mainstream" image of queer rights. We do not share this to further divide the community, but want to bring to light the notion that individuals who belong to marginalized communities are also implicated in the perpetuation of dominant narratives, which in some respect is a result of internalized stigma and oppression from the hetero- and cisnormative narratives that dominate our social and political world. Additional research is needed in this area to fully expand our understanding of these topics.

Overall, when conceptualizing treatment for LGBTQ clients experiencing minority stress, clinicians need to take into consideration techniques and modalities that address both individual concerns and choices that address the social environment for systemic change. The minority stress model is not designed to offer the clinician or client a direct map for treatment or support, but rather offers a framework to conceptualize treatment and care; it offers the creative arts therapist the opportunity to select appropriate levels of interventions given the type of minority stress experienced as well as a strengths- and needs-based assessment. Ultimately, there is a need for specific interventions to address minority stress.

In order to develop effective treatment interventions for LGBTQ clients, clinicians need to recognize the impact minority stress has on the health and wellness of their sexual and gender minority clients. It is furthermore important for clinicians to increase their own understanding of how minority stress impacts their clients, as well as how, as a clinician, they may be contributing to the minority stress of their clients.

Creative arts therapists need to develop specific interventions to assist their LGBTQ clients who seek therapy specifically for assistance in coping with challenges related to their sexual and gender minority status.

Therapist Self-Assessment

People are deeply and perpetually biased by nature (Ross, 2014) and tend to prefer those with whom there is a shared likeness, whether real or perceived. It can be challenging to acknowledge personally held discriminatory and biased beliefs; consequently, a prevalent defense against this tension is to deny any such prejudice. Audre Lorde (1984) once advised:

> Racism and homophobia are real conditions of all our lives in this place and time. I urge each one of us here to reach down into that deep place of knowledge inside herself and touch that terror and loathing of any difference that lives here. See whose face it wears. Then the personal as the political can begin to illuminate all our choices. (p.113)

Clinicians must be aware of their personal value and belief systems (Levitt & Moorhead, 2013) and should have an ongoing practice of acknowledging, exploring, and challenging biased beliefs towards ethical practice (Williams, 2017). Clinicians' intersections of identity, personal beliefs, and relationship(s) to power and privilege will impact their assumptions and assessments of clients. These writers contend that being mindful of these issues and an ongoing process of self-awareness is an ethical responsibility of the therapist. These authors suggest implementing self-assessment tools into one's practice as a way to identify, explore, and challenge rigid biases in support of just services.

Williams (2016), a drama therapist, developed an engaging and interactive curriculum designed to help therapists and others identify, explore, and challenge their biases. Building on the creative and embodied principles of drama therapy, the curriculum incorporates projective techniques including visual art, diverse images of people, and story to illuminate default mechanisms and unconscious biases. The curriculum is intended to highlight the ease with which we create stories about individuals and groups; furthermore, it encourages participants to take note of their default assumptions and biases and seeks to disrupt rigid and harmful narratives in a creatively engaged and embodied manner.

It also addresses the impact of societal, media, social, and cultural influences that impact individuals' assumptions and biased beliefs.

Hays (2008) developed the ADDRESSING framework, which invites clinicians to explore their relationship to power, privilege, and marginalization across several categories. Hays noted that experiencing marginalization in one or more identity categories does not exempt someone from holding power and privilege in others. Conversely, a person may hold power and privilege in one or more capacities while being marginalized in others. The categories outlined in Hays's ADDRESSING framework are: age and generational influences, developmental disability/disability acquired later in life, religion and spiritual orientation, ethnic and racial identity, socioeconomic status, sexual orientation, indigenous heritage, national origin, and gender.

Powell (2016), a drama therapist, expanded on Hays's model and developed an embodied multicultural assessment that is useful for the creative arts therapist. Powell combines the ADDRESSING framework (outlined above) with Landy's role taxonomy, a thorough distillation of roles from Western literature divided into six domains: somatic, cognitive, affective, social, spiritual, and aesthetic. Powell explains that Landy's taxonomy aligns with the ADDRESSING framework, because "each identity listed can be seen as roles we play as a result of family, society, and biology, some of which might change over time and experience" (p.116). Her embodied assessment invites clinicians to explore the roles that emerge for them within each category in a creative and engaged manner.

Powell (2016) noted that the goal of an embodied multicultural assessment is to encourage therapists "to consider their own intersecting identities, their relationships to privileges and power, and provide an embodied way to explore these in a group setting" (p.116). Williams (2017) builds on the exploration of self-understanding through her Relational-Roles Assessment Protocol (R-RAP) which allows clinicians to assess their beliefs, attitudes, and emergent roles in relationship to clients and explore the subsequent impact and influence on the therapeutic relationship. Williams's assessment tool also uses Landy's role taxonomy and offers embodied exercises to highlight the therapist's countertransference, increase empathy and awareness, and explore the intersubjective experience(s).

The tools outlined above have been developed to help therapists identify their relationships to power and privilege, disrupt rigid assumptions, and illuminate unconscious biases. It is crucial that therapists examine their personally held social and cultural belief systems as these influence every interaction and decision that one makes (Ross, 2014; Williams, 2017). This work can be challenging, and Hays (2008) observed that defensive responses may emerge in the therapist's process of self-assessment; she suggested using breath work and humor to navigate these feelings, which can be difficult and/or overwhelming to tolerate. Self-compassion and understanding are necessary components of therapists' consciousness (Williams, 2016) and a willingness to "boldly" encounter prejudiced and biased belief systems (Myers, 2014). It can be helpful within this practice to challenge the notion of cultural competence, which suggests mastery can be achieved. A more helpful frame, these authors contend, is striving for continual cultural understanding.

These writers endorse working with cultural humility, which entails "relinquishing the role of 'expert' and seeking to understand the other's perspective" (Martin, 2016, p.6). In so doing, clinicians release the idea that they can inherently know the experience(s) of another and are aware that they cannot know the story of another without that person's input. This way of working moves towards a process of understanding, and recognizes that the process is continuous.

In recognizing that we are inherently biased, it becomes necessary for clinicians to participate in dialogues that foster ethical and just practices. We assert that it is necessary to engage in conversations that allow for creative explorations of self and other and examining the impact of practices and processes on LGBTQ clients. To that end, we have offered a guide aimed at supporting discussions among clinicans on LGBTQ microaggressions and exploring the impact of oppressive systems on clinical practice.

A Guide for Queering the Conversation

This guide offers ways to engage in dialogue and discussion towards pushing against oppressive structures and challenging heteronormative and cisnormative narratives. Resources and questions to consider are offered for those facilitating dialogues, developing workshops or trainings, or engaging in self-study for professional growth and development. This is meant as a supportive tool and is not an exhaustive list of resources or topics. We encourage clinicians to expand on and add to the sections offered here as necessary.

Therapist's Own Identity

Exploring one's own multiple and intersecting identities helps clinicians deepen their awareness of their own lived experience and also their perception of others. It allows for an exploration of how cultural values and beliefs might impact how you view and treat others including within the therapeutic relationship and treatment process.

QUESTIONS TO CONSIDER AND EXPLORE

In which identity categories do you hold power and privilege?

In which identity categories do you experience marginalization?

How do the system and/or social world in which you live and work impact you and your identity?

SUGGESTED RESOURCES

Therapist self-assessment (Hays, 2008)

Embodied self-assessment exploration (Powell, 2016)

Exploration of Client's Identity

It can be helpful to explore not only your client's multiple and intersecting identities but also your perception and viewpoint(s) of their identity categories and how that intersects with your own identity composition, values and viewpoints. This type of self-assessment work can be helpful to illuminate unconscious biases and increase empathy and understanding.

QUESTIONS TO CONSIDER AND EXPLORE

Do you feel comfortable speaking openly with your client about their multiple and intersecting identities?

What are identities that you and your client share in common? How might this impact the therapeutic encounter and process?

What are identities that you and your client do not share in common? How might this impact the therapeutic encounter and process?

How does the system and/or social world in which you work impact your client?

SUGGESTED RESOURCES

Exploring client's identity (Hays, 2008; Hook *et al.*, 2017)

Embodied exploration (Hodermarska, 2013; Trottier & Hilt, 2017; Williams, 2017)

Benefits and challenges in embodying our clients (Landy *et al.*, 2012; Trottier & Hilt, 2017)

Exploration of the Political

The changing political climate has a direct impact on people's lives. An awareness and understanding of how current policies and social climate might impact your LGBTQ clients is an important part of fostering empathy and understanding.

QUESTIONS TO CONSIDER AND EXPLORE

How might the current political climate directly impact LGBTQ clients?

When there is political unrest there can be a shift seen in treatment spaces. How might these shifts be engaged and explored within treatment?

Who brings the conversation into the room? Do you bring into the room political issues that may impact your client or only address them if your client brings it up? What influences your thoughts about who should bring these discussions into the room?

Sharing Oversights, Missteps, and Ruptures

A practice of recognizing and owning oversights and microaggressions that occur in clinical practice fosters accountability. Furthermore, this practice is a necessary aspect of shifting and challenging unconscious biases and fostering just practices.

QUESTIONS TO CONSIDER AND EXPLORE

Do you discuss oversights, missteps, and ruptures in supervision or with your colleagues?

How do you practice self-compassion in the process of recognizing and owing oversights, missteps, ruptures, and microaggressions?

Do you feel comfortable addressing oversights, missteps, and ruptures with your client(s) when you recognize them, even if your client does not mention it?

SUGGESTED RESOURCES

Repairing ruptures (Hook *et al.*, 2017)

Cultural impasses (Gaztambide, 2012)

Considerations for Practice Assessment and Discussion

To create an affirming clinical practice, it is useful to develop a self-reflective and critically conscious practice assessment. The aesthetic of the therapist, their performance, and the therapeutic space should be assessed for the tools being utilized and the choices being made. The therapist who has thought critically about the fit or best practices of their clinical choices may develop an increased sense of flexibility and confidence in the delivery of affirmative care.

QUESTIONS TO CONSIDER AND EXPLORE

What does the therapist's space/physical environment communicate to LGBTQ clients (e.g. are books, bathrooms, and images LGBTQ representative and inclusive)?

What messages do the therapist's materials and resources send to LGBTQ clients (including intake paperwork and brochures)?

Are paperwork and other materials LGBTQ representative and inclusive?

What does the therapist's language communicate to LGBTQ clients (e.g. does the therapist use gender inclusive language, does the therapist make heterosexist assumptions)?

Considering the Voices That Are Missing

There is a depth and breadth to diversity and not all voices may be present or represented in dialogue. It is important to acknowledge those perspectives and lived experiences that may be missing. It may be useful to explore ways to incorporate additional narratives into your own self-reflective practice as well as when facilitating dialogues with other clinicians. "Who is missing?" is a historically queer question worth naming and exploring.

QUESTIONS TO CONSIDER AND EXPLORE

How do you create a space for people to have these conversations?

How can conversations be inclusive when those present do not represent the diversity of identity and experience?

How might story be used to represent voices that are missing? How can reading narratives of those whose identifiers are different than yours expand your understanding?

Continuing Education, Training, and Dialogue

Fostering a practice that is affirming, inclusive, and dedicated to just services requires an ongoing process of learning, self-reflection, and practice assessment.

QUESTION TO CONSIDER AND EXPLORE

What is your ongoing education, training, and self-assessment commitment and process?

Conclusion

In this chapter we highlighted the ways in which biases, microaggressions, and minority stress impact the lives of LGBTQ persons in the therapeutic encounter and also the larger world. Our review of literature underscored work and research that has been done in this domain. We also provided a guide for facilitating dialogues that challenge the perpetuation of and complicity with oppressive systems. It was our intention to underscore the necessity of clinicians tending to their own biases in support of ethical and inclusive care and to provide an engaging guide that supports this aim.

References

Alessi, E.J. (2014) 'A framework for incorporating minority stress theory into treatment with sexual minority clients.' *Journal of Gay and Lesbian Mental Health 18*, 47–66.

Balsam, K.F., Molina, Y., Beadnell, B., Simoni, J., & Walters, K. (2011) 'Measuring multiple minority stress: The LGBT People of Color Microaggressions Scale.' *Cultural Diversity and Ethnic Minority Psychology 17*, 2, 163–174.

Beauregard, M., Stone, M., Trytan, N., & Sajnani, N. (2016) 'Drama therapists' attitudes actions regarding LGBTQI and gender nonconforming communities.' *Drama Therapy Review 2*, 1, 41–63.

Bockting, W.O., Miner, M.H., Swinburne Romine, R.E., Hamilton, A., & Coleman, E. (2013) 'Stigma, mental health, and resilience in an online sample of the US transgender population.' *American Journal of Public Health 103*, 943–951.

Browne, D.R., Mickiewicz, E.P., & Firestone, C.M. (1994) *Television/Radio News and Minorities*. Queenstown, MD: Aspen Institute.

Chang, T.K. & Chung, Y.B. (2015) 'Transgender microaggressions: Complexity of the heterogeneity of transgender identities.' *Journal of LGBT Issues in Counselling 9*, 3, 217–234.

Crenshaw, K. (1993) 'Mapping the margins: Intersectionality, identity politics, and violence against women of color.' *Stanford Law Review 43*, 1241–1299.

Evans-Campbell, T. (2008) 'Historical trauma in American Indian/Native Alaska communities: A multilevel framework for exploring impacts on individuals, families, and communities.' *Journal of Interpersonal Violence 23*, 3, 316–338.

Frost, D.M., Lehavot, K., & Meyer, I.H. (2015) 'Minority stress and physical health among sexual minority individuals.' *Journal of Behavioral Medicine 38*, 1, 1–8.

Gaztambide, D.J. (2012) 'Addressing cultural impasses with rupture resolution strategies: A proposal and recommendations.' *Professional Psychology: Research and Practice 43*, 3, 183–189.

Goldblum, P., Testa, R.J., Pflum, S., Hendricks, M.L., Bradford, J., & Bongar, B. (2012) 'The relationship between gender-based victimization and suicide attempts in transgender people.' *Professional Psychology: Research and Practice 43*, 5, 468–475.

Grant, J.M., Mottet, L.A., & Tanis, J. (2011) *Injustice at Every Turn: A Report of the National Transgender Discrimination Survey*. Accessed on 11/8/2018 at http://endtransdiscrimination.org/PDFs/NTDS_Report.pdf.

Harper, I. (2012) 'No Asians, Blacks, Fats, or Femmes.' In K. Boykin (ed.) *For Colored Boys Who Have Considered Suicide When the Rainbow Is Still Not Enough: Coming of Age, Coming Out, and Coming Home*. New York, NY: Magnus.

Hays, P.A. (2008) *Addressing Cultural Complexities in Practice: Assessment, Diagnosis, and Therapy*. Washington, DC: American Psychological Association.

Hendricks, M.L. & Testa, R.J. (2012) 'A conceptual framework for clinical work with transgender and gender nonconforming clients: An adaptation of the Minority Stress Model.' *Professional Psychology: Research and Practice 43*, 5, 460–467.

Hodermarska, M. (2013) 'Body knowledge and living enquiry in clinical supervision.' *International Conference of Expressive Therapies and Psychotherapy Focused on Body and Psychosomatic Approach.* Olomouc, Czech Republic, Palacky University.

Hook, J.N., Davis, D.D., Owen, J., & DeBlaere, C. (2017) *Cultural Humility: Engaging Diverse Identities in Therapy.* Washington, DC: American Psychological Association.

Kelleher, C. (2009) 'Minority stress and health: Implications for lesbian, gay, bisexual, transgender, and questioning (LGBTQ) young people.' *Counselling Psychology Quarterly 22*, 4, 373–379.

Keppler Speakers (2013) *Laverne Cox on Bullying and Being a Trans Woman of Color.* [Video file]. Accessed on 11/8/2018 at www.youtube.com/watch?v=7zwy5PEEa6U.

King, M., Semlyen, J., Tai, S.S., Killaspy, J. *et al.* (2008) 'A systematic review of mental disorder, suicide, and deliberate self harm in lesbian, gay and bisexual people.' *BMC Psychiatry 8*, 70.

Lamda Legal (2010) *When Health Care Isn't Caring: Lambda Legal's Survey of Discrimination Against LGBT People and People with HIV.* New York: Lambda Legal. Accessed on 11/8/2018 at www.lambdalegal.org/health-care-report.

Landy, R.J., Hodermarska, M., Mowers, D., & Perrin, D. (2012) 'Performance as arts-based research in drama therapy supervision.' *Journal of Applied Arts and Health 3*, 1, 49–58.

Levitt, D.H. and Moorhead, H.J. (2013) *Values and Ethics in Counseling: Real-Life Ethical Decision Making.* New York, NY: Routledge.

Lockhart, S. (2012) 'Bathtubs and Hot Water.' In K. Boykin (ed.) *For Colored Boys Who Have Considered Suicide When the Rainbow Is Still Not Enough: Coming of Age, Coming Out, and Coming Home.* New York, NY: Magnus.

Lorde, Audre (1984) 'The Master's Tools Will Never Dismantle the Master's House.' In *Sister Outsider: Essays and Speeches.* Berkeley, CA: Crossing Press.

Martin, E. (2016) 'Cultural humility: Seeking another's perspective.' *Texas Nursing Magazine 90*, 4, 6–7.

McCarthy, M.A., Fisher, C.M., Irwin, J.A., Coleman, J.D., & Kneip Pelster, A.D. (2014) 'Using the minority stress model to understand depression in lesbian, gay, bisexual, and transgender individuals in Nebraska.' *Journal of Gay and Lesbian Mental Health 18*, 346–360.

McNair, R.P. (2017) 'Multiple identities and their intersections with queer health and wellbeing.' *Journal of Intercultural Studies 38*, 4, 443–452.

Meyer, I.H. (1995) 'Minority stress and mental health in gay men.' *Journal of Health and Social Behavior 36*, 38–56.

Meyer, I.H. (2003) 'Prejudice, social stress, and mental health in lesbian, gay, and bisexual populations: Conceptual issues and research evidence.' *Psychological Bulletin 129*, 5, 674–697.

Meyer, I.H. (2007) 'Prejudice and Discrimination as Social Stressors.' In I.H. Meyer & M.E. Northridge (eds) *The Health of Sexual Minorities: Public Health Perspective on Lesbian, Gay, Bisexual, and Transgender Populations.* New York, NY: Spring.

Meyer, I.H., Schwartz, S., & Frost, D.M. (2008) 'Social patterning of stress and coping: Does disadvantaged social statuses confer more stress and fewer coping resources?' *Social Science and Medicine 67*, 3, 368–379.

Myers, V. (2014) 'How to overcome our biases? Walk boldly toward them.' TEDxBeaconStreet, November 2014. Accessed on 11/8/2018 at http://linkis.com/ted.com/Verna_Myers_How_to_o.html.

Nadal, K.L. (2013) *That's So Gay: Microaggressions and the Lesbian, Gay, Bisexual, and Transgender Community.* Washington, DC: American Psychological Association.

Nadal, K.L., Issa, M., Leon, J., Meterko, V., Wideman, M., & Wong, Y. (2011) 'Sexual orientation microaggressions: "Death by a thousand cuts" for lesbian, gay, and bisexual youth.' *Journal of LGBT Youth 8*, 3, 234–259.

Nadal, K.L., Skolnik, A., & Wong, Y. (2012) 'Interpersonal and systemic microaggressions toward transgender people: Implications for counseling.' *Journal of LGBT Issues in Counseling 6*, 1, 55–82.

Perez, A. (2005) 'Internalized oppression: How it affects members of the LGBT community.' *The Diversity Factor 13*, 1, 25–29.

Powell, A. (2016) 'Embodied multicultural assessment: An interdisciplinary training model.' *Drama Therapy Review 2*, 1, 111–122.

Robinson, M. (2016) 'Five Things Providers Need to Know about Bisexual People.' In Z. Sharman (ed.) *The Remedy: Queer and Trans Voices on Health and Health Care.* Vancouver, BC: Arsenal Pulp Press.

Rood, B.A., Reisner, S.L., Surace, F.I., Puckett, J.A., Maroney, M.R., & Pantalone, D.W. (2016) 'Expecting rejection: Understanding the minority stress experiences of transgender and gender-nonconforming individuals.' *Transgender Health 1*, 1, 151–164.

Ross, H.J. (2014) *Everyday Bias: Identifying and Navigating Unconscious Judgments in Our Daily Lives.* Lanham, MD: Rowman & Littlefield.

Sharman, Z. (2016) *The Remedy: Queer and Trans Voices on Health and Health Care.* Vancouver, BC: Arsenal Pulp Press.

Shelton, K. & Delgado-Romero, E.A. (2011) 'Sexual orientation microaggressions: The experience of lesbian, gay, bisexual, and queer clients in psychotherapy.' *Journal of Counseling Psychotherapy 58*, 210–221.

Smalley, K.B., Warren, J.C., & Barefoot, K.N. (2015) 'Barriers to care and psychological distress differences between bisexual and gay men and women.' *Journal of Bisexuality 15*, 2, 230–247.

Spengler, E.S., Miller, D.J., & Spengler, P.M. (2016) 'Microaggressions: Clinical errors with sexual minority clients.' *Psychotherapy 53*, 3, 360–366.

Sterzing, P.R., Gartner, R.E., Woodford, M.R., & Fisher, C.M. (2017) 'Sexual orientation, gender, and gender identity microaggressions: Toward an intersectional framework for social work research.' *Journal of Ethnic and Cultural Diversity in Social Work 26*, 1–2, 81–94.

Su, D., Irwin, J.A., Fisher, C., Ramos, A., *et al.* (2016) 'Mental health disparities within the LGBT population: A comparison between transgender and nontransgender individuals.' *Transgender Health 1*, 1, 12–20.

Sue, D.W. (2010) *Microaggressions in Everyday Life: Race, Gender, and Sexual Orientation.* Hoboken, NJ: Wiley.

Testa, R.J., Sciacca, L.M., Wang, P.A., Hendricks, M.L. *et al.* (2012) 'Effects of violence on transgender people.' *Professional Psychology: Research and Practice 43*, 5, 452–459.

Trottier, D.G. & Hilt, L. (2017) 'I don't feel naked: The use of embodied supervision to examine the impact of patient clothing on clinical countertransference on an inpatient psychiatry unit.' *Drama Therapy Review 3*, 2, 261–283.

Velez, B.L., Watson, L.B., Cox, R., & Flores, M.J. (2017) 'Minority stress and racial or ethnic minority status: A test of the great risk perspective.' *Psychology of Sexual Orientation and Gender Diversity 4*, 3, 257–271.

Viehl, C., Dispenza, F., McCullough, R., & Guvensel, K. (2017) 'Burnout among sexual minority mental health practitioners: Investigating correlates and predictors.' *Psychology of Sexual Orientation and Gender Diversity 4*, 3, 354–361.

Williams, B.M. (2016) 'Minding our own biases: Using drama therapeutic tools to identify and challenge assumptions, biases and stereotypes.' *Drama Therapy Review 2*, 1, 9–23.

Williams, B.M. (2017) 'Role power: Using role theory in support of ethical practice.' *Drama Therapy Review 3*, 1, 131–148.

3

Therapist as Guide

Role Profiles, Metaphor, and Story to Understand the Parallel Hero's Journey of the Queer Therapist and the Straight Client

DANA GEORGE TROTTIER

Once upon a time, there was a young boy who would freeze. He was not always frozen, but when he froze it took a lot to thaw out. He was different from most of the other kids at school, but did not have the words to express his otherness. You see, the other boys would often call the boy names like fag or homo. Unaware of how to respond to their taunts, the different boy would freeze. The boy did not know what these names meant, but the intensity with which the words were thrown indicated to the boy that he was not accepted. He was being labeled other, before he understood his otherness. The frozen boy tried his best to behave in a similar way to his peers, but he could never fully commit to a role that felt unnatural. The frozen boy knew that in order to not freeze in the presence of the other boys, he would need to learn how to respond to the names, to the roles he was being asked to play, in a way that would allow him to continue to move rather than freeze.

The Hero's Journey

As a drama therapist, I conceptualize my work with patients through the metaphor of a journey. Together, we embark on a collaborative journey; while separately, we embark on two different, yet parallel journeys. More recently, I have been interested in exploring this parallel journey in an effort to better understand myself, my clients, and the therapeutic relationship. More specifically, I am interested in the parallel journey of the queer therapist and the straight client. How can I use my theoretical frame and practice as a drama therapist to understand this unique, yet common relationship that I find myself actively participating in? How can I use my tools as a creative arts therapist to build role responsiveness to reduce the potential for freezing in the therapeutic relationship?

Predominantly, I work with adults in acute inpatient psychiatry, where I utilize the frame of Landy's hero's journey (2009), adapted from Joseph Campbell (1949), to assist clients in moving through their stay on the psychiatric unit. This metaphoric frame helps me to better understand the clinical narrative, and, perhaps, the same frame can help me understand the parallel journey alongside the patient. Often when clients arrive at the psychiatric unit, depending on symptomatology and the numerous ways of being labeled a danger to themselves, or a danger to others, they will isolate and withdraw, spending long periods of time in their rooms, or they may present with larger performances (symptoms of mania, disorganization, or aggression) that lead others to disengage or avoid. Patient shame performs in a multitude of ways, with the universal goal of disconnecting from others. Further complicating the presentation, the personal narrative of the client in acute care is often incoherent and not readily understood due to an inability to sustain internal dialogue. An inability to hold an internal dialogue results in a disorganized structure and "can lead to a singular inflexible or to a chaotic narrative" (Lysaker, Lysaker, & Lysaker, 2001, p.255). Using the frame of the hero's journey offers a grounding, organized structure and agency, which allows for reconstruction of the story, rebuilding internal dialogue through external dialogue. The goal of the therapist is to help the client see themselves in a larger societal context where they are connected to others. Growth does not develop in isolation; rather, it develops through relationships (Robertson & Lawrence, 2015), where the individual can gain perspective, make meaning, and interact with the world in a different way.

My practice as a drama therapist is informed by the theoretical orientation of Landy's role theory, holding the assumption that each individual is made up of a multitude of roles that can be accessed to assist the individual in organizing their everyday interactions with other individuals and objects, and within themselves (2009). For example, I am queer and a drama therapist: two roles that can be found in my role system (Landy, 1993); two roles that enter into my daily sessions with clients; two roles that have not yet fully integrated with each other. Within role method, treatment is conceptualized as a journey that involves four roles, or characters: the hero, the destination, the obstacle, and the guide (Landy, 2009). Each role on the journey is a part of the individual's personality and gives information as to how they view and interact within themselves and their world. From Landy's iteration of the hero's journey, and much like the greatest stories told, the hero starts out on a journey towards a destination and, while on that journey, encounters an obstacle. Faced with said obstacle, the hero calls upon a guide who assists the hero in moving through the obstacle to arrive at the destination.

In the context of my work in acute care, the patient's (as hero) arrival to the psychiatric unit can be likened to a *call to adventure* (Campbell, 1949). The patient then has the choice to answer or decline the call. If the call is accepted, the patient embarks on a journey towards some destination, which is often physically represented by home and psychologically represented by psychiatric stability; either way, the hope is that the hero ends their journey with a new perspective, or an integration of roles, that allows them to transition back to and live more successfully in the outside world (Landy, 2008; Lawson, 2005; Robertson & Lawrence, 2015). Patient choice in acute care is rare; the hero's journey creates space for choice. Ultimately, by using the hero's journey as a metaphor, the therapist and patient are able to collaborate and make meaning of each other and, in turn, the current situation.

An individual most often comes to therapy when an effective guide is not available. At the onset of the therapeutic work, the therapist typically holds the role of guide until an intrapsychic guide becomes available for the client (Landy, 2009). At the beginning of treatment, the client may cast the therapist into the role of a guide that they think they need, which may be a different role from what the therapist thinks the client needs. Additionally, the role the client casts the therapist in may align or misalign with the therapist's personality, or the performing of the role may not serve the client well. The therapist must find a way to respond, given the clinical information available in the moment; the only information truly available to the therapist in these moments is how they feel in the presence of the client. Although I am made up of a multitude of roles, this chapter focuses specifically on two significant roles: the Queer Person and the Drama Therapist.

Queer Therapist in Performance

Living and moving in a heterocentric society, as a white, cisgender, male therapist, clients often assume I am heterosexual as they cast me into a role of quintessential masculinity: "You must play basketball; you must be a lady killer." In these moments, I am passing. Goffman (1963) first conceptualized the idea of passing, or covering, as a way to refer to individuals who appear as if they do not possess the stigma in question and perform as "normals" (p.5), or, in my case, heterosexual. The act of passing encompasses two defining factors: fit and energy. Fit is the extent to which an individual believes they are conforming to role expectation, whereas energy marks the effort needed to pass (Kanuha, 1999). Passing requires more energy in certain situations than others.

Some clinical situations may indicate a need for me to be "straighter," where I try to intentionally pass (Goffman, 1963)—for example, how I may choose to engage a client who presents with symptoms of paranoia rooted in the reality of a family member identifying as gay; I am less comfortable in these interactions, despite my ability to pass. On the other hand, some clinical situations may indicate a need for queerness, as with a client who has difficulty coming out to their family due to familial and cultural beliefs, or religious affiliations; I am more comfortable in these interactions, while acknowledging the challenge of this work. Moreover, in clinical practice, I feel more comfortable when interacting with queer clients than I do with straight male clients; after all, matching the therapist–client sexual orientation for gay and lesbian patients is mutually beneficial to treatment (Kronner & Northcut, 2015; Liddle, 1996; Porter, Hulbert-Williams, & Chadwick, 2015). In these moments, queerness is working in service of the client—an LGBTQ client sitting across from a therapist who embodies the queer experience offers an understanding and comfort. It creates a coming together, rather than a coming out. Likewise, I feel more comfortable and relaxed when working with straight female clients than straight male clients, and it has been explored that straight female clients feel more comfortable with a self-disclosing gay male therapist than a straight counterpart (Haldeman, 2010). Nonetheless, the clients I serve belong mostly to the heterosexual majority.

Within this chapter and within my life, I identify as queer, which I believe captures not only my sexual orientation but also the intersection of my sexuality and my gender performance as a queer person; I also use queer in an effort to reclaim the word from its archaic, pejorative connotations. In order to provide ethical care, I need to be aware of and acknowledge my intersections, biases, privileges, and limitations (Powell, 2016; Williams, 2016). Although sexual orientation is viewed as an invisible minority, being gay, or queer, does not necessarily equal invisibility. My performance of queerness is visible; the performance can be quiet and it can be loud. I like to think I have become proficient in regulating my queer performance. When individuals interact, social cues offer a way of organizing and understanding the individuals we interact with; this can include body language, physical appearance, choice of dress, and speech (Fuller, Chang, & Rubin, 2009). Clients infer a great deal about the therapist not only from verbal exchanges (explicit) but also from the therapist's physical performance (implicit) (Kronner & Northcut, 2015). These markers offer ways to organize individuals within a social space. An individual may want to hide these markers in an effort to be viewed differently by those they interact with, or an individual may unintentionally pass as a member of the majority (Fuller *et al.*, 2009).

When I trained to be a drama therapist, there was a lack of available resources to speak to the experience of being a queer therapist. Even in my cross-cultural counseling course the focus seemed to be on training heterosexual therapists to work with LGBTQ clients. Work culture certainly influences the therapist's choice to be out (Falzarano & Pizzie, 2015). "Oppressive forces, such as homophobia, heterosexism, and internalized homophobia influence the level of identity synthesis for the therapist regardless of client's sexual orientation" (Satterly, 2006, p.245). The duality of identity that comes with being queer and a therapist requires self-reflection—a level of self-analysis: how the therapist sees themselves versus how the world sees the therapist. Through identity synthesis, or integration from a role theory perspective, the synthesized therapist presents a more authentic self, reducing the experience of internal struggle, or paradoxical dissonance.

Being a queer-identifying therapist working with LGBTQ clients comes with its own unique territory to traverse, but acceptance is not typically one of those challenges. As a queer therapist working with straight clients, however, there are potential complications around acceptance. Satterly (2006) posited that the performance of oppression between a gay therapist and straight client presents itself in three forms: "heterosexism (client assumes therapist is straight), negative comments (a client makes disparaging remark about gay people), and therapist projection of homophobia onto the client" (p.245). These performances of oppression lead the queer therapist to discover alternative ways of responding in terms of self-disclosure. When it comes to disclosure, the therapist develops theories about which situations are risky for disclosure, but risk is not the only factor; intimacy with another can lead to disclosure, or to feelings of guilt for not disclosing (Goffman, 1963).

For example, when asked specifically by a straight client about sexual orientation, I struggle with maintaining authenticity while also preserving the real relationship (Satterly, 2006). There is not a prescriptive response that I can give to these questions, nor would I truly want one. Each of these moments is unique, and the therapist makes the determination to disclose or not, neither right nor wrong. I have directly answered questions around my sexuality, and other times I have not. I have even become defensive and told the client it was too personal a question ("Have you ever been asked if you're straight?"). I have used humor as well as exaggerated facial expressions or embodiment to create confusion or imply a level of discomfort. I have also deflected the question as well as responded with "If you can connect that question back to the topic at hand, perhaps we can both understand the need for knowing the answer." Moreover, I have used the question to create immediacy: "I am wondering if what you really want to know is if I can understand your experience." Again, these moments span the spectrum of being handled with ease and seemingly feeling as if I failed; navigating tough questions in treatment does not come with a guide map. I still get caught up at times when asked directly about my sexual orientation.

On the other hand, when a client assumes I am straight, I can often play out the role that is projected, or seemingly needed. When the straight client, who initially assumed a shared identity, discovers the contrary, however, a shift of sorts can occur in the relationship, which may result in mistrust (Kronner & Northcut, 2015), as their assumption is shattered. When a client assumes I am gay and they are LGBTQ affirming, my queer performance confirms their assumption, aligns our shared worldviews, and therapeutic rapport typically develops more quickly. Research demonstrates that individuals perceive the disclosing gay and lesbian counselor as more trustworthy than their nondisclosing counterparts (Carroll *et al.*, 2011). A client utilizing knowledge of my queerness in an effort to join me often signifies a level of trust between the two of us; whether I join back, signifying some level of admittance or self-disclosure can be challenging to navigate.

Therapist self-disclosure can take many forms. Self-disclosure can be deliberate, unavoidable, or inadvertent (Barnett, 2011) as well as verbal, nonverbal, or unconscious (Carroll *et al.*, 2011). Moreover, Kooden (1991) created six categories of self-disclosure: philosophical (sharing of perspective or facts), countertransference (reactions to client), emotional (emotions conveyed in session), relational (experience of client in session), fantasy (fantasies stimulated during impasse), and historical (explicit information specific to the therapist's life). Disclosures may not only be verbally articulated by the therapist to the client, but also through the dynamic relationship the client is able to deduce from the therapist's behavior in session (Carroll *et al.*, 2011; Russell, 2006). In my clinical practice, I have become acutely aware of the qualities of certain behaviors or performances that clients utilize to form their understanding of my queerness: posturing, affected expression, clothing, voice quality, among others. In order to reduce the potential for stumbling blocks in the clinical relationship, the therapist needs an adaptive model for decision making of therapist self-disclosure, given the dynamic nature of the identity of the LGBTQ therapist.

Therapist Role Responsiveness

Looking through the lens of role theory, the client may cast the therapist into a role that may be aligned with the therapist's personality, or role repertoire, or it could be disconnected from the therapist. By taking on the projected role, the therapist communicates something about themselves into the therapeutic relationship, which can be viewed as a form of self-disclosure. In drama therapy, the client and the therapist will take on and play out roles. "The roles that each chooses to play create a boundary from the other... Both players in the one-on-one cast the other in various roles and act toward the other as if he or she was in role" (Landy, 1996, pp.88–91). I refer to the action of the therapist taking on the role cast by the client, or a role in response to a client's chosen role, as therapist role responsiveness; therapist role responsiveness is a reflexive, spontaneous reaction that may result in acceptance of the role, declination of the role, or transformation of the role into a complementary role response; ultimately, role responsiveness is anchored by the level of service it will offer the client. Therapist role responsiveness speaks to the question proposed by drama therapist Bruce Howard Bayley, "'Who am I being, at this moment?' and also, 'Who am I experiencing the therapist or client as being'" (1999, p.6).

To a large extent, therapist role responsiveness holds a strong relational component in the therapeutic encounter.

Moreover, the therapeutic relationship, or working alliance, is rooted in collaboration and attachment (Gelso & Mohr, 2001). Collaboration implies a co-created experience between client and therapist, and collaborative attachment implies safety. A contributing factor in the therapeutic relationship is the therapist's congruence. Congruence is both the therapist's genuineness (mindful self-awareness) and their ability to communicate their experience with/of the client to the client. Previous research demonstrates that clients in congruent relationships with a therapist view themselves as capable and worthy of time; moreover, that they are a person with strengths and weaknesses, which results in acceptance of the problems they face as well as hope in their efforts to make change (Kolden *et al.*, 2011). Positive transference can contribute to the development of the working alliance in the early stages, which often shifts to a real relationship as the therapist takes on the role of supportive double. Attachment, congruence, and genuineness inform therapist role responsiveness.

We can also speak of therapist role responsiveness as a form of therapeutic presence, as presence implies simultaneously the therapist balancing their contact with their own experiences and contact with the client's experience resulting in an internal and external connection. "From a role theory perspective, empathy is the ability to identify roles in ourselves that connect to roles in others" (Williams, 2017, p.135). The embodied stance of the therapist being with their experience serves a function for attachment as well as role function within the therapeutic relationship (Kolden *et al.*, 2011). From a drama therapy perspective, the therapist will build upon their role responsiveness, including flexibility and spontaneity, by integrating the roles they play out for and with clients. These roles become part of the therapist's clinical role repertoire. By expanding the clinician's role system, therapist role responsiveness increases and the therapist is better able to respond to the needs of their clients.

Clinical Moments of Therapist Role Responsiveness

As a queer therapist, I have been on the receiving end of role projections that have aligned with my identity and those that have misaligned with my identity. For example, a client who enters the therapeutic space and begins to engage me in a hostile manner in the role of *Faggot* will receive role responsiveness in the form of declination. The role of Faggot is not grounded in quality or a shared reality, but rather exists solely in the client's singular reality; a faggot being someone they think they have seen, but does not exist. In other words, for this client, their projection of the role of Faggot is rooted mostly in their hateful and stereotypical perception of how a homosexual performs in the social world. More often than not, this is not an exchange rooted in psychosis, but rather one rooted in hate and hostility. Additionally, it is important to differentiate between countertransference and dislike; transference is a phenomenon specific to the co-created experience of the therapist and the client, which is different from all therapist reactions to a client (Gelso & Mohr, 2001)—a homophobic client eliciting a negative response in the queer therapist may not be rooted in transference but in realistic dislike for the client, given the client's views and biases towards LGBTQ individuals. To play out this role, I would communicate to the client that this quality of person exists within my community, confirming for them an inaccuracy or prejudiced perspective of queer people.

Further confounding the working alliance of a queer male therapist and the heterosexual male client is the spectrum of masculinity. Some heterosexual male clients, already feeling the incongruence between masculinity and psychotherapy, when faced with a queer male therapist come to feel more threatened, especially given the shifting power dynamic (Porter *et al.*, 2015). I discontinued treatment with a client who, in the two sessions (initial assessment, group therapy), could not move beyond or work with my queerness, as he said to me multiple times, "You will not get inside of me"—a reference to both the intimacy involved in the therapeutic relationship and also a fear of physical intimacy with a man. Additionally, my own defenses could certainly present themselves, which would be a disservice to the client. Being aware of my limitations, I find grounding for ethical practice; I cannot work with everyone. As a result, given the short nature of acute care and the need for long-term dynamic treatment to address these specific biases, it made sense to refer this client to another creative arts therapist on the unit.

Different from the aforementioned examples, when clients communicate their acceptance or understanding of my queerness, they do so in unique and creative ways. On several occasions, clients utilized socially acceptable pop culture representations of queer performance to indicate their understanding of my queer identity and to organize our relationship. These moments occurred as fleeting therapeutic encounters, brief milieu exchanges, and other times carried out and informed the duration of treatment. When recalling one of the more fleeting moments, a common theme presented itself in relationship with straight female clients. Three different clients over the past year told me that they either personally knew RuPaul, designed clothes for RuPaul, or partied with RuPaul in the West Village in the 1980s. The first time this happened, I had no idea how to respond; a similar freezing action occurred, much like when a client would call me a derogatory name. This was my mind's response; my body, however, left me feeling dissatisfied as it did not ring as true as those moments of oppression.

In order to understand these encounters, I spent time reflecting on these moments and on the client communicating these statements; I came to view this exchange as more of an attempt to join and build rapport. The intention of each statement came from a place of acceptance and a desire to communicate this acceptance of me to me; what is more, these references were utilized to organize the dynamic relationship that was developing, with the therapist representing a good object. After identifying the intention, I was better able to respond and would do so with a playful acceptance of their role projection, in role responding verbally with "yasss," or "you betta work," phrases in queer culture that have become synonyms with RuPaul, drag culture, and the ball scene. The result was a shared secret, a self-disclosure that aligned their perspective of me with who I am; intimacy was developed and relationship was forged, which contributed to the working alliance, ultimately elevating the clinical work (Gelso & Mohr, 2001). As a result, I was building necessary role responsiveness to understand the shared, clinical performance.

More recently, I worked with a straight cisgender female client who upon arrival into acute care was disorganized and internally preoccupied. When she spoke, she did so in the dialogical structure of a monologue (Lysaker *et al.*, 2001), which was challenging to interrupt. Select aspects of the monologue were decipherable, but most were incoherent to me. Despite the seemingly bizarre performance of the client, I tried to attune myself to her; I cued in to find a dialogical path, a point of entry to build relationship and expand communication. I discovered that when I was in her presence, she would refer to me directly, casting me in a role, as one of three specific gay icons: George Michael, Elton John, and Boy George. She seemed to be communicating what she needed, but only a select few would be able to join in the shared reality. In the beginning, when she would refer to me in these ways, I would often not engage around the topic as it did not seem connected to me; in retrospect, perhaps this was my own way of trying not to self-disclose my queerness. As I considered these references and processed the working relationship, I discovered that just as much as I was trying to organize my image of her, she was trying her best to organize her image of me. I began to see this as a non-threatening attempt at connecting and that the success of our relationship would be rooted in my ability to respond to the roles being cast.

Initially, it took the form of recognizing the characters she was calling out for. "[A]cting in the projected client's best interest tends to increase connectivity, which in turn, reduces the time necessary to establish a therapeutic alliance" (Satterly, 2006, p.244). As I built my role responsiveness, I was better equipped to respond; it could be with a song lyric indicating my acceptance of the role, or a simple invitation to join in role: "If I am Elton John, who are you?" I received the response, "Marilyn Monroe," "Norma Jean," and, at times, "Madonna." She began to enrole me from the moment she saw me arrive at the unit, using the name of the character, rather than my given name; and, in response, I would take on the role, serving as a supportive double, or a guide, who would help her organize to the environment and build necessary roles to meet the world outside of our co-created reality. We worked in this way for months, until she was ready to refer to me by my name. As she became healthier, and our conversations became more rooted in socially approved reality, she started to bring other staff into her treatment. At times, as if indicating a moment of missing, she would refer to our days as gay pop culture icons. During our course of treatment, I transferred to a different position and left the unit, leaving her behind. At this point, she was engaging with other clinical supports on the unit as we worked through separation–individuation. When I returned for our weekly session, she would challenge me by feigning disorganization and make some reference such as "I killed Madonna on the moon yesterday." Rather than rejecting the feigned delusion, a sign to me of creativity, insight, and adaptability, I responded with "Elton John misses Marilyn as well." Our working alliance was dynamic and congruent.

Therapist role responsiveness will ultimately result in the client viewing the therapist as a real person with beliefs, thoughts, feelings, opinions, as well as a sense of humor; it can be modified and tailored according to the performance of the client. The therapist works to develop role responsiveness in the same way they may process transferences: by studying their own internal reactions, gaining insight into how the client impacts others, and how others react to the client. The therapist ultimately utilizes this information to make choices about interventions. There are those clients who come in to treatment and accept the therapist's sexuality as if it is a non-issue, those clients who are not necessarily aware of the dynamics in relationship, and those who are curious and ask many questions. It can be challenging responding to these exchanges, and practice in anticipation of these moments can assist in developing necessary therapist role responsiveness. The queer therapist needs a model that allows them to think ahead and come from a place of embodied knowing to make informed decisions in the context of the therapeutic alliance.

Hermeneutic Self-Study of the Queer Therapist

In an effort to answer the question "How can the queer therapist make meaning of the roles a client cast on them to build role responsiveness?" I conducted a hermeneutic, arts-based self-study. I seek to understand the nature of this phenomenon by collecting information about my lived experience as a queer therapist. For this project, the philosophical aspects of phenomenology are used rather than the suggested procedure to construct a specific phenomenological study. As a result, this self-study takes to heart one specific goal of phenomenology, which is "to construct a possible interpretation of the nature of a certain human experience," holding closely the notion that this individual's experience is also the possible experiences of others (van Manen, 1990, p.41). This notion of interpretation implies a specific approach of phenomenology known as hermeneutical phenomenology. Hermeneutics, by definition, is "the theory and practice of interpretation" (van Manen, 1990, p.179). In the case of this project, then, hermeneutic self-study implies an interpretation of my life texts as a queer therapist. "The phenomenological ethnographer, trained as a drama therapist, uses intuition, sensation and metaphorical thinking to infer meaning from verbal and non-verbal cues" (Landy et al., 2012, p.51). Hermeneutic phenomenology values the description of the act of living in an experience, as well as the reflection on the lived experience that makes the experience have special significance; it is the retrospective nature of hermeneutics that brings quality and meaning to an experience.

Self-Study: Role Profiles, Metaphor, and Story

Over the course of this chapter, I have provided just a few examples of the ways clients communicate their understanding, approval, or disapproval of my queerness. I have also shared ways in which I have responded and called for the development of therapist role responsiveness. In the remaining sections, I share with you a protocol that I have found useful to process these unique clinical moments. First, I illustrate the theoretical underpinnings of this self-study as well as the procedural methodology. Additionally, my own processing in the form of art making, metaphor, story, and writing are shown as an example and sample of the extent to which this protocol can be utilized. Specifically, I process the work between myself and the straight cisgender female client who consistently cast me in the role of Elton John. Ultimately, the goal is to assist other therapists in developing a method to process the therapeutic work in an effort to build therapist role responsiveness.

FINDING OUR ROLES: SESSIONS 1 AND 2

As an assessment tool in drama therapy, Role Profiles is a card-sort instrument that allows the taker to organize a specific set of 58 roles from Landy's (1993) taxonomy of roles into four distinct categories: This Is Who I Am, This Is Who I Want To Be, This Is Who Stands in My Way, and This Is Who Can Help Me (Landy & Butler, 2013). In terms of story, the four categories match with the characters in the hero's journey: hero, destination, obstacle, and guide, respectively. This sort is designed with the intention to aid in the transition from assessment to action in story. There is a four-step process to completing the Role Profiles assessment (Landy & Butler, 2013). First, the individual completes the card sort as a way to explore personality. Next, a discussion occurs between the administrator and taker that involves a series of questions; for this study, these questions are explored by the individual and include the following derived from the list provided by Landy and Butler: What do you see? Does anything surprise you? Do you see any connections among the roles? After discussion, the assessment moves into results, where the individual looks for balance or imbalance among the roles. Finally, an analysis is conducted which attempts to make meaning of the role sort as a reflection of the individual's role system.

For this self-study, I completed a Role Profile assessment for myself while thinking specifically about the therapeutic work with the identified client (Session 1). Next, I embodied the client and completed a Role

Profile in role as the identified client (Session 2). It is recommended that the role sort and client embodiment be completed in the presence of a peer therapist to provide a witness and a mirror for reflection. Also, if available, the therapist can use an actual role sort completed with the client in treatment to accomplish Session 2. The profiles below in Table 3.1 and Table 3.2 display the results of the two role sorts. It is clear that both the client and the therapist bring roles into relationship, as well as mutual roles. The shared roles are highlighted below and may suggest attunement in terms of both parties identifying the same roles. Of particular interest to these sorts, you can see that the greatest number of shared roles exists in the obstacle column, suggesting an aligned understanding of the presenting problems in achieving wellness. For the therapist's sort, the column with the least number of roles is the destination, which may imply my uncertainty around where I see the relationship going, or what the end results of treatment may look like. For the client's sort, if we were to remove the roles that were not originally in the taxonomy of roles (Landy, 1993), there would be a clearer imbalance among the categories specifically within the guide role (indicated with a *); this seems to further support the notion that when a client comes to treatment guideless, the therapist takes on the role of guide. The incorporation of the roles played out by the therapist appearing in the guide column of the role sort indicates an acknowledgment of the supportive double the therapist plays in treatment while the client develops an intrapsychic guide. You can see some shifts across the sorts that suggest some level of balance between the therapist and client. For example, the roles of George Michael, Boy George, and Elton John appear under the hero role for the therapist, and under the guide role for the client, indicating a role match.

Table 3.1 Role Profile of Therapist in Reflection of Identified Client

Therapist Role Profile			
Who I Am	Who stands in way	Who can help me	Who I want to be
Elton John*	Zombie	Outcast	Dreamer
Rebel	Critic	Artist	Adult
Villain	Adolescent	Optimist	Calm Person
Son	Sick Person	Saint	Elder
Witness	Fearful Person	Average Person	Visionary
Mother	Vampire	Beast	Hero

Husband	Slave	Clown	Believer
Helper	Poor Person	Orphan	Healer
Boy George*	Sister	Wise Person	Warrior
George Michael*	Angry Person	Innocent	Free Person
Healthy Person	Perfectionist	Survivor	
Friend	Doubter	Lover	
Special Person	Rich Person		
Pessimist	Victim		
Child	Egotist		
Beauty			

Not sorted: Brother, Suicide, Ignorant Person, Wife, Killer, Daughter, Sinner, Father.
* Indicates roles added by the client.

Table 3.2 Role Profile of Therapist in Role of Identified Client

	Client Role Profile		
Who I Am	**Who stands in way**	**Who can help me**	**Who I want to be**
Angry Person	Sick Person	Optimist	Calm Person
Elder	Adolescent	Artist	Wife
Doubter	Sister	George Michael*	Lover
Adult	Sinner	Saint	Survivor
Dreamer	Zombie	Helper	Average Person
Outcast	Norma Jean*	Believer	Beauty
Warrior	Ignorant Person	Child	Healthy Person
Visionary	Pessimist	Elton John*	Rich Person
Slave	Mother	Victim	Marilyn Monroe*
Beast	Poor Person	Clown	Innocent
Rebel	Critic	Friend	Special Person
Villain	Wise Person	Father	Free Person
Witness	Vampire	Boy George*	Hero
Orphan	Fearful Person		
Egotist			
Killer			

Not sorted: Perfectionist, Suicide, Brother, Husband, Daughter, Healer, Son.
* Indicates roles added by the client.

IDENTIFYING THE OBSTACLE AND GUIDE: SESSIONS 3 AND 4

Initially, the guide exists in the social world outside of the client and may take on many forms from family to pop culture icon. "The guide is a transitional figure that stands between the role [hero] and CR [obstacle] and is used by either one as a bridge to the other. One primary function of the guide is integration" (Landy, 2009, p.68). One goal of treatment, from a role theory perspective, is to assist the client in internalizing an intrapsychic guide; the therapist is viewed as a companion on the journey (Halstead, 2000). The guide role is utilized to assist the client in moving through the obstacle on the journey towards the destination. The obstacle, originally conceived in role theory as the counterrole (Landy, 1993), is "the figure that lurks on the other side of the role, the antagonist" (Landy, 2009, p.68). In simpler words, the obstacle blocks the hero from reaching their destination. From Campbell (1949), the obstacle can be viewed as a series of tests the hero may encounter while on their journey—tests that may be physical, spiritual, emotional, or mental. The goal, from a role theory perspective, is not to destroy the obstacle, but rather to find balance between the hero and obstacle with support of the guide, understanding that each character is a part of the individual who holds them. After all, "these various roles and counterroles combine to create an individual's role system" (Landy & Butler, 2013, p.150).

Within this protocol, the therapist utilizes metaphor and image as a tool to make meaning of this phenomenon. Metaphors are more than just linguistic tools; metaphor represents how a person makes sense of their world (Lawson, 2005; Wickman *et al.*, 1999). Following this logic, the therapist can use metaphor to connect to the client's world, and when attuned to the client's metaphoric expression, the relationship becomes congruent. I chose to explore the obstacle and guide through image.

Figure 3.1 The Obstacle (see color plate in the center of the book)

To create the obstacle (Figure 3.1), I utilized the list of the roles that appear in the obstacle column (This Is Who Stands in My Way) for the client as well as for the therapist. It was important to acknowledge barriers I bring into the relationship that may not align with the client's identified obstacles—barriers that may impact my therapist role responsiveness. Additionally, I am curious about the similar roles in the obstacle column. Therefore, I created role cards for each role and utilized a pre-made mask and glued the role cards on to the mask. The mask provides a concrete image for containment of the variety and number of obstacle roles. Reflecting on the piece, I am overwhelmed by the sheer number of roles that appear on the mask; in list form, the task of overcoming the obstacle seems more manageable, whereas presented on the mask you can see how the obstacle roles may team up together in an effort to hinder the client's journey. Viewing the obstacles in this way, I am also aware of the roles in my hero category that are identified obstacles for the client. Specifically, I identify with the role of Mother as a hero role for myself, whereas the client sees this role as an obstacle. It is also clear that the obstacles may come in many forms and qualities. I can already see the narratives that are playing out just by reviewing the parallel journey of the therapist and client.

Figure 3.2 The Guide (see color plate in the center of the book)

For the guide (Figure 3.2, Session 4), I focused in on a guide role that the client specifically projected on to me, which is Elton John. This role is one that appears in the hero category for the therapist and the guide category for the client, which indicates a clear role match, the beginnings of a shared narrative. For this step, I recommend selecting an image for the guide and then expanding upon it. I selected an image of an Elton John album cover and explored the image through painting. Reflecting on it, the image is striking to me as I see a vibrant guide character stepping out on to a path and clearing aside the darkness to bring forth a guiding light. The shared role of the Clown seems present in the guide figure's costume, as well as the role of the Optimist clearing away the dark skies. If you were to view the image and the list of guide roles simultaneously, the impact of each seems present in the image. In the distance of the image, I noticed two structures. The image directly at the end of the path is a shelter of some sort. To the left-hand side of the shelter, there is a towering building coming out of the darkness. When connecting this image to the work with the client, this client was initially slated for transfer to long-term psychiatric hospitalization, and this may be represented by the towering image in the shadows. As the guide, holding the roles of the Optimist, Artist, and Saint, the goal is to work towards a destination that fits the health of the client. It was challenging in this relationship to communicate the health I saw in the client to other treatment providers; what they were able to see, however, was the healthy relationship that carried through her care.

My queerness is present in both images. It is most clearly identifiable in the guide role image by the rainbow symbol on the back of the guide's jacket. It also seems present in the bright colors that adorn the human figure in the image. The character seems a bit more androgynous than I anticipated, which speaks to my gender performance. In the obstacle image (Figure 3.1), my queerness seems represented by the roles I anticipated would be obstacles due to my queerness such as Perfectionist, Sinner, Ignorant One, Adolescent; these roles outline the sides of the mask, which, in retrospect, seems to demonstrate that these roles are less present than anticipated for the client.

CONCEPTUALIZING THE DESTINATION: SESSION 5

The destination is the newest character to enter into role theory and method, and therefore has the least information available about the use of this role. Most common, the destination takes the form of home (Landy, 2012). Moreover, Landy & Butler (2013) refer to the destination as the part of the hero's journey that reflects the statement "This Is Who I Want To Be." For me, the destination is a representation of the integration of the hero and obstacle by the guide—the triadic relationship of hero–guide–obstacle. For this project, the destination is explored in the form of letter writing (Session 5). The therapist in the role of guide writes a letter to the hero (the client) about how they conceptualize the destination for the client given all of the previously acquired information in the preceding steps. The following is an excerpt from the fantasy letter I wrote to the identified client:

Dear Hero,

I see you. I see both the healthy and sick parts of you. I am aware of your obstacles, and I am also aware of the obstacles I am bringing into our relationship. I will try my best to protect you from my obstacles, the obstacles that do not belong to you... I am queer and I think you know that already; I appreciate the way you have communicated your acceptance of me and that you have been able to use this aspect of who I am to help guide you on your journey... Your obstacles are many. I will not be able to help you with all of them, but I will certainly help you with some and hopefully leave you with the skills to move through the others. It is clear to me that Norma Jean, although you hold on dearly to this role, seems to be holding you back from reaching your destination. Norma Jean seems to encompass some of your other obstacles including the adolescent, sick person, zombie, poor person, fearful one. Norma Jean, the birth name of Marilyn Monroe, something I may not have known if I did not know my queer history. It is clear that your destination is Marilyn Monroe, not in actuality, but in your iteration of her. The Marilyn Monroe from the movies: the beauty, the healthy person, the innocent, the free person, the wife (multiple times), the survivor, the lover, the rich person; they are all Marilyn, and one day, hopefully, they will all be you... I hope I can guide you to a place where you are able to embrace all parts of you, all of your roles, as they serve you in a variety of ways and you are who you are and who you will become with them.

Take good care,

Your guide

PARALLEL JOURNEY PERFORMED: SESSIONS 6 AND 7

The final steps in this project are to create a piece (Session 6) that is performed for a supervisor, or colleague (Session 7). Ultimately, this performance piece aims to achieve aesthetic distance, "a balance state of affect and cognition, wherein both feeling and reflection are available" (Landy, 1993, p.25). Aesthetic distance implies a creation of flow that allows for spontaneity and builds flexibility. Through sharing this work, the therapist will discover a deeper emotional and cognitive understanding of their therapeutic work through embodiment. Maria Hodermarksa, a drama therapist, wrote: "Embodiment is verification… We create emotional intimacy with the client through theater, but the process is indeed mutually constructed out of treatment" (Hodermarska, 2015, pp.193–194). In other words, the artistic process, specifically performance, allows the therapist the space to make meaning of their clinical encounters and ultimately increase empathic understanding of the clients they serve and of themselves. Extending from this, performing the created monologue, or story, is a useful tool in developing embodied knowledge through embodied verification in performance. This body knowledge, in the form of roles, ultimately translates into therapist role responsiveness as the queer therapist integrates the performed roles into their clinical role repertoire.

The following is a sample of a monologue from a larger performance piece I wrote entitled *Marilyn, Norma Jean, and Me: An Embodied Case Narrative* and demonstrates an achievement of aesthetic distance and embodied knowledge:

> Her resilience was evident in her brilliant use of pop culture references as a way of organizing her current environment: an inpatient psychiatric ward. A unit. To even the strongest of minds, words often escape in an effort to explain the happenings of a psychiatric unit. Some of her references were immediately clear: someone perhaps looked like a famous person. Yet, others were harder for me to understand. Of course, it wasn't necessary for me to fully understand her efforts, but to join in them… Myself, George Michael, Boy George, Elton John: each a gay man, her understanding and acceptance of my sexuality; her way of organizing me as a non-threatening entity. It was her way of categorizing me in a way to know that I would first do no harm, as harm had been done in her past. It took months before she called me by name, and rather than correct her, which is typically not my wont, I joined her and assumed the role she cast me in. I didn't ignore her calls of "Boy George" from down the hallway, and I certainly never missed a beat each manic Monday when greeted with, "Hello George Michael." She knew I was not these people, but it created a sense of safety, for the both of us, to meet each other in this creative space. We share similar references, often speaking of Princess Di, Elton John, Madonna, Marilyn Monroe, icons of

the gay persuasion; she entered my reality as much as I entered hers. Our camp was strong and it facilitated our trust... (Trottier, 2017)

Conclusion

As a queer therapist, it has been valuable to explore the clinical relationship with the straight client. Using the dynamic frame of the hero's journey, combined with my artistic exploration and reflection, I have developed a rich understanding of the therapeutic relationship, expanded my clinical role repertoire, and built on my therapist role responsiveness. It is my hope that queer creative arts therapists, as well as other therapists, will utilize this protocol to make meaning of their experiences in practice, becoming consciously aware of who they are, who they work with, and the intersubjective space in between. By developing an awareness, the queer therapist will be able to expand and respond to their clients as needed.

Protocol: Role Profiles, Metaphor, and Story to Make Meaning and Develop Role Responsiveness

Goal

To identify and strengthen the role system of the therapist to develop optimal role responsiveness in clinical practice.

Objectives

- *Objective 1.* The therapist will identify the roles that make up their current role system that can be utilized in clinical practice as evidenced by completing a role profile.

- *Objective 2.* The therapist will develop at least two techniques to process transference and countertransference through the use of metaphor, letter writing, art making, storytelling, and performance.

- *Objective 3.* The therapist will be able to identify how the roles cast on the therapist can be utilized to inform clinical interventions, as evidenced by metaphor and story making.

- *Objective 4.* The therapist will be witnessed by another therapist to validate their clinical work and achieve aesthetic distance (balance of cognition and affect) to develop insight into the clinical relationship through embodied verification.

Duration

Duration is based on the therapist's schedule. Each session could be completed in one sitting or over the course of multiple sittings.

Materials

- Role cards

- Paper and pencil

- Art materials, as preferred

Curriculum

SESSION 1: WHO AM I? ROLE SORT OF THE THERAPIST

The purpose of this exercise is to assist the therapist in identifying the roles that make up their role repertoire as a clinician specifically in reference to their work with the identified client. Ultimately, select one role for each category: This Is Who I Am, This Is Who I Want to Be, This Is Who Stands in the Way, This Is Who Can Help. It is highly recommended to have a witness to share in reflection.

SESSION 2: WHO ARE YOU? ROLE SORT OF THE CLIENT

The purpose of this exercise is to take on the role of the client and complete a role profile as the client to better understand your image of the client through their role profile. Ultimately, select one role for each category: This Is Who I Am, This Is Who I Want to Be, This Is Who Stands in the Way, This Is Who Can Help. (This may also be completed by the client's role sort done in session, if available.) Observe and reflect on the two sorts side by side. It is highly recommended to have a witness to share in reflection as well as support the therapist in stepping in and out of role.

SESSION 3: WHO STANDS IN OUR WAY? IDENTIFY THE OBSTACLE

The purpose of this exercise is to identify the obstacle that stands in the way for the therapist and the client. For this step, identify a metaphor to represent the obstacle, or barrier. Utilize the following prompts, write out the roles and qualities of the obstacle, and create an image to represent it. (How would you describe the size, color, texture, smell of the barrier? Do you want to move towards or away from the barrier? Can you see a way around the identified barrier? What associations do you have of the barrier? How might the client view this barrier? Are your views aligned/attuned with each other? What role does queerness play here?)

SESSION 4: WHO DO YOU WANT/NEED ME TO BE? THERAPIST AS GUIDE

The purpose of this exercise is to identify the specific guide role the client places you in. The client may offer you a role, or metaphor, to play out specifically as guide, which is a true gift. This session allows you to further explore that role through metaphor, image, or writing in an effort to find the qualities that you share with the identified guide. You may discover through this process that the role cast on the therapist is not a supportive one, which could still be viewed as a guide; it may be difficult to understand the less positive projection as guide and this may demonstrate some challenges for the relationship. It may be helpful to start from the guide roles identified in the parallel profiles from Sessions 1 and 2. What role does queerness play here?

SESSION 5: WHERE ARE WE GOING? WRITING THE DESTINATION

The purpose of this exercise is to explore the destination. Through letter writing, as the guide role, write a letter to your client—a letter that you do not intend to send. The message you share is a reflection of where you hope the client will be at the end of your work together. An end is not necessarily marked by termination; an end can be an achievement of a specific objective in treatment or a milestone in relationship. What role does queerness play here?

SESSION 6: WHAT IS OUR HERO'S JOURNEY? PARALLEL JOURNEY OF THERAPIST AND CLIENT

The purpose of this exercise is to write the hero's journey with a relational marriage of the client's journey and the therapist's journey (the parallel journey). This writing can be as short or as long as the therapist needs. It can take the form of a story, monologue, dialogue, or other. What role does queerness play in this story?

SESSION 7: WHO CAN WITNESS? PERFORM THE JOURNEY
The purpose of this exercise is to perform your story in the presence of a supervisor or fellow colleague(s) as a final integration of the clinical work. This session results in aesthetic distance, where the therapist has a balance of cognition and affect in an effort to gain insight into the therapeutic process.

References

Barnett, J.E. (2011) 'Psychotherapist self-disclosure: Ethical and clinical considerations.' *Psychotherapy 48*, 4, 315–321.

Bayley, B.H. (1999) 'Feeling queer in dramatherapy: Transformation, Alice, and the caterpillar.' *Dramatherapy 21*, 1, 3–9.

Campbell, J. (1949) *The Hero with a Thousand Faces*. Princeton, NJ: Princeton University Press.

Carroll, L., Gauler, A.A., Relph, J., & Hutchinson, K.S. (2011) 'Counselor self-disclosure: Does sexual orientation matter to straight clients?' *International Journal of Advanced Counseling 33*, 139–148.

Falzarano, M. & Pizzi, M. (2015) 'Experiences of lesbian and gay occupational therapists in the healthcare system.' *Journal of Allied Health 44*, 2, 65–72.

Fuller, C.B., Chang, D.F., & Rubin, L.R. (2009) 'Sliding under the radar: Passing and power among sexual minorities.' *Journal of LGBT Issues in Counseling 3*, 128–151.

Gelso, C.J. & Mohr, J.J. (2001) 'The working alliance and the transference/countertransference relationship: Their manifestation with racial/ethnic and sexual minority clients and therapists.' *Applied and Preventive Psychology 10*, 51–68.

Goffman, E. (1963) *Stigma*. London: Penguin.

Haldeman, D.C. (2010) 'Reflections of a gay male psychotherapist.' *Psychotherapy: Theory, Research, Practice, Training 47*, 2, 177–185.

Halstead, R.W. (2000) 'From tragedy to triumph: Counselor as companion on the hero's journey.' *Counseling and Values 44*, 2, 100–106.

Hodermarksa, M. (2015) 'Body knowledge and living enquiry in clinical supervision.' International Conference of Expressive Therapies and Psychotherapy Focused on Body and Psychosomatic Approach. Olomouc, Czech Republic, Palacky University.

Kanuha, V.K. (1999) 'The social process of "passing" to manage stigma: Acts of internalized oppression or acts of resistance?' *Journal of Sociology and Social Welfare 26*, 4, 27–46.

Kolden, G.G., Klein, M.H., Wang, C.C., & Austin, S.B. (2011) 'Congruence/ genuineness.' *Psychotherapy 48*, 1, 65–71.

Kooden, H. (1991) 'Self-Disclosure: The Gay Male Therapist as Agent of Social Change.' In C. Silverstein (ed.) *Gays, Lesbians, and Their Therapists.* New York, NY: W.W. Norton & Company.

Kronner, H.W. & Northcut, T. (2015) 'Listening to both sides of the therapeutic dyad: Self-disclosure of the gay male therapist and reflections from gay male clients.' *Psychoanalytic Social Work 22*, 162–181.

Landy, R. (1993) *Persona and Performance: The Meaning of Role in Drama, Therapy, and Everyday Life.* New York, NY: The Guilford Press.

Landy, R. (1996) *Essays in Drama Therapy: The Double Life.* London: Jessica Kingsley Publishers.

Landy, R. (2008) *The Couch and the Stage: Integrating Words and Action in Psychotherapy.* Lanham, MD: Jason Aronson.

Landy, R. (2009) 'Role Theory and the Role Method of Drama Therapy.' In D.R. Johnson & R. Emunah (eds), *Current Approaches in Drama Therapy* (2nd edn). Springfield, IL: Charles C. Thomas.

Landy, R. (2012) 'Destination Germany: Drama therapy part 3.' Blog post, July 18. Accessed on 11/12/2018 at www.psychologytoday.com/blog/couch-and-stage/201207/destination-germany-drama-therapy-part-3.

Landy, R. & Butler, J. (2013) 'Assessment through Role Theory.' In D. Johnson, S. Pendzik, & S. Snow (eds) *Assessment in Drama Therapy.* Springfield, IL: Charles C. Thomas.

Landy, R.J., Hodermarska, M., Mowers, D., & Perrin, D. (2012) 'Performance as arts-based research in drama therapy supervision.' *Journal of Applied Arts and Health 3*, 1, 49–58.

Lawson, G. (2005) 'The hero's journey as a developmental metaphor in counseling.' *Journal of Humanistic Counseling, Education, and Development 44*, 134–144.

Liddle, B.J. (1996) 'Therapist sexual orientation, gender, and counseling practices as they relate to ratings of helpfulness by gay and lesbian clients.' *Journal of Counseling Psychology 43*, 4, 394–401.

Lysaker, P.H., Lysaker, J.T., & Lysaker, J.T. (2001) 'Schizophrenia and the collapse of the dialogical self: Recovery, narrative, and psychotherapy.' *Psychotherapy 38*, 3, 252–261.

Porter, J., Hulbert-Williams, L., & Chadwick, D. (2015) 'Sexuality in the therapeutic relationship: An interpretive phenomenological analysis of the experiences of gay therapists.' *Journal of Gay and Lesbian Mental Health 19*, 165–183.

Powell, A. (2016) 'Embodied multicultural assessment: An interdisciplinary training model.' *Drama Therapy Review 2*, 1, 111–122.

Robertson, D.L. & Lawrence, C. (2015) 'Heroes and mentors: A consideration of relational-cultural theory and "The Hero's Journey."' *Journal of Creativity in Mental Health 10*, 264–277.

Russell, G.M. (2006) 'Different ways of knowing: The complexities of therapist disclosure.' *Journal of Gay and Lesbian Psychotherapy 10*, 1, 79–94.

Satterly, B.A. (2006) 'Therapist self-disclosure: From a gay male perspective.' *Families in Society 87*, 2, 240–247.

Trottier, D.G. (2017, October) *Marilyn, Norma Jean, and Me: An Embodied Case Narrative*. Performance presented at the meeting of the North American Drama Therapy Association 38th Annual Conference, Danvers, MA.

van Manen, M. (1990) *Researching Lived Experience: Human Science for an Action Sensitive Pedagogy*. Albany, NY: SUNY.

Wickman, S.A., Daniels, M.H., White, L., & Fesmire, S.A. (1999) 'A "primer" in conceptual metaphor for counselors.' *Journal of Counseling and Development 77*, 389–394.

Williams, B.M. (2016) 'Minding our own biases: Using drama therapeutic tolls to identify and challenge assumptions, biases and stereotypes.' *Drama Therapy Review 2*, 1, 9–23.

Williams, B.M. (2017) 'Role power: Using role theory in support of ethical practice.' *Drama Therapy Review 3*, 1, 131–148.

4

Some Considerations Regarding the Path to Parenting for Lesbian Couples

JUDITH LUONGO

Will modestly discover to yourself
That of yourself which you yet not know of.

William Shakespeare, *Julius Caesar*, Act 1, Scene 2

As a therapist, an artist, and a parent, the challenges of listening to, attempting to understand, and finding a way to express the inner voices of both others and of myself are exciting and, at times, anxiety-provoking. In all three areas, I may be faced with the possibility of ever-expanding self-knowledge, not all of which is comforting. As I was listening to a discussion recently between Katherine Bradford and Chris Martin, two courageous artists, Katherine shared, having realized early on in her journey, that she found her work to be "embarrassing." She added that she had finally arrived at the place where she simply accepts that. The audience laughed both gleefully and a bit anxiously. What was magical for me was how safe I felt, with all of the insecurities that being an artist stirs, in this group of like-minded others.

The experience of belonging and the hope that is engendered by being seen can allow for a sense of heightened aliveness to be derived when something honest and commonly denied or hidden is revealed. The best lines of comedians provide us with mirrors by speaking aloud the thoughts or feelings we all relate to, but would not easily admit to.

My work as an artist, therapist, and parent is to be open to the unthinkable in both myself and in the other. I consider it to be my task to create an atmosphere of safety within which one's "true" self (Winnicott, 1965, p.140) can be revealed, experienced, and accepted.

My focus for this chapter will be on my work with lesbian clients and in particular with these clients' paths to becoming parents. In order to set the framework, I would like to look back briefly at some significant developments in the understanding of child development, which led to the increasing complexity attributed to the role of the caretaker in that unfolding process.

In his early thinking about development, Sigmund Freud (1924) envisioned the psyche as a closed system within which the three functions of the mind that we are all familiar with—id, ego and superego—evolve as a working system to enable the developing person to cope with the demands of the external world. The early representations of this external world are the parents, who make the ordinary demands needed for the child to adapt to the requirements of society. An important shift occurred, with a later understanding of the paper "Mourning and Melancholia" (Freud, 1915). In this writing, Freud described the loss of a significant other as bringing about a mourning process which culminates in that "lost other" being held on to, so to speak, through the process of identification.

This view of the ego, which posits that its development includes an identification through psychic internalization of others with whom we have had significant emotional ties, shifted the role of caretakers to a much more prominent position in regard to ego development. Heinz Hartmann, seen as the father of ego psychology, took this further by hypothesizing that an "average expectable environment" was necessary for the healthy unfolding of the developing ego (Mitchell & Black, 1995, p.36). This elevated the role of parents from mere representatives of reality to the providers of the circumstances necessary for the developing ego's capacity to negotiate the demands of the outside world.

Theories provide a framework for consideration of what we observe. Anna Freud (Freud & Burlingham, 1943) was very influenced by the theories developed by Ego Psychology and by the actual catastrophic losses inflicted upon children during and after World War II. She and Dorothy Burlingham initiated the establishment of a center for infants and children who had been orphaned or separated from their families due to the war. The Hampstead War Nurseries, as they were named, provided residential child care and became a center for child study and research (1941–1945). As their observational approach became more widely known, further efforts to understand children's development were undertaken.

René Spitz (1945) is well known for his finding that infants who were provided with the basics of physical care but received a minimum of interaction and stimulation from caretakers suffered with what he termed *anaclitic depression*. The symptoms were severe and devastating, and correlated with the loss or absence of a caretaker's emotional availability.

As evidence mounted determining the critical role played by parents in their child's emotional as well as physical survival, interest was drawn to the psychological and emotional development of the parents themselves. Therese Benedek's (1959) paper, "Parenthood as a developmental phase," elucidated her observations that parenthood itself is a developmental process for adults. She proposed that as our children move through their own developmental phases, there are conscious and unconscious memories and fantasies evoked in parents. Thus, parenting inevitably means being continually confronted with one's own past, simply through the act of caring for offspring. This can afford all parents an invitation to review aspects of the past from a new vantage point. Through the lens of identifying with our children, a level of empathy can be experienced for our own inevitable history of injuries, allowing for new opportunities to heal and to consolidate our individual potentials and evolve towards increased personal authenticity.

The threads that connect the task of nurturing to the ultimate growth of the nurturer affect all of us who are part of the larger group we call society. Society is a container for the individuals who inhabit it, much as parents are for their developing infants. When any of these individuals or groups within the whole experience rejecting and discriminatory attitudes rather than a secure "holding" environment (Winnicott, 1965), it becomes a problem for every individual in that society.

The awareness of the challenges facing all parents can be our own path, as a culture, towards providing the support that Winnicott (1965) referred to in his descriptions of the attachment between the "good enough" caretaker and the infant. We don't have to be perfect in our understanding, but we do have to be "good enough."

The decision to become a parent is a unique one for each individual. It is my feeling that for those of us who have the desire to parent, there is an innate, if not always conscious, drive to transcend our individual needs. Erik Erikson (1950) referred to this as a drive towards "generativity." He was also one of the first theorists to posit the continuing development of the human psyche through the entire life cycle. He juxtaposed "generativity" with "stagnation" as opposing polarities. The drive to continue evolving in new ways through one's life is at odds with the drive to withdraw from new challenges and find comfort in playing out pre-ordained roles assigned by families, work, partners, or societal norms. Seen through this lens, parenting can be a role which is taken on as a given—one that is simply an automatic expectation passed along from others—or it can be taken on with thoughtfulness and intentionality.

When I was a young teacher of art therapists who were pursuing their graduate training, I had a student whom I will never forget. She was already in her mid-60s when she decided to pursue her master's degree. I will refer to her as Millie. Millie was a reserved and thoughtful woman. I was aware that something had recently occurred in her personal life which was upsetting, but I had not felt invited to pursue further inquiry into what the event was. However, during one of our individual supervision sessions she quite uncharacteristically broke down, first in tears and then into a state of inconsolable sobbing. The following story unfolded.

Millie was married to a professional man for 25 years, with whom she had a child, who had just completed his college studies. In addition, she added that she had a very close female friend for almost that same number of years. This close friend had a catastrophic accident which resulted in her sudden death. At this point Millie looked at me with a mixture of painful despair and hope. She then shared that she and this friend had been lovers for all of those years, without anyone's knowledge. Having been brought up in a conservative home, Millie had felt that her sexual orientation, which she had been aware of from early adolescence, would have been unacceptable to her family, so she proceeded to live a life in partial hiding. At the age of 25, Millie decided to enter into a marriage with a man who was a close friend and was also gay. They both very much wanted to have children and agreed that their close friendship and common struggle with hidden aspects of their identities would allow them to have a compatible union as they pursued family life. Now, however, the fact that Millie could not mourn publicly, and was therefore deprived of the support of community as she struggled with the profound nature of her loss, was causing her to question the way she had gone about constructing her entire life.

If we view society as a container of both shared values and shared traumas, Millie's experience and the experiences of others who have been in her situation affect us all. Selma Fraiberg's poignant article entitled "Ghosts in the nursery" (Fraiberg, Adelson, & Shapiro, 1975) poetically brings our attention to the harm that can be done when unremembered, past, damaging experiences, specifically with significant others, interfere with an individual's well-being. This interference inevitably enters into all of our relationships including, of course, with our own children.

In a sense, Millie's experience represents a potential "ghost" in the nursery for a whole segment of our society. When we look at other marginalized groups, it is easy to see how acknowledgment of the losses and exclusions of all kinds that they have endured can create pathways to healing. This is extremely well portrayed in the work of a brilliant and creative pioneer, lawyer, and social activist Bryan Stevenson. As the founder of the Equal Justice Initiative, he advocates for and has been creating a memorial to commemorate the history of violence towards African Americans. Stevenson addressed this in his momentous TED talk (2012) and in his book *Just Mercy* (2015), by driving home the point that no one in a society is truly free when there has not been an acknowledgment by the larger community of the violence experienced by any subgroup.

The construction of a space for public memorializing of traumatic histories is known to be an element in healing that history and, perhaps more importantly, ensuring that it doesn't repeat itself. For Freud (1914) "what is not remembered is repeated" (p.147). The traumas experienced by the LGBTQ community are held by that community, but have not necessarily been acknowledged within the larger heteronormative culture. This lack of acknowledgment may continue to breed hate from the majority and begin to become internalized by the LGBQ community. Internalized homophobia, a term introduced in the 1970s (Weinberg, 1972), is a concept used to identify the various forces of self-hatred that homosexuals may experience through absorption of and identification with the culture that generally promotes a heteronormative attitude. As a result of being socially stigmatized, this internalization of hate and discrimination may result in perpetual shame and minority stress which may hinder LGBQ individuals from living their full potential, maintaining healthy relationships with their partners, and, specific to this chapter, becoming parents.

Ideally, an individual begins life by experiencing the self within the context of an attuned and emotionally available caretaker (Bowlby, 1988). This attachment can foster a sense of security through the experience of being know-able, understood, accepted, and loved in the eyes of the caretaker. Ultimately, this facilitates the capacity for an enthusiastic exploration of the world beyond the confines of the home, and an overall sense of trust in the predictability of one's positive effect upon others. When the environment presents an individual with a "bad fit," meaning that the individual's nature is experienced as foreign or unacceptable, the resulting distortion in mirroring may leave one to engage in self-blame and irrationally driven self-doubt.

In a culture in which heteronormativity predominates and discrimination against the LGBTQ community has not been publicly acknowledged, there is fertile ground for the continuation of internalized homophobia. It is important to note that over the past two decades there have been very effective efforts initiated by the LGBTQ community. There are safe spaces for young LGBTQ individuals seeking support, the Supreme Court ruled that the Defense of Marriage Act is unconstitutional, and the number of LGBTQ couples taking the road to parenthood has increased remarkably, making the availability of support systems infinitely more available than had been the case for Millie. In spite of this, there is still a tentative wariness among many about the security of these monumental gains.

Our heteronormative culture exerts its effect upon us as clinicians and upon our LGBQ clients. In an article written by John E. Pachankis and Marvin R. Goldfried (2013), entitled "Clinical issues in working with lesbian, gay, and bisexual clients," it is stated that:

> Even when homosexuality is not viewed as pathological, mental health professionals need to consider the distress that antihomosexual bias can cause LGB individuals. Disregarding such factors may lead to erroneous and unfortunate attributions of the sources of distress in an LGB person who is seeking therapy. (p.45)

The authors include the following in identifying some important core tenets of LGB-affirmative therapy:

- encouraging clients to establish support systems with other LGB individuals

- facilitating the raising of clients' awareness regarding how oppression has affected them

- helping to alleviate the shame and guilt surrounding homosexual thoughts, behaviors, and feelings

- normalizing clients' expression of anger in response to being oppressed.

Furthermore, Shannon and Woods (1991) suggested that therapists of LGB clients must act as advocates for them in helping them to face the challenges inherent in possessing a sexual minority status.

I would like to share some observations from my private practice which draw attention to some of the more covert manifestations of problematic tendencies which may not be identified by the client as emanating from having absorbed and internalized an attitude towards the self, based upon a heteronormative frame of reference. As a clinician, I am aware that my focusing upon some of my clients' difficulties as being related to unresolved trauma attributable to living in a heteronormative society may be emanating, at least to some degree, from my own guilt as a member of the heterosexual community. On this I must be constantly checking in with myself. In addition, I invite clients to let me know if they feel I am missing something or seeing it from a point of view which they find is reflective of my own heteronormativity. Overall, I attempt to approach this work with a sense of humility and self-reflection.

Some Clinical Vignettes

A client, whom I shall call Liz, reports that she is fearful when about to engage in social interactions because she feels she will have nothing of value to contribute. She accepts this as simply the way she has always felt for as long as she can recall. She generally speaks with guarded warmth about her family of origin. When I asked her to speak about her experience of coming out as lesbian to her family, she revealed that she first moved to the other side of the country and told them over the phone since she was so frightened of their reaction. Liz had always viewed this as her own problem. Once she talked more openly about it, she was flooded by memories of how much of herself she had learned to hide and cover, fearing the disapproval of those around her. In session, we experimented with using unfamiliar art materials and daring to do art with no agenda. Taking risks in art making has been challenging, but has introduced a metaphor for creating one's own safe space and for generating and appreciating one's own uniquely individual mark making.

Another client, whom I shall refer to as Beth, expressed the continuing fear that any new partner would sooner or later find her to be unlovable. She felt it was somewhat "irrational" since she knew that she was seen as being attractive, intelligent, and accomplished. Despite that, however, she felt it was always just a matter of time before she would be found to be too unacceptable in some way to stay emotionally involved with. She had never spoken about her coming out as she reported that her family had always been totally accepting of her sexual orientation. Nonetheless, I asked her to revisit the time in her life when she began to be aware of being gay. This opened up a deeply protected self-experience of utter aloneness and isolation which she reported with shame. She was raised in a family which was extremely high-functioning, and great pressure was exerted upon her to maintain composure and an attitude of self-reliance.

During one session, Beth spontaneously took notice of the fantasy sand tray figures I keep on a bookcase. We laughed together at the thought of playing with these and then entered the fantasy place they so invitingly evoked. Through creating scenarios between a seductive mermaid figure and a monstrous ogre, she began to articulate these two characters as representing her attraction to girls when she was a young teenager and her fear of this being something monstrous and out of her control.

A third client, whom I shall call Carrie, began to have phobic fantasies of developing a disfiguring illness upon preparing for a public event with her partner of ten years. When we hypothesized this as a possible experience of "coming out" all over again, she revisited the time as a young teenager when she began to admit to the fear that she could never live up to her perfectionistic mother's picture of who she would be. Carrie proceeded to work on a series of art pieces using found objects and was able to enjoy creating evocative rather than beautiful images.

Some of these difficult-to-articulate experiences reveal themselves in the transference. A recently divorced lesbian client, whom I shall refer to as Anne, admitted after missing a session that she had imagined that I was now hoping she would find a man to be in a relationship with. In exploring this further, it became clear that this client was carrying an extra burden of failure after her divorce and experienced it as a punishment, on some level, for having dared to transgress heteronormativity. She also saw it as a more painful failure in that the wish to prove that gay marriages are inherently good and can work, within a prohibitive environment, induced the feeling that she had let her entire lesbian community down.

In this particular case, I had to think carefully about her feeling that I wished she could now find a male partner. I was aware that I had a protective, maternal countertransference with this client. As I pondered further, I was forced to confront my own wish for her to have the "protection" of a man now that she was single. This was reflective of my own traditional upbringing with a father whom my siblings and I saw as a hero and a protector. I made use of this information by inquiring about Anne's new sense of herself as a single person. This opened up a level of awareness regarding feelings of vulnerability that had been safely hidden under a "toughing it out" demeanor. Anne worked on a series of quickly molded figures using Model Magic. In reflecting upon these figures, she saw them as embodying openness and receptivity within their vulnerability.

Another client, whom I shall call Sandra, took quite a while to reveal that she had developed an attraction to me, as she feared I would "kick her out of therapy." When I asked her to tell me more about these feelings, she hesitatingly shared that she felt I would find her to be repulsive, annoying, and unlovable. Attachment may take the form of a little girl expressing her passionate love for her mother by the expressed wish to "marry" her. In a child's mind, "marry" does not necessarily carry the usual sexual or romantic notion it does for adults. It can be an expression of healthy attachment and the wish not to have to share the love object.

Due to the fact that some parents' own heteronormative biases are unconscious and/or condoned by the culture at large, it is not uncommon for a little girl's loving overtures towards her mother to be rebuffed or for a little boy's similar passionate stance towards his father to be met with anxiety and negativity. I viewed this client's anxiety regarding my imagined reaction to her attraction to me as an indication that she had experienced shame regarding her normal feelings of attachment as a child. Indeed, she did have a relationship with her mother that was fraught with fears and ambivalence which continued to play out with me in the transference.

A breakthrough occurred when Sandra brought a camera to her session. She insisted upon taking photos of me, although I requested, true to my analytic training, that she put this wish into words instead of acting it out. When I realized that she couldn't put this impulse into words, I simply went along with the picture taking. Sandra was able to share, the following week, that she kept these photos in a drawer at work and looked at them when she experienced the anxiety she had been feeling when one of her bosses, who had been highly critical of her work, was about to approach her.

Sandra had, up until then, devalued her own artwork and was sure that it could never please me. Her inhibitions extended to many aspirations regarding forms of self-expression in which she thwarted herself before even trying. The one area she now felt safe enough to pursue was her singing. She started working with a teacher and derived great satisfaction from this passionately expressive use of her voice. In this instance, my thoughts about the early thwarting of her attachment needs allowed me to see beyond my analytic stance regarding her taking the photos of me. She was thus free to provide her own art therapy experience through which she was able to create a soothing presence or transitional object (Winnicott, 1965).

Through my clinical experiences, the working hypothesis that has evolved is that some past experiences of my clients may not have been previously viewed as traumatic because they had been seen through a heteronormative lens. By revisiting these experiences in an atmosphere of safety and collaboration, a new level of integration can be facilitated and the possibility for the fulfillment of one's aspirations can be viewed with freedom and enthusiasm.

My student Millie engaged in her wish to have her own biological child in the way that, at that point in time, was felt to be the only viable route. It is now estimated that 3 million LGBTQ individuals have likely had a child and that about 2% of Americans have an LGBTQ-identifying parent (Rosswood, 2016). These statistics seem to indicate that when a lesbian couple is considering parenting in the 21st century, the options are very different.

Opening Space for the Couple

Nowadays, there are more choices available to lesbian couples who choose to become parents, which require careful consideration and which can stimulate hopes, fears, and conflicts within the couple relationship. To begin with, two women present two people, both of whom may be biologically able to conceive and give birth. Therefore, the decision whether to adopt or have a biological child may be followed by the decision as to which partner will carry baby: The two partners may not necessarily be in agreement about these options. For some lesbian couples, one of the partners may have a long-standing wish to be pregnant and to experience giving birth. For the other, who may have no such wish, the idea of her partner being biologically related to their child can stimulate powerful fears around feeling excluded. If the biological mother nurses, this feeling of being excluded can be further exacerbated.

For a client, whom I shall call Gail, whose wife is passionate about becoming pregnant and giving birth, the search for donor sperm became a source of tremendous anxiety. As they both scrolled through different possible donors, Gail became overcome with jealousy. The sperm donor had the equipment she was lacking to make her partner happy. She was angry at her own inability to do this and began to see it as simply unfair that she and her wife's biology required involving another person in such an intimate expression of their love as making a baby together.

We were able to consider the possibility that this was an expression of her internalized heterosexism. In viewing it from this vantage point, she was able to see that her partner had chosen her and indeed greatly needed her presence as support through her efforts to become pregnant, through her pregnancy, and into parenting together. Once past the initial flood of anger, she was able to move into and through her own mourning process related to the "hoops" she felt they had to go through because she and her partner are not heterosexual. These "hoops" were viewed as a punitive consequence for being gay in a heteronormative culture. In looking back upon this difficult moment, I can picture having asked this client to work on a series of hoops using drawing materials, paint, or collage. We could then have visually observed what other meanings may have been embedded in this image.

Helping couples to view their decision making as a unique and exciting experience of bonding in itself can allow for the making of these decisions to reveal areas of vulnerability perhaps never experienced before, and thereby open new levels of trust and growth for the couple.

Making the decision to adopt, as opposed to pursuing a pregnancy, can also present a couple with painful emotional hurdles. The process of adoption can entail a level of scrutiny that can easily be experienced as intrusive and critical in addition to feeling interminable. Even after a couple is found to be acceptable, there is an unknown period of time to wait, which can stimulate many feelings of frustration and rejection. This in itself can cause stress between partners and evoke feelings of failure. With increased awareness and self-reflection, however, this can become a time when couples can negotiate sharing the burden or taking turns in the anticipatory anxiety of waiting for baby to arrive. This can happen when partners are mindfully open and accepting of their feelings of vulnerability. For example, "I'll hold the anxiety for both of us today; you make dinner, okay?" can be a strategy to help detoxify a situation over which neither partner has control. This struggle can provide a potent opportunity for partners to empathize with and enable each other to transcend the potential triggering of feelings around being "good enough."

The working out of roles is another challenge for the couple waiting for the birth or adoption of baby. Since the stereotypical roles assigned to most heterosexual couples do not have to apply, there is room for fluidity. This, however, can be experienced by some partners as just more difficult decision making and can evoke fears about one partner being the "preferred" parental figure for baby. This issue of roles will also be related to and tap into conscious and unconscious templates taken on by each partner from her family of origin.

In my work with couples, I try to create a safe space within which partners are willing to enter a path towards discovery. They need to feel seen and heard by me, by each other, and by themselves in order to stay true to this path. The continuing development of empathy and self-awareness in partners promotes both generativity and creativity. The use of self-reflection and mindfulness are of tremendous value in creating this space.

In the work of Laury Rappaport and Debra Kalmanowitz (2014) there is a wonderful metaphor used to explain the essence of mindfulness. In photos of huge storms involving high winds and precipitation of many kinds, which can have destructive impacts upon the surrounds, there is an opening at the center. This is, as we all know, referred to as the eye of the storm. It has a stable and calm appearance within the seemingly random frenzied motion of the energy that surrounds it. "Mindfulness practices help us to find a center (eye or 'I') within ourselves to bear witness to the storm of thoughts, feelings, sensations and all aspects of our experience, with acceptance" (p.24). I will add to this, that this maintaining of the "I" allows for a stance of objectivity to be accessed more readily when differentiating one's inner voice from the noise of our surrounds. These authors also astutely bring our attention to the balance needed between experiencing and mindfully witnessing. We need both to work in tandem, so that we do not simply exploit mindful practices as a way to distance from challenging circumstances and their attendant emotions.

The use of spontaneous art making can become a route that allows for safe access to the energy and meaning of the various "storms," while mindfully witnessing it as a return is made to a calm center of ourselves. I think of this as the dance we engage in as therapists and as artists. In both of these practices, we have to fully enter the experience of the "other" or of our creative endeavors, while also being prepared and intuiting when to emerge. Each time we emerge, something new is experienced. We attain a point of view we never could have come upon had we allowed ourselves to stay embedded in the familiar.

When I meet with couples and I hear one partner say, "Oh, she *always* has to do that," I am immediately clued in to a lack of mindfulness which may have become normalized in the relationship. The opposite of mindfulness is mindlessness. I do not mean to use this in a pejorative way. We all engage in a certain amount of mindlessness for the purpose of short-cutting and categorizing our experiences in life that otherwise may be too overwhelming to make sense out of, and therefore to feel capable of addressing. In relationships, however, it is important to become aware of tendencies towards organizing experience in predictable ways at the expense of maintaining a more open and receptive stance towards our partners. A lack of mindfulness in relationships means reacting as opposed to responding; it means assuming rather than discovering; it means thinking we "know" rather than being able to tolerate not knowing and waiting to find out. When we impose expectations upon one another based upon our internal drive to organize past experiences and therefore predict and/or categorize current behaviors, we miss the potential for engaging authentically and allowing something new and perhaps unexpected to emerge in the present moment.

I was recently involved in a theater initiative which used improvisation and thus meant that we were not given scripts when the time came for us to perform in front of an audience. It brought into sharp focus for me how seductive it is to buy in to the illusion that we can rely upon presumptions and falsely imposed roles to guide our behaviors, and how truly terrifying it is to be on stage in front of an audience and not know beforehand what will actually emerge.

Choosing a life partner is a major commitment. Choosing to have a child with a partner is often felt to be an even deeper and more profound connection. It is an entrance into territory in which both partners will continue to grow and evolve in many ways that are not predictable. For lesbian couples, there are more limitations regarding role models in our culture than there are for heterosexual couples. Therefore, they can become the authors of their own script. Art therapy can support the development of new life scripts.

Here I would like to propose a way to think about a series of structured sessions using art materials and gentle directives. Working in this way has the potential to open unexpected spaces facilitating the deepening of intimacy—trust and emotional depth so important for facing the developmental tasks ahead. Each of the four sessions I will outline below begins with the following:

Opening Ritual

Partners are asked to sit on the floor with legs crossed or in chairs if that is more comfortable, facing each other. They are then asked to close their eyes and are led through a short relaxation exercise. This is followed by breathing deeply and paying attention to the breath and to any lingering tensions in their body. Eyes are now opened and partners are asked to look deeply into each other's eyes for three minutes. They are asked to pay attention to how they feel, to urges to look away, or to anything else interfering with maintaining each other's gaze. After three minutes they are instructed to take turns saying to each other whatever comes to mind. We then spend a few minutes processing this interaction, talking about the feelings this evoked in each partner, with each having the chance to describe her own and respond to the other's experience.

First Art Experience
Discovering Oneself/Discovering the Other

Now art materials are put out and we all sit together at a table. Each partner is asked to create a self-portrait in whatever way it feels right to do this. It can be representational, it can be when one was a baby or child, it can be abstract or done with collage. There are 15 minutes allotted to this art making. When this time has been reached, partners are asked to find closure with their art piece and then to give the completed piece to their partner.

Witnessing

In this last phase of the session, each individual is asked to witness her partner's work. This involves looking at the work with an intentional attitude of non-judgment, of observation, and of caring contemplation. This contemplation of each other's art is followed by each partner's writing whatever comes to mind about the work, for five minutes.

Finally, partners take turns reading aloud their writings in response to each other's work.

This experience of being attended to, through the metaphor of spontaneously produced art, can provide a sense of renewal, the opening of new perceptions of one another, and the building of tolerance and compassion for feelings related to self-exposure and vulnerability.

Second Art Experience
Envisioning Beginnings

We begin again with the ritual of relaxation, breathing, and three minutes of gazing into each other's eyes. We then sit at the table with art materials and partners are asked to draw a portrait of parents. This can be one's own parents, someone else's parents, parents from a novel or film—whatever image of parents comes to mind spontaneously. This again can be done representationally or abstractly. The images are exchanged, then witnessed, and the writings read aloud to each other.

In creating this parental presence, the most feared and wished for aspects of one's inner parental imagoes can be revealed, allowing for conscious processing. Roles that are revealed may be part of one's embedded or unconscious expectations of a heteronormative ideal, and can be witnessed and mindfully considered. Shared mourning for what each partner will never or can never be, as well as shared empathy and joy in the unfolding of new potentialities, can be opened for exploration.

Third Art Experience
Envisioning Context

After our relaxation and gazing ritual, partners are asked to create a family engaged in something together. This can be done representationally or abstractly and, again, can be based upon one's own family or one's fantasy family. There is time for witnessing each other's work and for reading the writing aloud to each other.

For this exercise, partners are asked to decide for themselves whether they wish to witness their own or each other's art. This shifts an important decision about processing in-the-moment experiences to the couple and away from the therapist.

In creating images of a family, the underlying dynamics of familial relationships are given visual form. It becomes a powerful way to explore issues around control, inclusion or exclusion, dominance or submission, closeness or distance, and other unprocessed feelings around the transition from being a couple or dyad to becoming a group. Again, the images provide a safe place within which partners can respond mindfully both to what they see and to what is being evoked in them by what they see. Allowing fears and anticipatory anxieties to be safely explored together can be an extremely important practice in preparation for parenting with one's partner.

Fourth Art Experience
Generating, Building, Transcending

Following the relaxation and gazing ritual, partners are given a variety of materials with which to construct a three-dimensional piece. They are given the simple open-ended directive: "build something together." Once they come to closure with the piece, they are each asked to write their witnesses and to read them aloud. We then process together what came up for each during this collaboration.

By working on a three-dimensional piece, partners are facing the task of "not knowing" together in a safe space. In addition, they are sharing the excitement and challenge of joining their needs, perspectives, and desires together for the good of the whole. The act of making spontaneous art not only opens vulnerabilities, but stimulates improvisation, introduces surprises, challenges assumptions, facilitates new ways of looking at life, and deepens one's presence in the moment. Practicing this type of mindfulness allows us to tolerate not knowing, sensitizes us to the extraordinary in the ordinary, and allows us to see the difference between what is generated from within oneself and what is being imposed from outside of oneself.

It is my intention to offer new ways of seeing each other and themselves to a lesbian couple facing the unique challenges of their path to parenthood, while living within a culture that does not readily provide the "holding" or "mirroring" conducive to growth through this generative life phase.

References

Benedek, T. (1959) 'Parenthood as a developmental phase: A contribution to libido theory.' *Journal of the American Psychoanalytic Association* 7, 3, 389–417.

Bowlby, J. (1988) *A Secure Base: Parent–Child Attachment and Healthy Human Development*. London: Routledge.

Erikson, E.H. (1950) *Childhood and Society*. New York, NY: W.W. Norton & Company.

Fraiberg, S., Adelson, E., & Shapiro, V. (1975) 'Ghost in the nursery: A psychoanalytic approach to the problems of impaired mother–infant relationships.' *Journal of the American Academy of Child and Adolescent Psychiatry 14*, 3, 387–421.

Freud, A. & Burlingham, D. (1943) *Infants Without Families*. London: Allen & Unwin.

Freud, S. (1914) 'Remembering, Repeating and Working Through (Further Recommendations on the Technique of Psychoanalysis II).' In *Sigmund Freud Standard Edition* Volume XII, trans. J. Strachey. London: Hogarth Press.

Freud, S. (1915) 'Mourning and Melancholia.' In *Sigmund Freud Standard Edition* Volume XIV, trans. J. Strachey. London: Hogarth Press.

Freud, S. (1924) 'Further Recommendations in the Technique of Psychoanalysis: Recollections, Repetitions and Working-Through.' *Collected Papers Vol. II* (trans. J. Riviere).

Mitchell, S. & Black, M. (1995) *Freud and Beyond: A History of Modern Psychoanalytic Thought*. New York, NY: Basic Books.

Pachankis, J.E. & Goldfried, M.R. (2013) 'Clinical issues in working with lesbian, gay and bisexual clients.' *Psychology of Sexual Orientation and Gender Diversity 1*, 45–58.

Rappaport, L. & Kalmanowitz, D. (2014) 'Mindfulness and the Arts Therapies: Overview and Roots.' In L. Rappaport (ed.) *Mindfulness and the Arts Therapies Theory and Practice*. London: Jessica Kingsley Publishers.

Rosswood, E. (2016) *Journey to Same-Sex Parenthood*. Far Hills, NJ: New Horizons Press.

Shannon, J.W. & Woods, W.J. (1991) 'Affirmative psychotherapy for gay men.' *Counseling Psychologist 19*, 197–215.

Spitz, R.A (1945) 'Hospitalism—An inquiry into the genesis of psychiatric conditions in early childhood.' *Psychoanalytic Study of the Child 1*, 53–74.

Stevenson, B. (2012) 'We need to talk about an injustice.' TED talk, March 2012. Accessed on 12/7/2018 at www.ted.com/talks/bryan_stevenson_we_need_to_talk_about_an_injustice.

Stevenson, B. (2015) *Just Mercy: A Story of Justice and Redemption*. New York, NY: Spiegel & Grau.

Weinberg, G. (1972) *Society and the Healthy Homosexual*. New York, NY: Grune & Stratton.

Winnicott, D.W. (1965) 'Ego Distortion in Terms of the True and False Self.' In *The Maturational Processes and the Facilitating Environment*. London: Hogarth Press.

5

Attuning to the Needs of LGBTQ Youth

Trauma, Attachment, and Healing Relationships

MARK BEAUREGARD AND KRISTIN LONG

Introduction

LGBTQ (lesbian, gay, bisexual, transgender, queer) youth have reported feeling that they must go outside of the community in which they live in order to be accepted and seek out families of choice beyond their family of origin in an ongoing effort to feel understood. Misattunement and relational traumas occur within the families of origin for LGBTQ youth, and this can be replicated or played out time and time again in school and social service systems, even when they are meant to offer a safe space. This chapter will provide readers with an understanding of this cycle from a trauma-informed relational viewpoint. We will highlight how creative arts therapy treatment assists in developing interpersonal attunement and secure attachments in the therapeutic dyad, thus helping readers find ways of mitigating trauma's impact on LGBTQ youth in order to deliver more affirming care.

Sexual and Gender Identities: To Infinity and Beyond...

We recognize that individuals with diverse sexual orientations and gender identities have existed across time and cultures, long before language and/or systems acknowledged them. Myths and stories from all over the world include accounts of gender fluidity and LGBTQ relationships, including those from ancient Chinese, Hindu, Japanese, Greek, and

Roman cultures. Modern language can be limited in its ability to capture and give form to identity, and is constantly shifting and developing to better fit people's experience as sexual and gendered individuals in the world. Today, we find ourselves in an expansive era where binaries and rigid concepts of sexuality and gender identity are being broken down and expanded upon. We are quite literally queering the language lexicon to create copious identity labels, thus providing numerous possibilities of defined experience. We recognize and celebrate the need to have a word or label that defines one's self, while also appreciating that sexual and gender identities are groupings which are not so easily categorized and simplified; they are unique to individuals and exist upon continuums of abundant opportunity and variability.

Our challenge, as therapists, is to define and communicate about concepts that are not fixed. What do we mean when we speak about sexuality or gender? And how do we understand the need for definition in a society where spoken language is the privileged form of communication, but the language itself is limited? Sexual orientation is defined as an "enduring pattern of emotional, romantic, and/or sexual attractions" to others (American Psychological Association, 2008, para. 2) that are "tied to the intimate personal relationships that meet deeply felt needs for love, attachment and intimacy" (American Psychological Association, 2008, para. 4). In attempting to define the term *gender*, we lean into Adrienne Harris's (2009) concept of gender as a "soft assembly." She writes, "I have come to see gender as an increasingly multiple and layered experience, drawing on attachments that need to be deconstructed to expose both fantasy and preconscious and conscious organizations of genderedness" (pp.125–126).

For our work, gender is indeed a "soft assembly," not an immovable or rigid structure meant to hold solid throughout one's lifetime, but rather a robust and fluid construct. Holding on to both "identity and multiplicity or difference" (Aron, 1995, p.202) allows us a range of language and identity options, while keeping in mind what Salamon (2010) warns when they say how important it is to not lose the person in the midst of trying to code the body. We find that clinicians may encounter youth who identify as agender, asexual, bisexual, bigender, cisgender, demigender, demisexual, gay, heterosexual, feminine or masculine of center, fluid, genderqueer, gender non-conforming, gender creative, gender-expansive, intersex, lesbian, non-binary, neutrois, omnisexual, pansexual, pangender, queer, questioning, skoliosexual, trans/transgender, transmasculine, transfeminine, two-spirit, and many other terms referring to one's sexual orientation and/or gender identity. The use of language and knowing how to talk/inquire about sexual orientation and gender identity in treatment can be challenging for therapists of all skill levels, particularly when youth and their families are not in alignment around identity and language (Brill & Pepper, 2008; Nealy, 2017; Ryan, 2009).

The two vignettes below illustrate that there can be disconnects between how youth identify and how their parents and other adults may acknowledge them, requiring flexibility and validation on the part of the therapist to affirm the youth's language and sense of self, while maintaining compassion for parents/caregivers. Throughout this chapter, we have decided to not identify which story comes from which clinician as a way to maintain the anonymity of our patients as much as possible.

SLADE

Slade walked into the office, wearing a cat-eared headset with pink glitter, a tail from their feather scarf trailing behind. At 20 years old, Slade was more interested in fashion than almost anything else, except their close group of friends and an ongoing Snapchat streak that's over 300 days long. Slade's mother had called the week prior, concerned that her daughter had schizophrenia. "She's becoming split personalities. I can't keep them all straight and she gets really upset when I make a mistake. I think there is something seriously wrong and I need help figuring out what to do." I assured Slade's mom that this gender expression wasn't new to me, and, if needed, I could certainly assess for some deeper pathology as well.

In the latter part of our first session, Slade announced they were "cisgender, pansexual, and demisexual." From their direct stare my way, it was clear they were wanting to challenge me as well—testing how I would respond to their announcement. "Sounds like you have a clear idea of who you are," I offered. Slade smiled, and then gleefully suggested that most of our work would be around explaining this to their parents, who "insist on using female pronouns to describe me. I am getting tired of correcting them!"

JORDAN

I met with Jordan's parents the day before meeting Jordan, listening while this well-intentioned but scared couple told me what prompted them to seek a therapist for their tween daughter. Jordan, assigned female at birth, began questioning his gender identity and was becoming increasingly more distressed. Jordan's parents were not using his preferred name or pronouns (he/him/his) and openly shared with me that they were "not ready for that." They were hurt that Jordan began to tell friends and be more public about his new name, expressing they could accept if Jordan was gay, but were not prepared to have a transgender kid. Jordan's parents were struggling but wanted him to have a place to talk to someone who could understand and help, outside the family.

My first meeting with Jordan came and a gentle tween artistic kid entered my office. I warmly greeted him with my hand and introduced myself. He instantly looked down awkwardly at the floor and then apprehensively up at me. "I don't know what to say, I'm not sure how my parents have already introduced me to you." "Ah," I said. "Well, how would you like me to know you? What name and pronouns would you like me to use?" He took a breath, smiled shyly, and said, "Jordan, and I guess he/him. I'm fairly certain I'm trans, I think," as if trying to convince me. "Nice to meet you, Jordan." I emphasized, "I don't expect or need you to know exactly who or how you are forever, more just right in this moment." Almost immediately after saying that, I felt a concern I may have come across as dismissive, fearing that in my efforts to connect I could also have gone wrong right out of the gate and repair might be needed.

I looked at him for a moment. He seemed relieved and then began to tell me the story of how he came to pick his name and the other options he wound up not choosing. He moved on to how, although he knew his parents were "trying," he wished they would call him by the name and pronouns he identifies with. "How does it feel when people do that?" I asked. "Great! Like they know me." The current and constant misgendering in his family was extremely difficult for him. When the session came to an end, I made sure to say, "Goodbye, Jordan. See you next time."

Best practices around inclusive and affirming language usage recommend that clinicians mirror the language that patients use and prefer with regard to sexual and gender identity, including names and pronouns (American Psychological Association, 2011; Whitehead-Pleaux et al., 2012; WPATH, 2011). Although it can be challenging, clinicians can work with parents and families around education, as moving toward affirming language practices is vital. Psychoeducation for parents and other family members is often a crucial part of this work, and resources available online such as the Genderbread Person can help give language and form when clarifying spectrums of gender and sexuality (The Genderbread Person). Offering parents research on how supportive practices by family members have significant positive outcomes for the mental health and development of queer and trans youth is essential. These behaviors, such as using pronouns that match a child's gender identity, supporting a child's gender expression, and taking time to talk with a child about their gender identity and/or sexual orientation, can dramatically increase self-esteem and reduce risk of negative outcomes later in life (Nealy, 2017; Ryan, 2009; Ryan et al., 2009; Ryan et al., 2010; Travers et al., 2012).

Trauma and Queer and Trans Youth

While we live in a seemingly increasingly accepting place where great strides have been made for equality and acceptance of LGBTQ individuals, it remains true that the world can be a dangerous place for queer and trans youth, threatening their safety, their relationships, and their ability to live authentically in the world. An article published in *The New York Times* (Park & Mykhyalyshyn, 2016) just after the mass shooting at the Orlando Pulse nightclub examined research from the FBI stating that LGBT people are the most likely minority group to be targeted for hate crimes. Ironically, as they note, increased targeted violence has much to do with social justice and strides made in equality. As equality increases and society is seen to become more tolerant, there are subsections of individuals who fight harder against it, increasing in violent reaction to oppose this change. In 2017, there were a total of 52 reported hate-related homicides of LGBTQ people in the United States, an 86% increase from 2016 (NCAVP, 2018). LGBTQ people of color experience disproportionally higher rates of violence across age groups as a result of anti-LGBT discrimination combined with persistent structural racism. This is especially true for trans women of color (Grant et al., 2011). Queer and trans youth of color experience significant hardship as a result of cumulative stress that occurs from being targets of harassment and abuse around gender, sexuality, and race-based discrimination. Higher levels of stress have also been reported by queer and trans youth when their experience included intersections of gender, sexual orientation, and religion (Diaz & Kosciw, 2009).

LGBTQ people are living in a world of duplicity that involves both increased acceptance and visibility and continued struggles with backlash toward gains in equality, safety, and visibility. Traumatic experience is all too common for queer and trans individuals, particularly queer and trans people of color. An intersectional lens in treatment is imperative, and, as mental health professionals, we must consider the impact trauma has on the ability of queer and trans youth to form relationships, and understand the power of therapeutic relationships to help them creatively, confidently, and successfully move through their lives.

Trauma

In the field of behavioral health, trauma is often divided into two categories: big "T" trauma and little "t" trauma (Bromberg, 2011; Corbett et al., 2014; Parnell, 1999). Big "T" traumas, sometimes referred to as "simple" traumas, are specific, time-framed events. A bookend can be put around start and end times. Examples of these traumas include earthquakes, airplane crashes, rape, exposure to a violent act, and terrorist attacks. While we recognize that big "T" traumas are significant in the lives of many queer and trans youth, we are not focusing on these traumas in this chapter. Rather, we will focus more specifically on the little "t" traumas, also referred to as relational, complex, or developmental traumas.

In 2005, Bessel van der Kolk, a psychiatrist who is well known for his research around traumatic stress, neurobiology, and attachment, started to discuss trauma in a relatively new way. He noted that internal ongoing trauma states, which he labeled developmental trauma disorder, were occurring in the patients that he was treating. While there was a substantial movement from the mental health community for this diagnosis to be accepted into the American Psychiatric Association's *Diagnostic Statistical Manual*, 5th Edition, it was eventually denied (van der Kolk et al., 2009). While this was a major disservice to people who suffer from relational traumas, clinicians can still consider it a useful diagnostic framework to use when understanding developmental traumas. The children van der Kolk and others were treating had experienced trauma but did not meet the diagnostic criteria for post-traumatic stress disorder (PTSD), and therefore were given the damaging labels of oppositional defiant disorder or conduct disorder (van der Kolk, 2014). Throughout our career as therapists, we have seen this occur repeatedly in outpatient and inpatient mental health systems in New York City. Using a medical model for diagnostic purposes, youth who were dealing with ongoing relational traumas were admitted to psychiatric hospitals/clinics and were discharged with detrimental diagnoses that followed them into their home and school settings.

In general, relational traumas include being bullied, experiencing emotional neglect, ongoing parental or teacher disapproval, repeated exposure to a family member with a severe mental illness or substance abuse problems, and other relational issues.

Relational Traumas Experienced by Queer and Trans Youth

In queer and trans communities, relational traumas often take the form of an erasure or disavowing of one's true self. This disconfirmation, a trauma of unrecognition, happens by parents, by friends, and sometimes even by oneself in a society steeped in heteronormative assumptions and microaggressions. Queer and trans youth often feel a need to keep silent about their identities, for fear of being teased or bullied, or even beaten. A survey of more than 10,000 LGBT-identified youth across the United States by the Human Rights Campaign (2013) highlights frequent relational traumas that LGBT youth experience in their families and communities, often resulting in feelings of alienation, fear, and compounding ruptures. When youth were asked to identify the biggest problem facing their lives, the top three responses were: non-accepting families (26%), school/bullying problems (21%), and a fear of being out or open (18%). Nearly half (42%) of the youth reported feeling they must leave the community in which they live in order to be accepted. Thirty-three percent of youth reported their families were not accepting, with youth hearing discriminatory comments in their home about LGBT identity frequently (Human Rights Campaign, 2013).

Youth report significant trauma experiences in school environments as well. In a survey conducted by Kosciw and colleagues (2016) of 10,528 LGBTQ-identified youth across the United States, over half of the students (57.6%) stated they felt in danger at school because of their sexual orientation, and 43.3% felt unsafe because of their gender expression, resulting in frequent avoidance and absence from school. A staggering 85.2% of students surveyed described experiencing verbal harassment in school, frequently hearing homophobic and transphobic remarks by peers and, sadly, even from teachers and staff. Many of the LGBTQ-identified students reported experiencing physical harassment and assault as a result of their sexual orientation or gender identity or expression. Sixty-three percent of students who reported discrimination in their schools stated that school staff did not respond (Kosciw *et al.*, 2016). As therapists, we can imagine the impact this can have on a student's sense of self-worth and the likelihood that they will struggle to trust adults in the future.

We have all had relational traumas, but many of us find repair in later, more secure relationships. This may occur with friends, with partners, or with mentors who validate our sense of reality. Queer and trans kids who are kicked out of their homes, who are neglected, who are beaten for spoken or unspoken identity performances are all at risk for ongoing developmental/relational traumas. This is when therapy can literally be life-saving. Bromberg (2011) beautifully describes the relationship between little "t" and big "T" traumas, and the importance of repair:

> When a child suffers consistent nonrecognition and disconfirmation of her self-experience—the cumulative nonrecognition of entire aspects of self as existing—what happens is that the developmental trauma and vulnerability to massive trauma become interwoven. In adulthood, the capacity to then live a life that is creative, spontaneous, stable, and relationally authentic requires an extraordinary natural endowment, and, probably, a healing relationship with some person who enables the adult to *use* [their] natural endowment. This other person is often a therapist, but need not be. (pp.4–5)

The vignettes below show how a relational trauma may start, for a queer youth, to be established within a family system:

ROB

Rob's parents called to set up an intake appointment at the beginning of the school year. They were concerned that he had "lost his imaginative self" and noted that he was starting to withdraw from activities that he previously enjoyed. I met with his parents and obtained additional developmental history, all which was on par with normal physical and psychological growth. His parents were at a loss as to why their 15-year-old son seemed to "change overnight" and, rather suddenly, was showing signs of despair. He still attended tennis practice, but stopped his other extracurricular activities. As our intake session was winding up, I asked if there was anything else that felt important for the family to share with me. As an afterthought, Rob's dad said that their son recently told them that he "thinks he is gay." I asked how, as parents, they took this information. Both parents felt that, if their son "really was gay," they would be fine with it. But they quickly added that they didn't think he was and, of course, "it was too soon to tell."

This brief description of their son's identity stayed with me, long after I met their child. When Rob first entered the room, I was aware that I coded him as gay. When Rob and I met, I held on to the idea that he was questioning his sexuality, and it wasn't until weeks into our treatment, once we had developed a therapeutic relationship, that I asked him directly about it.

"Rob, when I first talked to your parents, they told me you were questioning if you were gay or not. I realize you and I never talked directly about this." Rob looked like he was going to jump off the couch. His eyes were big; his hands gesturing. "No! I told them I AM gay—they added the 'not sure' part." He seemed to be waiting for me to challenge him, but instead we held the gaze for a moment, as if solidifying this new information between the two of us. "I got it," I firmly replied, holding a moment of eye contact for a few extra beats.

Several family sessions followed, as well as meetings with just Rob's parents in an ongoing effort to provide psychoeducation and support of their own experience.

Sustaining a stance of empathy for parents is essential when doing systems work, as many parents go through their own process of mourning the child's perceived identity when their child's gender and/or sexual orientation is different to what they envisioned or planned. However, the importance of affirming parents is key for children to feel safe.

Families who are conflicted about their child's LGBTQ identity can often feel they should help their child assimilate with heterosexual and/or cisgender peers, or deny access to other LGBTQ peers and resources as a means of protection, acting out of a protective stance to keep their child safe from a potentially dangerous future (Nealy, 2017; Ryan, 2009; Travers *et al.*, 2012). However, this can often be perceived by the child as rejection of who they are, that their parents do not love them, and this can have significant consequences. Research sheds light on the dramatic impact family relationships and behavior have on both protective and risk factors for LGBTQ youth health and mental health outcomes. Family rejection is linked to low self-esteem, increased isolation, increased risk of drug use, increased risk of HIV and STI infection, and higher rates of depression and suicide (Ryan, 2009; Ryan et al., 2009). Family rejection is, of course, connected to the alarming statistic that 40% of homeless youth in the United States identify as LGBT (Human Rights Campaign, 2013), and that rejected and vulnerable queer and trans youth often seek out families and communities of choice where they feel they will be more accepted and able to meet their relational needs.

In contrast, specific family accepting behaviors toward LGBTQ youth are found to be protective measures against suicide, depression, and substance use. Youth who experience higher levels of family acceptance have significantly higher levels of self-esteem, social support, and general well-being compared with those who experience low levels of acceptance (Ryan et al., 2010; Travers et al., 2012). Support and acceptance in schools shows dramatic improvements in the lives of queer and trans youth as well (Kosciw et al., 2016). Parent and caregiver engagement is obviously crucial in fostering resiliency in youth and increasing relational understanding and bonds. As therapists, we have found the concept of attunement to be fundamental in working with LGBTQ youth in creating healing relationships with our patients and their families.

Attunement and Secure Attachment

Attunement is a crucial component in all relational dyads. Most research in this area is around parent–infant relations, and the applications to adult psychotherapy treatment (Beebe & Lachmann, 2014). Attunement is one of the most basic tools we have as therapists, and yet our experience is that it is rarely explained or discussed in much detail in training programs. Stern (1985, 1995) was interested in attunement from an intersubjective, bi-directional infant–parent relationship. Drama therapist Pitruzzella (2017) describes Stern's notion of "affect attunement," explaining that it included cross-modal correspondences, which means that expressions through different modes of communication can be engaged and comprehended due to the synchronization of the senses.

Attunement isn't the act of imitating or replaying another person's behaviors or movements. Attunement is less of an action and more of an affective state; we internally know when we feel attuned to, or when misattunement happens. More than anything, attunement is a somatic experience. In thinking about somatic experiences, especially with trans and queer youth, their own body has not always been a container that feels trustworthy. Therefore, recognizing attunement may be more difficult for our queer and trans patients, and, for them, trusting a new therapeutic relationship may take additional work on the part of the clinician. Positive attunement can actually regulate our nervous system and we can settle physically into a sense of being held, being kept in mind. As therapists, we work to notice how our emotions and our bodies respond to messages from our patients—both implicit and explicit. We also understand the importance of mentalization, and for our patients to feel "held in mind" beyond our specific session time (Fonagy & Target, 1996).

The goal here, both for parents and therapists, is not to be perfect and never to misattune. Clearly, we cannot always resonate with others. Rather, the goal is awareness with an ongoing attempt to offer repair(s). As Winnicott (1971) coined the term "good-enough mother" (p.10), so we want to aim to be good-enough therapists. Without attunement, validation, and secure attachment, the potential for emotional repair is lost (Schore, 2001, 2003). In discussing ways to heal damaged attunement systems, van der Kolk (2014) mentions the importance of rhythmicity and reciprocity. Integrating body senses allows us to be attuned to our own self-states, as well as those of others. This idea is not a new one for creative arts therapists. Schore (2003) wrote:

> [T]he attuned, intuitive clinician, from the first point of contact, is learning the nonverbal moment-to-moment rhythmic structures of the patient's internal states, and is relatively flexibly and fluidly modifying her own behavior to *synchronize* with that structure, thereby creating a context for the organization of the therapeutic alliance. (p.52)

Cross-Modal Attunement

Cross-modal attunement, which allows one to feel most attuned to by another (Stern, 1985), is especially of interest for creative arts therapists. With an understanding of attunement, we can begin to imagine what it means to attune across sensory modalities. In terms of a developmental model, this was thought of as voice to gesture, or movement to sound. For example, a baby waves their hands in the air, and their parent vocalizes, "Weeeeeeeeee!" As creative arts therapists, we often do this already by helping patients take information from movement into language, or the other way around. However, we want to consider expanding this to include attunement across the creative arts modalities as well. When collaborating, we might take a two-dimensional piece of artwork and create a piece of music from it. Or take a dance and create a sculpture. While this isn't specifically a crossover of sensory modalities, future creative arts therapy research might want to consider exploring this further. We are left wondering: Might patients feel even more attuned to when experiencing this deep comprehension across artistic modalities?

Attachment

In his foreword to Bowlby's book titled *Loss: Sadness and Depression*, Daniel Stern (1980) wrote: "Today it seems incredible that, until Bowlby, no one placed attachment at the center of human development" (2000, p.xiii). Breaking the word down, and imaging or co-creating what it is to be "attached," seems to be at the core of our work as clinicians. In therapy, group or individual, what transpires is attaching: connecting, bridging, linking, joining. Traditionally, there are four main attachment patterns. For the scope of this chapter, we wanted to acknowledge that these patterns exist, but focus more on the disruption of attachment that often occurs when a queer or trans child isn't accepted in their family of origin. As Bromberg (2006) noted, little "t" traumas are significant because they form "the attachment patterns that establish what is to become a stable or unstable core self" (p.6). From a developmental stance, parents and children form attachments, often from pre-birth. This attachment includes a profound, unconscious understanding of safety, love, fear, closeness, anxiety, and other affect states. When the attachment pattern is secure, children grow up with a sense of feeling attuned to, which leads them to believe the world is a mostly safe, welcoming space.

Creative Arts Therapy: Creatively Developing Attunement and Attachment

As creative arts therapists, we identify the immense power of the arts in assisting youth with identity development and coping when spoken words are not always accessible or enough. Queer and trans youth often need to work harder to find opportunities for emotional repair, due to a lack of understanding of the repetitive traumas they are susceptible to, such as when their belief about their core self is brought into question.

As therapists working with this population, we have an opportunity to offer these reparative experiences. These are chances for a patient to have a new experience of a caring adult, often in the form of a therapist.

The repair starts to happen when the therapist not only listens and validates, but also attunes to the patient, verbally and nonverbally, and helps them to not fall back into the pattern of repeating past traumatic experiences (Atlas, 2016; Beebe & Lachmann, 2014; Bromberg, 2011; Fonagy & Target, 1996; van der Kolk, 2005). By attuning to the needs of our patients who are struggling to have validated coherent self-narratives, we can offer them a space to explore their own identities and carefully, safely, articulate what they know about their own self-states. Green (2003) writes:

> [T]he gay child often has no help in regulating affect states, in processing information, or in verbally decoding experiences. It is only after a "witness" listens to his experiences that the boy is able to integrate, as part of his developmental narrative, and understand who he is and what these experiences mean to him. Thus, the dissociation is gradually overcome and the individual's self can be integrated. (pp.180–181)

Beauregard and Moore (2011) discuss this concept in a similar way, encouraging therapists to create a permissive and safe atmosphere to "use the therapeutic space as a laboratory for identity exploration" (p.307). Inspired by drama therapist Renee Emunah (1994), Beauregard and Moore (2011) conceptualize the therapeutic space as being a gender/sexuality lab where youth can playfully try on and take off identity roles at will, ultimately working toward an increasingly integrated sense of self through creative and embodied experiences.

Creative arts therapy processes allow for the unfolding of healing relationships where therapist and patient encounter one another while growing together through witnessing and mirroring, and by providing sensory-based experiences where patients can have their various self-states acknowledged and validated. Versaci (2016) writes: "As sensory and embodied methodologies, the creative arts therapies have a unique ability to promote attachment and heal the wounds of insecure attachment" (p.225). The concept of sensory-based attunement is essential to creative arts therapy practice. As Malchiodi (2016) points out:

> The unique sensory nature of the "expressive arts therapeutic relationship," first and foremost, is what differentiates it from verbal

therapies in its impact and role in intervention and healing... The expressive arts therapies emphasize senses, feeling and non-verbal communication, establishing a different type of attunement between the practitioner and the individual or group less dependent on words. (para. 3)

She points out that it is the alchemy between the therapist, patient, and the artistic process that is what contributes to healing and change.

The following case illustrates how creativity becomes a catalyst and bridge for attuning and being with another in a new way. It is less a complete picture and more a collage of moments of a developing therapeutic relationship. It is a story about the creative moments that propel us forward. The creativity our clients bring, the creativity we as therapists bring, and how that creativity is used in the therapy space to support youth and families find inroads to being and expressing their authentic selves.

DEVAN

I started seeing Devan when he was nine years old. His mother was seeking therapy to help him in part with managing executive functioning difficulties, but primarily out of concerns related to his social skills, self-esteem, and difficulty coping with intense bullying from peers around what was perceived as more feminine gender expression. Devan was an energetic, talkative Trinidadian American kid whom his mother described as very "expressive." She worried about how badly he was picked on and that he was having trouble connecting with others, especially peers.

I remember his face and look of excitement when he came into my office, loving the art and play supplies, as if he had walked into a candy store. We began using paints, exploring feelings in color on paper, mixing colors, and reflecting together how fun it was. He shared how he didn't get to be so "colorful in public," how he often felt different to other kids. I myself understood this feeling. I also knew what it meant to try to dull your own colors so you are not seen as "too much." In my office, I offered, we can be as colorful as we want to be. That began as our initial contract about our work— to be as expressive and playful as possible together. Color and play were the language we established first, witnessing and mirroring while we explored boundaries of expression in our co-created therapy play space.

Devan loved puppets. One session he created a pink puppet. Color was now taking shape and form. In the session, we explored the puppet's character through an interview format, with me getting to know the puppet. At the end of the session I invited him to take it home. He very quickly said, "I can't take that home; boys don't like pink!" That one sentence told me so much. Ironically, I was wearing a pink shirt that day. I countered the idea: "I love pink, I'm wearing a pink shirt." We laughed. We decided we would keep the pink puppet in the office for us to use in future sessions and to hold safe for him.

Over the course of several sessions, improvised play took us on a journey that began in an imaginary restaurant and led us to face bullies. Devan was drawn to playdough, and we began creating food and improvising long sessions of the two of us as wait staff in restaurants serving demanding customers. Cue music. The kitchen music was always Donna Summer hits, his and his mother's favorite singer. It was the perfect soundtrack to allow us to get in role as our most powerful diva-wait-staff-selves. A shift began to happen where the customers became offensive, saying derogatory things, and we would process it in role: "Did you hear what they just said to me??" "I can't believe that!!" "Well, what should we do?" We created signs that said, "Bullies not welcome here in our restaurant!" and we practiced what we would say to them in response to their derogatory remarks.

This fictional, thinly veiled world led us into the reality of his everyday life. We had been seeing one another for some time and Devan was ready to process and talk about his real-life bullying encounters, fears, and even times when his own inner "Diva" helped him to stick up for himself— at times also making him a target. As we continued to work together, we frequently checked in, processed, and rehearsed real-life situations through use of an empty chair where we could both address and confront the bullies. We engaged in puppetry and role plays to problem solve, and continually identified supporters and allies at school and in the community where he lived. I worked with his mom, his biggest ally of all, to help find a school and community that they felt more supported by before our work came to a close. On our last day, he went home with the colorful images, and the pink puppet.

The fact that Devan and his caretakers were Trinidadian and lived in and went to school in predominantly Caribbean communities was an important piece of the family's experience. Throughout the treatment I was keenly aware of the potential conflicts between cultural beliefs and norms and Devan's gender expression, and the family's need to find safe and supportive care and environments. This dynamic was definitely an undercurrent always in my mind throughout the process.

Interestingly, though, while I felt it was also on their minds (both Devan's and his mother's), I do not believe it was ever spoken outright between any of us. As I recollected back to this case and considered that, I wondered about that happening and what role that silence played in our treatment. Was it too hard to speak about? Were we all just afraid to bring it up, or was I too afraid to bring it up? Was our silence around the specific cultural dynamic also akin to the silence and worry they experienced in public and community encounters, their fears of bullying and retaliation? In thinking back, I wonder what could have been gained in really locating and bringing those intersectional elements outright into our dialogues.

A few years later Devan's mother reached out to me, wanting to share that things were going well, and that Devan had recently come out to her as gay and was doing quite well with the support of a therapist in his school. I was very glad to hear that. Our work was not about whether he was gay, but so much more about being comfortable in his skin, in how he expresses himself, his true colors, and finding the adults and peers that validated him.

Conclusion

Van der Kolk (2014) wrote: "As we grow up, we gradually learn to take care of ourselves, both physically and emotionally, but we get our first lessons in self-care from the way that we are cared *for*" (p.112). When this first lesson in self-care is less than optimal, people may seek therapy, and, on some fundamental level, hope for a new experience around how someone cares for them. As therapists, it is important that we recognize the fundamental healing power of relationships, and, in the influence and responsibility that we have as therapists, provide affirming and corrective experiences to LGBTQ individuals and their families. Attunement and validation, combined with artistic intervention, become valuable tools which we use to help develop and strengthen bonds that have been ruptured or tested by relational trauma.

References

American Psychological Association (2019) 'Understanding Sexual Orientation and Gender Identity.' Accessed on 2/12/19 at https://www.apa.org/topics/lgbt/ orientation.

American Psychological Association (2011) 'Practice Guidelines for LGB clients: Guidelines for Psychological Practice with Lesbian, Gay, and Bisexual Clients.' Accessed on 7/12/17 at www.apa.org/pi/lgbt/resources/guidelines.aspx.

Aron, L. (1995) 'The internalized primal scene.' *Psychoanalytic Dialogues 5*, 195–237.

Atlas, G. (2016) *The Enigma of Desire*. New York, NY: Routledge.

Beauregard, M. & Moore, D. (2011) 'Creative Approaches to Working with Gender Variant and Sexual Minority Boys.' In C. Haen (ed.) *Engaging Boys in Treatment: Creative Approaches to the Therapy Process*. New York, NY: Routledge.

Beebe, B. & Lachmann, F.M. (2014) T*he Origins of Attachment: Infant Research and Adult Treatment*. New York, NY: Routledge.

Bolby, J. (1980) *Loss: Sadness and Depression*. New York, NY: Basic Books.

Brill, S. & Pepper, R. (2008) *The Transgender Child*. San Francisco, CA: Cleis Press.

Bromberg, P.M. (2006) *Awakening the Dreamer: Clinical Journeys*. Mahwah, NJ: The Analytic Press.

Bromberg, P.M. (2011) *The Shadow of the Tsunami and the Growth of the Relational Mind*. New York, NY: Routledge.

Corbett, K., Dimen, M., Goldner, V., & Harris, A. (2014) 'Talking sex, talking gender—a roundtable.' *Studies in Gender and Sexuality 15*, 4, 295–317.

Diaz, E.M. & Kosciw, J.G. (2009) *Shared Differences: The Experiences of Lesbian, Gay, Bisexual, and Transgender Students of Color in Our Nation's Schools*. New York, NY: GLSEN.

Emunah, R. (1994) *Acting for Real: Drama Therapy Process, Technique, and Performance*. New York, NY: Brunner/Mazel.

Fonagy, P. & Target, M. (1996) 'Playing with reality: I. theory of mind and the normal development of psychic reality.' *International Journal of Psychoanalysis 77*, 217–233.

Genderbread Person (n.d.) 'The Genderbread Person v4.0.' Accessed on 3/28/2019 at https://www.genderbread.org.

Grant, J.M., Mottet, L.A., Tanis, J., Harrison, J., Herman, J.L., & Keisling, M. (2011) *Injustice at Every Turn: A Report of the National Transgender Discrimination Survey*. Washington, DC: National Center for Transgender Equality and National Gay and Lesbian Task Force.

Green, J.A. (2003) 'Growing up hidden: Notes on understanding male homosexuality.' *American Journal of Psychoanalysis 63*, 177–191.

Harris, A. (2009) *Gender as Soft Assembly*. New York, NY: Routledge.

Human Rights Campaign (2013) *Growing up LGBT in America: HRC Youth Survey Report Key Findings*. Washington, DC: Human Rights Campaign.

Kosciw, J.G., Greytak, E.A., Palmer, N.A., & Boesen, M.J. (2016) *The 2015 National School Climate Survey: The Experiences of Lesbian, Gay, Bisexual and Transgender Youth in Our Nation's Schools*. New York, NY: GLSEN.

Malchiodi, C. (2016) 'Expressive arts therapy and self-regulation.' *Psychology Today*. Accessed on 7/28/17 at www.psychologytoday.com/blog/arts-and-health/201603/expressive-arts-therapy-and-self-regulation.

National Coalition of Anti-Violence Programs (NCAVP) (2018) *A Crisis of Hate: A Report on Lesbian, Gay, Bisexual, Transgender and Queer Hate Homicides in 2017.* Authors: Emily Waters, Larissa Pham, & Chelsea Convery. New York, NY: New York City Anti-Violence Project.

Nealy, E. (2017) *Transgender Children and Youth: Cultivating Pride and Joy with Families in Transition.* New York, NY: W.W. Norton & Company.

Park, H. & Mykhyalyshyn, I. (2016) 'LGBT people are more likely to be targets of hate crimes than any other minority group.' *New York Times,* June 16, 2016. Accessed on 11/13/2018 at www.nytimes.com/interactive/2016/06/16/us/hate-crimes-against-lgbt.html.

Parnell, L. (1999) *EMDR in the Treatment of Adults Abused as Children.* New York, NY: W.W. Norton & Company.

Pitruzzella, S. (2017) 'Between innocence and experience: Variations on Robert Landy's Persona and Performance (1993).' *Drama Therapy Review 3,* 1, 101–112.

Ryan, C. (2009) *Helping Families Support Their Lesbian, Gay, Bisexual, and Transgender (LGBT) Children.* Washington, DC: National Center for Cultural Competence, Georgetown University Center for Child and Human Development.

Ryan, C., Heubner, D., Diaz, R.M., & Sanchez, J. (2009) 'Family rejection as a predictor of negative health outcomes in white and Latino lesbian, gay, and bisexual young adults.' *Pediatrics 123,* 1, 346–352.

Ryan, C., Russell, S.T., Huebner, D., Diaz, R., & Sanchez, J. (2010) 'Family acceptance in adolescence and the health of LGBT young adults.' *Journal of Child and Adolescent Psychiatric Nursing 23,* 4, 205–213.

Salamon, G. (2010) *Assuming a Body: Transgender and Rhetorics of Materiality.* New York, NY: Columbia University Press.

Schore, A.N. (2001) 'Minds in the making: Attachment, the self-organizing brain, and developmentally-oriented psychoanalytic psychotherapy.' *British Journal of Psychotherapy 17,* 3, 299–328.

Schore, A.N. (2003) *Affect Regulation and the Repair of the Self.* New York, NY: W.W. Norton & Company.

Stern, D. (1985) *The Interpersonal World of the Infant.* New York, NY: Basic Books.

Stern, D. (1995) *The Motherhood Constellation.* New York, NY: Basic Books.

Travers, R., Bauer, G., Pyne, J., Bradley, K., Gale, L., & Papadimitriou, M. (2012) *Impacts of Strong Parental Support for Trans Youth: A Report Prepared for Children's Aid Society of Toronto and Delisle Youth Services.* Toronto, ON: TransPulse. Accessed on 11/13/2018 at http://transpulseproject.ca/research/impacts-of-strong-parental-support-for-trans-youth.

van der Kolk, B.A. (2005) 'Developmental trauma disorder: Toward a rational diagnosis for children with complex trauma histories.' *Psychiatric Annals 35,* 5, 401–408.

van Der Kolk, B.A. (2014) *The Body Keeps the Score: Brain, Mind, and Body in the Healing of Trauma.* New York, NY: Penguin.

van der Kolk, B.A., Pynoos, R., Cicchetti, D., Cloitre, M. *et al.* (2009) *Proposal to Include Developmental Trauma Disorder Diagnosis for Children and Adolescents in DSM-V.* Accessed on 2/25/2018 at http://cismai.it/wp-content/uploads/2013/11/DTD_papers_Oct_095eb2.pdf.

Versaci, R. (2016) 'Attachment performs: Framing attachment theory within the dramatic worldview.' *Drama Therapy Review 2,* 2, 223–227.

Whitehead-Pleaux, A., Donnenwerth, A.M., Robinson, B., Hardy, S. *et al.* (2012) 'Lesbian, gay, bisexual, transgender, and questioning: Best practices in music therapy.' *Music Therapy Perspectives 30,* 2, 158–166.

Winnicott, D.W. (1971) *Playing and Reality.* London: Routledge.

World Professional Association for Transgender Health (WPATH) (2011) *Standards of Care for the Health of Transsexual, Transgender, and Gender Nonconforming People, Version 7.* Accessed on 11/8/2018 at www.wpath.org/publications/soc.

6

Seeing and Meeting the Other...Clearly

A Case Study Examining How Unconscious Bias Can Get in the Way in Treatment with a Transgender Teen

CARA A. GALLO-JERMYN

Introduction

This chapter is an examination of a therapeutic process that I, a dance/movement therapist, engaged in with a transgender teenager. It was an imperfect course of treatment, one where I was fallible. I believe some of my missteps were as a result of my unconscious bias as a cisgendered, heterosexual, white woman. It is the story of a therapeutic relationship wherein important shifts occurred in the patient during treatment. Upon reflection, I think our work could have been richer had I had more knowledge and understanding of my own bias and blind spots, in addition to knowledge of the psychological and emotional experiences of the transgender person in the adolescent stage of development (Levitt & Ippolito, 2014). Throughout this chapter it is my hope that by naming and exploring my own process, including the identification of some blind spots, insight might be gained into how more thoughtful work can be conducted in the future. This transparent examination of myself might have implications for examining difference when working with various other marginalized and oppressed populations. Despite these limitations, the relationship did support the patient in the work of separation-individuation, and of moving away from self-harm, towards the externalization of anger and pain. The therapeutic relationship fostered the beginnings of productive self-expression, empowerment, and the development of an authentic self. These changes became manifest both in the teenager coming out as transgender and in a slow, but consistent shift away from dealing with intense emotions through self-injurious behaviors, towards an outward expression of anger and hurt.

In spite of my limited experience working with transgender youth in private practice, I am a highly experienced therapist who has spent many years working with the adolescent population in inpatient and outpatient psychiatric settings, therapeutic educational settings, and private practice. My theoretical grounding is based in dance/movement therapy and relational as well as humanistic psychotherapy. I place a high value on in-depth exploration in the relationship, as well as playfulness in the moment. I believe that it is the relationship that facilitates healing in treatment. My experience has led me to understand that it is these elements that are of most use in the consulting room.

As I write this chapter, our therapeutic relationship has terminated. Having distance from the case has given me space to consider the mistakes I made. I will begin by outlining the course of treatment, which took place over two school years, beginning in November of the patient's freshman year of high school and terminating and transitioning into an intensive outpatient program at the beginning of the patient's junior year of high school. During these two years, there were two psychiatric hospitalizations in quick succession which followed an incident of running away from home for ten days just before the close of the patient's sophomore year of high school. In my exploration of this case, I will include the issues that brought the patient to therapy, discussion of the material addressed during treatment, and the patient's decision to terminate treatment.

Adolescent Development

Frankel (1998) states in his work *The Adolescent Psyche* that the period of development that begins at around age 12 and continues well into the early 20s is a time marked by constant change in the development of the human psyche. Siegel (2013), in his work *Brainstorm*, talks about the neural pruning which is the literal cutting away of neural pathways that are underutilized in childhood, and the surges of neural pathway and neural myelination development that occur during this period of life. Siegel argues that these biological surges in development underpin the shifts in adolescent personality, emotion, and behavior. I have spent almost 15 years working with adolescents and I feel that

I have intrinsically understood this phenomenon without knowing what was happening biologically. It is this sense of possibility, of novel thought and innovative creative approaches to problems, that has drawn me to work with teenagers. As Siegel so aptly points out, "Adolescence is not a period of becoming 'crazy' or 'immature.' It is an essential time of emotional intensity, social engagement and creativity" (p.4). In my experience of the adolescent population, they enter the consulting room each week with variations on their identities, values, interests, dress codes, friends, and lovers. Developmentally, questions of who am "I" in the world and what will "I" pursue as a growing person and eventual adult are at the fore. These are the essential, existential questions the adolescent is grappling with. In therapy, drastic changes can occur in their perspective almost weekly. It is necessary for them to explore, experiment, destroy, and reconstruct their view of reality during this period of life. The adolescent challenges all that they were as children, including attachments to family and friends from that period of life. The teenager will sometimes approach these matters in a mature and insightful manner, and at other times like a destructive toddler, all the while vacillating between the permutations of these extremes. These ideas are illustrated and supported by Siegel:

> There are changes in the fundamental circuits of the brain that make the adolescent period different from childhood. These changes affect how teens seek rewards in trying new things, connect with their peers in different ways, feel more intense emotions, and push back on the existing ways of doing things to create new ways of being in the world. Each of these changes is necessary to create the important shifts that happen in our thinking, feeling, interacting and decision making during adolescence. (2013, p.7)

Conflicts and questions about self, creativity, and relationships can be further complicated in the cases of transgender teens. These are not the only challenges being faced (Levitt & Ippolito, 2014). In the case of the transgender teen, there is the additional work of developing a coherent gender identity (Fraser, 2009). A research participant elucidates in Levitt and Ippolito's 2014 research study by saying that "it is a question of how do I deal with the fact that my anatomy tells people I'm somebody else?"(p.1742). In her memoir *Trans*, Juliet Jacques (2015) also discusses the challenge of developing a coherent gender identity. She writes:

If I'd been allowed to transition in my early teens then my adolescent and adult life would have been much easier... I said in the *Guardian* that transitioning was about "re-launching" the symbiotic relationship between my body and mind from a starting point that felt right. (pp.305–306)

This concept of a complex integration of the self is further supported in research conducted on transgender adolescent development by Grossman and D'Augelli (2006). Factors they found adding to the complex challenges of identity integration in transgender youth include positive identity development, cultural and ethnic backgrounds, personal characteristics, and family circumstances. Many of these factors played a role in the work with this patient, as we will see.

Beginnings

When Dunne came to treatment, he was using his birth name, Astrid, and gender pronouns, zie, zir, zirself. He came out as transgender later in the course of treatment. However, to affirm his prefered gender, he will be referred to as Dunne, and I will use the gender pronouns "he," 'him," 'himself" throughout this chapter. These decisions were in line with the affirmative model of mental health therapy (Danoff, Daskalakis, & Aberg, 2013). Also of note, the use of preferred pronouns is required by law in New York State.

Dunne was 14 years old and starting freshman year of high school when we began our work. He had been cutting himself at the start of the school year. Dunne later told me that he had a history of cutting himself in middle school, during periods of high stress and anxiety. Dunne's mother discovered these most recent incidents of self-harm after observing scratches and scabs on his arm and, being understandably concerned, sought treatment.

Throughout our work Dunne was resistant to therapy in general and especially to movement. He outright refused to engage in any overt movement process. I joined his resistance by following his lead. Thus, we spent a great deal of time getting to know one another through talking. I observed and attuned to Dunne's micro and macro movements; I would subtly attune to and mirror his rhythm of breath, posture, tone of voice, language, and gesticulation. Dunne was quite shy about his body and in many ways seemed ambivalent about being seen by me. I was acutely conscious in my mirroring and attunement not to be intrusive, and would respond to any sign of discomfort by reducing my mirroring and/or completely backing off from it when Dunne's nonverbal communication indicated even the slightest sign of discomfort or shutting down.

In the first months of treatment, Dunne's physical presentation at times appeared almost fragile. Dunne was tall and very thin; he moved with a great deal of light effort (Bartenieff & Lewis, 2002) and thus at times it seemed his feet almost didn't touch the floor. Dunne was fair-skinned and had piercing blue eyes. His wardrobe generally consisted of baggy jeans and large baggy T-shirts, usually worn with an even baggier sweatshirt over them. When I first met Dunne, I felt his physical presentation and attire was quite androgynous as his female sex characteristics were not visible because of his attire and how Dunne held his body. Following our first session I wondered if he was transgender.

I would like to note that I use the word "wonder" very intentionally here, and not "assumption," as I did not want to make any assumptions about Dunne's gender. Rather, I did wonder and was curious about this aspect of Dunne's life, as Dunne's mother had described Dunne as gender questioning, and Dunne defined himself as gender questioning and gay. A dance/movement therapist (DMT) is trained to be acutely aware of the patient's body. This includes posture, rhythm, gesticulation, and use of space. I am acutely aware of all of my patients' bodies in this way. This type of body awareness and attunement affords me knowledge about the patient and where they are at in the moment, in addition to facilitating the patient being "fully" seen and received by me in the relationship. Lots of DMTs have written about what can be gained from movement observation, and to write this chapter from that perspective would make it something else entirely. For the purposes of this chapter, I add this movement observation because this was the subtle way in which movement was integrated into our sessions, since we did not move or dance overtly.

Dunne came into session each week with a base of bleached blond hair, and almost every week changed the dyed color on top. He would usually sit on the floor of my studio with the support of a back-jack (this is a small folding chair that allows one to sit comfortably, directly on the floor of the studio). Dunne has very long, thin limbs. In one of our first meetings his legs were drawn up at the knees, with his arms encircling them and his hands clasped just below the knee joint. I remember thinking that Dunne's torso was blocked, and that he had sufficiently protected himself, perhaps from me. To empathically attune, I drew my body up into a similar posture, sensing in myself the need to protect and keep the torso, guts, and emotional center safe. My initial induced experiences indicated to me that relationships were perhaps dangerous for Dunne. From speaking with both Dunne and his mother, I knew that there were several instances of emotionally painful separations with his mom, dad, and older brother. Building a relationship would require my being gentle and open.

Despite Dunne's continued reticence with regard to therapy, he was curious about me, smiling and easily laughing at my playfulness and generally answering direct questions without prodding or difficulty. When I asked about why Dunne thought he was in therapy, he replied without hesitation that "it's because of my mom," and if not for that, "I would not be here." He thought that "therapy is a waste of time and money." That said, Dunne didn't seem to withhold information from me, although he would only respond to direct questions. He would completely shut down and become resistant when I asked more open-ended questions. I felt, at the time, that Dunne required a lot of structure and that open-ended questions were far too lacking in structure and were anxiety-provoking. I adjusted my approach by providing a great deal of structure to our sessions.

In the first weeks of treatment, Dunne disclosed being gay and polyamorous. When I asked what "poly" meant, he described having several partners and that each of these relationships were open; Dunne was free to date and/or hook up with others. This kind of relationship constellation was somewhat new to me, and showed some of my ignorance. I remained open and curious, asking questions of Dunne when I didn't understand something. Looking back, my questioning felt innocent enough and seemed part of getting to know one another; I wonder now if this fell into one of the categories described in Mizock and Lundquist's (2016) study of mistakes made by psychotherapists in the treatment of transgender patients. They describe this as education burdening. This psychotherapy barrier refers to the participant feeling the need to educate the psychotherapist on transgender and gender non-conforming (TGNC) issues for psychotherapy to proceed. Participants of this study indicated that the lack of psychotherapists trained in TGNC care contributed to the burden of educating their psychotherapists, taking them out of the client role.

At this time, Dunne's relationship constellation did not seem to be in any way connected to his gender identity. My reliance on the patient to describe how polyamory works may have been a form of education burdening. Dunne alluded to his older brother also being poly, and there seemed to be some vague knowledge that at some point his parents had been involved in polyamorous relationships too. I quietly noted this information to myself and opted not to explore it further just then, as it seemed too early to ask more about this revelation. In retrospect, I wonder if I was leading us away from the material that mattered most. I also noted the cavalier manner in which Dunne divulged it. I found it quite surprising. I also filed that away to be explored later, once trust and a firmer foundation had been established in the relationship. Dunne's apparently intimate knowledge of his parents' sexual relations during their marriage loomed quite large in our work together. The implications of this were not entirely clear yet. He talked about it with a simmering anger and disdain.

Despite outward statements of resistance to therapy, Dunne returned each week. Some weeks were more interactive than others. Much of our early conversation centered around his choice of hair style or color for the week, what he was focusing on in school, and how his relationships with girlfriends were getting along. As our relationship progressed Dunne was more open and shared more of himself, but there was a continuing block—a sense, felt in me, of distance in sessions between us. I recall processing in my supervision group that I certainly was not an expert in working with transgender clients, but felt that we were making progress and building a relationship, even though Dunne would intermittently say that he felt therapy was a waste of time and something that his parents "made him do."

Family Perspective

I feel it important to add a bit about Dunne's mother's impression of her child upon seeking treatment for him. I believe this will add some context and background to Dunne's experience, and give a view into my processing and understanding of the case and how the family and my personal identity lens shaped my view. In my view, in work with children and teenagers, the familial perspective is very important. It has a real day-to-day impact on the young person, partly because children and adolescents are usually so completely embedded in the family structure with all of its attendant rules. In the case of adolescents, separation and individuation are the primary goals (Siegel, 2013). Since they are not yet fully independent, their parents' role continues to be vitally important, and so to my mind it is essential that the family be involved in the therapy work for patients in this age group. I recall a former supervisor from my days working on an adolescent inpatient psychiatry unit referencing Bonomi (2006) and saying that it's not just the teenagers walking into the room for group therapy but also the influence of their mom, dad, sister, brother, grandparent, aunt, uncle, or whoever the caregiver is in the home environment.

During my first meeting with Dunne's mom, she told me that Dunne was having difficulty at home. He seemed sad, depressed, and hopeless, was having outbursts of anger and tantrums, in addition to being irritable and engaging in acts of self-injury. As in all cases with children and teenagers, I find it useful to ask both the parents and the child what they believe the challenges to be. I also think it's important to do this as a way of exploring whether family therapy might be a more effective treatment or an important addition to individual treatment. For this family, I felt that family therapy would have really enhanced Dunne's individual treatment, but unfortunately it was a financial impossibility.

Dunne's mom was, at this point, the primary caretaker, as Dunne's father lived several hours away, making a meeting with both parents quite difficult. Dunne's mom began our first meeting by describing a rather complex family system. Dunne's parents had separated several years prior to Dunne beginning treatment with me. Dunne lived with his mother, his mother's current partner, and his five-year-old half-sister. Dunne had a full biological brother who had moved out of the home several years previous to this and had minimal contact with his mother and inconsistent contact with Dunne. When his parents separated, the father became the primary caretaker of Dunne and his brother. However, once an apartment large enough to house the family was found, Dunne's mother had the children move in with her and her new partner, and it was then that she became the primary caretaker. Dunne then split time between the two homes. Several years into this familial constellation and structure, Dunne's father lost his job and moved several hours from his children for both work and a lower cost of living. This move was very difficult for Dunne, who deeply valued their relationship. Dunne's mother said that once Dunne's dad moved away he became inconsistent in his visits and calls. This shift, according to Dunne's mother, was at the root of the distress that had been building in Dunne for several years. Dunne did eventually echo similar feelings in session. It took several months, a visit to the emergency room for increased depressive symptoms, and Dunne stating that he wished to kill himself before this material was revealed and we were able to begin working with it.

During our initial meeting, Dunne's mother mentioned that Dunne was gay, was questioning gender and preferred the pronoun "zie." At this point, Dunne was engaged in a long-distance relationship with a young person he had met online. Dunne's mother expressed concern over his online activity, and feared that Dunne could unwittingly put himself in unsafe situations this way. After hearing Dunne's mom's concerns, I agreed to meet Dunne for a consultation. I emphasized that it was of the utmost importance that we follow Dunne's lead, and if he felt the connection between us was good enough, we would go forward with meeting once a week for therapy.

At the end of this meeting, Dunne's mother wondered aloud what Dunne would make of me. I asked what she meant by this and she answered, "Astrid will likely think of you as square, so I wonder if zie will be able to engage with you." I replied with something to the effect of "We will have to see how it unfolds, how zie feels about it, and proceed from there." I shared a similar fear, although I felt confident in my experience as a therapist and in my ability to handle this work with the same care and attention I strive for in all my work. I believed my bi-monthly supervision group and weekly personal therapy would be great assets in this regard. I had worked with transgender people and teenagers who were questioning their gender identity many times before, in my work at Bellevue Hospital and at a therapeutic school for children with severe mental illness. This new relationship felt different, however. All of my previous work occurred either within the therapeutic mode of group therapy or in institutional settings, not in the mode of individual therapy as in my private practice.

Gender and Sexuality in Individuals and Families

As mentioned earlier, Dunne seemed to know quite a bit about his family's history and his parents' divorce. From Dunne's point of view, their divorce involved stress, conflict, and complexity for the whole family. Dunne described a very close relationship with his father but was hurt when his mother moved out. This anger, sadness, and hurt loomed large in Dunne's experience and, from my perspective, continued to go largely unexpressed. I frequently directed our conversation towards this material, in an effort to support the processing and metabolization of these feelings. This is where I believe some of my unconscious bias came into play and influenced our work; I wonder if I was, in fact, engaging in gender-avoiding behavior? Mizock and Lundquist (2016) describe gender avoidance as "lacking focus on issues of gender in psychotherapy with transgender clients" (p.151). As I examine this course of therapy with some distance, I can see the importance of the family material and how the work we did around family dynamics was vitally important in helping Dunne feel more stable in his family relationships. In moving us toward the family material on a regular basis, however, I believe I was neglecting other pieces of Dunne's experience. I wasn't regularly checking in with Dunne on how he was managing feelings and experiences around gender identity.

A possible example that illustrates this misstep is when Dunne shared with me that he had asked his dad about the divorce. Instead of explaining to Dunne what had happened from his perspective, he encouraged Dunne to talk with a friend of his. Dunne made contact with this friend and was told that his mom and dad had been involved in a brief polyamorous relationship with the man who was now Dunne's mother's partner, and the father of his half-sister.

When Dunne recounted this family story, he showed almost no outward affect, but just below the surface there seemed to be a great deal of emotion. It felt as though Dunne was almost daring me to feel something. I remained quite calm, present, and open, listening to each piece of the experience as Dunne unfolded this detailed tapestry to me. Dunne seemed, at least on the surface, to be unperturbed that he had learned this sensitive information from a family friend and not from his dad directly. I believe Dunne was incredibly hurt and confused by this experience, but shut down these feelings entirely, and so I spent a great deal of time directing us towards it, perhaps mistakenly.

In the session that included this disclosure, and several sessions thereafter, Dunne expressed a great deal of anger with his mother and called her a "homie hopper." A "homie hopper" is a person who has sex with one person after another within the same group of friends, or homies (Urban Dictionary, 2018), and in Dunne's description there were also no breaks in between. When I would gently attempt to explore the role that Dunne's father may have played in the dissolution of the marriage, Dunne was unable to consider this possibility. He felt that his dad was a victim in this situation. It became clear to me, around then, that Dunne's relationship with his dad was, crucially important to him and needed to be protected in the therapeutic relationship. Dunne was questioning his gender identity and his dad was the parent providing vitally important gender mirroring or what Fraser (2009) terms "gendered reflection" (p.131) for Dunne.

My countertransference towards Dunne's dad following the disclosure of this material moved between deep confusion, sadness, and anger. I felt protective of Dunne, given the level of exposure his dad had facilitated, and due to the fact that Dunne was left to manage his feelings and responses alone. Since Dunne was receiving important gendered reflection (Fraser, 2009) in the relationship with his dad, I felt that I needed to handle the feelings induced within me with the utmost care.

It is likely that much of the anger I felt towards Dunne's father was the displaced, unexpressed anger that Dunne felt. I contained this experience and worked with it by sometimes asking questions of Dunne about his feelings toward his dad and their relationship. These lines of inquiry often gained little or no traction in our sessions. In hindsight, I may have been missing the point. Dunne certainly has unresolved feelings about his dad, but what I see differently now is the function of that disclosure in our relationship. In retrospect, the stories of the family's sexual relationships and questions around gender identity were really about Dunne's own struggles with self and gender identity. When Dunne brought this material into the therapeutic relationship, instead of asking about his internal feelings about gender and sexuality, I asked about feelings he must have been experiencing towards his dad because he had exposed him to his own questions about gender and sexuality. In this, I missed Dunne, thoroughly and completely. I was blind to the possibility that Dunne may have been bringing his gender identity material into the conversation through this disclosure.

Around the time of these disclosures about the family, Dunne became increasingly irritable and depressed. He was brought to the psychiatric emergency room by his mom from school, one afternoon in the winter of his freshman year, after reporting to the school guidance counselor that he was having thoughts of self-harm. At the psychiatric emergency room, Dunne was given antidepressant medication as well as a referral to a psychiatrist.

Following this first visit to the emergency room, Dunne was more open to discussing some of the feelings around the relationship with his father. This was especially true when it came to unexpressed hurt and anger about his father's inconsistencies and unreliability with visits and calls. Since Dunne was opening up about these feelings, it seemed appropriate to call for a family therapy meeting. Dunne and I agreed that the goals of this meeting would be to get both parents on the same page with regard to his treatment, and to discuss what had led Dunne to a point where he felt so hopeless and depressed.

As a result of Dunne's hard work in our individual sessions, he was able to directly express feelings to his mom and dad during the family session. Dunne openly shared how hurt he was by his dad's inconsistent visits and calls. His mom and dad were able to take in what Dunne was sharing, and to work towards shifting the family dynamic by together developing a daily phone call and monthly visit schedule. This collaborative development of a consistent schedule for daily calls and regular visits with his dad supported a positive shift in Dunne; he was less irritable, had fewer outbursts of anger at home, and was more focused on school work.

Coming Out

Following this family session, the material in our individual therapy shifted. It seemed to me that as the relationship with Dunne's dad became more stable with the structured calls and visits that had been set up during the family meeting, our work began to move more directly towards identity and sexuality. Dunne began to openly share about the various romantic relationships he had in school and on the internet. At this time he also began chest binding with a large torso ace bandage. Experimentation with how to relate to alcohol and drugs came up in our discussions too. Some weeks Dunne proclaimed that he was "straight edge," never doing drugs or alcohol, while at other times he claimed to drink and use marijuana regularly on the weekends. We discussed using substances responsibly and safely, and Dunne was very open to this.

This period following the family meeting was one of great progress for Dunne, emotionally, psychologically, and academically. It lasted from his visit to the psychiatric emergency room in the winter of freshman year to the summer break between freshman and sophomore years of high school. During the summer break between freshman and sophomore years, Dunne came out as transgender. The day he came out in session to me, Dunne's mom, step-dad, and younger sister were away on a trip out of town, one that Dunne had refused to go on because he "wasn't going to travel without Dad." He was staying with his maternal aunt. They had spent the afternoon playing Pokémon Go all around Manhattan and visited a large chain makeup store. While there, Dunne made his face up similar to the character of the Joker from *The Dark Knight*. The mask and the metaphor of both being seen and not seen simultaneously were all feelings palpable in the room during this session. This disclosure felt like an important moment in the process. Dunne was delivering his true self into the room. When I asked what this meant for Dunne personally, he shared that he intended to continue chest binding and wanted to explore hormone treatment. Dunne added that when he mentioned this possibility to his mom and dad, they both said, "no," that he could not begin hormone treatment until he was 18 years of age. I was saddened to hear this as I felt Dunne may have experienced this as a rejection. Coming out as transgender was very important to Dunne, and I felt, as the research states, that he needed to be deeply supported by his family (Russo, 2015).

It was during this session that Dunne shared that he no longer wished to be called by the name Astrid, and was choosing to be called Dunne with the corresponding male pronouns: he, him, his. I felt so pleased that Dunne felt safe and seen enough to share himself so honestly and openly in our relationship.

Following this session, Dunne came out to his long-time, long-distance girlfriend who, Dunne said, told him that her family was uncomfortable with his gender identity. This left him feeling incredibly rejected. Following Dunne's coming out to his girlfriend there were several instances of them breaking up and getting back together. According to both Dunne and his mom, they would get into many hours of heated arguments on the phone and on Facetime. During this period, I often couldn't keep up with whether they were together or not. I felt quite confused and, at times, bewildered by this relationship, and wondered if this was an experience Dunne was displacing on to me.

Dunne's eventual return to school, after summer break, and how he would come out to peers and teachers at school was something we spent quite a bit of time working on. Upon his return to school, he reported that there was one teacher in particular who had a very difficult time calling Dunne by the correct name and using the preferred gender pronouns. This raised some concern. In Grossman and D'Augelli's 2006 study, a transgender youth talks about the social impact that occured when a teacher repeatedly misgendered him. One student in the study talks about how a teacher's repeated misgendering of him would lead to conflict and bullying by peers that would at times lead to his having to physically defend himself. I worked with Dunne's mother to speak with the teacher, and we developed a plan for informing other teachers and staff, with varying levels of success.

Often, however, Dunne was unresponsive to exploration and inquiry about how it all was going in school, so that made it difficult to verify the success of those efforts. During this time, there was a growing disconnection in our relationship. Dunne was consistently late for sessions, leaving little time for us to talk. When I would ask him about this, he would say that he needed to stay later at school, that it was hard to get to my office via public transit, and that he preferred his mother driving him to sessions.

Dunne's coming out and returning to school that fall coincided with some new determinations he made, mainly to taper off antidepressant medication and to end treatment with me. He expressed wanting to "deal with stuff on his own." This time was marked by a great deal of conflict and negotiation in our relationship. I wanted to honor Dunne's wishes but I also wanted to make sure that there was a healthy transition out of therapy and off medication. Dunne's psychiatrist, with whom I was in close contact throughout treatment, shared similar feelings. She felt it important that Dunne have agency over his own treatment, but was clear that we should support a gradual transition towards termination and not have an abrupt ending, which was how Dunne had initially envisioned the process. Dunne begrudgingly agreed to this plan and felt it made sense that he not let go of all of his support systems at once, especially given that he had recently come out and that this was a big transition in his life. Reluctantly, he agreed, repeatedly stating he wanted to "deal with stuff on his own."

By mid-December of his sophomore year, Dunne was off all medication and continued to meet with me once a week and with his psychiatrist once a month. As time went by, he again started to show signs of irritability and resistance in our work. He expressed anger and resentment that he still needed to be in therapy after coming off the antidepressant medication. He was more shut down than ever, continuing to arrive late, leaving only 10–15 minutes for sessions. Sometimes, at the last minute, he would request that we meet by phone, claiming that he got out of school late and would not make it to the office on time.

I wondered about this increased distance and resistance that was building in our relationship, and I was curious that this was happening after Dunne came out as transgender. I wondered if he wasn't feeling supported enough in our relationship and I felt saddened by this. I cared a great deal for Dunne, but felt I was losing him rather quickly in the relationship. In our sessions I would bring up this distance and ask what Dunne felt might be happening. His new mantra was "You don't help me; you helped me once with my dad but since then you do nothing and you don't help at all." I attempted to join Dunne in these moments, playing with the idea that I wasn't very good at my job, and he would agree and say, "Yes." I would usually follow this up by asking him what material might be helpful to explore now. This was usually met with "I don't want your help; I can do all of this on my own. You are a waste of my time and my mom's money." I would even go as far as suggesting that I help to find him a new therapist who might be more suited to his needs, but even this was met with "NO, I don't want to be in therapy! I want to deal with stuff ON MY OWN!" Yet each week Dunne returned if even for ten minutes, either in person or on the phone. I believe that it was at this juncture in the relationship that my lack of understanding of the interiority of the teenage transgender experience, coupled with my not placing significant enough emphasis on the things that were most important to Dunne, may have enabled this growing distance.

Our relationship continued like this from December until early March. Each session was a similar permutation of the last, with Dunne telling me that I wasn't helpful anymore and that he wanted to deal with things on his own. Dunne's mother, his psychiatrist, and I all felt deeply concerned about Dunne's well-being. He was increasingly angry, depressed, cutting classes, failing courses, and, at times, outright refusing to attend school. Occasionally, this anger manifested in a physical acting out both at school and at home (punching and kicking walls, the latter of which led to breaking his toe at school). On the strong recommendation of Dunne's psychiatrist, he resumed antidepressant medication, albeit with fury and reluctance. The medication certainly helped to even out Dunne's mood, but his position on therapy was immovable. We began to seriously discuss finding him a new therapist since seeing a therapist was a prerequisite of being on the medication, according to his mom. This conversation was brought to an abrupt halt at the end of May, just before Dunne's 16th birthday. He ran away from home and was gone for nearly ten days.

Running Away

I haven't felt as scared or concerned for a patient as I did during those ten days. I reviewed the case many times, wondering whether there was something I'd missed or overlooked that might provide a clue as to his plan. Eventually, Dunne showed up at his school. From there he was brought to the psychiatric emergency room and his mother was notified. He was then psychiatrically hospitalized for approximately one month, because he was determined to be a danger to himself. During the hospitalization, Dunne reported material that he had never mentioned to me. He claimed that he was experimenting with hard drugs, including intravenous heroin, and he reported hearing the voice of a man who yelled at him to harm himself. Following his initial hospitalization, Dunne returned home for approximately two weeks and was then re-hospitalized as he reported a wish to kill himself and felt he could not control this impulse.

It was during this second hospitalization that the therapist on the psychiatric unit suggested to Dunne that he might do well in the hospital's intensive dialectical behavioral therapy (DBT) day treatment program. Dunne was resistant at first, but agreed. His mother initially wanted him to continue his individual therapy with me, in addition to the outpatient program. I discussed this possibility with Dunne in one of our family therapy sessions and "No" was his resounding answer. He would do the DBT program and would end treatment with me. There was clarity and finality to this statement, and attuning to him in this moment seemed particularly important. I agreed that we would terminate treatment and shared with him that at some point I really did miss him in the work, and that as a result of this the treatment had become stagnant. I added, however, that there would need to be parameters to the termination of our relationship. Even though Dunne's desire was to discontinue treatment that day, I explained that while I understood this impulse, it would be far more useful for us to take our time, so that we could review everything and say goodbye in a conscious and intentional manner. He reluctantly agreed.

Termination

During this time in the work with Dunne and in my own supervision process, I took a deep look at where I may have gone wrong. I considered the places where I missed attuning to him emotionally, as an individual.

I asked Dunne what he felt was missing in our work together, and he offered very little information, just that same old mantra he'd been reciting for months: "You don't help me; you helped me once with my dad, but you don't help and it's a waste of my time and my mom's money." He did, however, add to these statements that "I think you are a good therapist, I just don't think you are a good therapist for me." I was quite surprised by this change in Dunne's ability to express positive feelings towards me. He was not one to offer up empty compliments, and I shared with him that I was thoroughly impressed by his candor and insight.

One afternoon, after much consideration, I shared with Dunne that I was working on a theory about our work together and wondered aloud if he would like to hear it. He begrudgingly agreed. I shared that I felt that there were ways in which I thought I made some unknowing mistakes in our work, and that I was just now beginning to see them clearly. I shared that I felt I might have influenced the energy and direction of our work. I told him that I may have spent too much time on what I saw as the complicated dynamic between him and his family. I went on to tell him that I was now considering that I may have unwittingly ignored his experiences and feelings around the complexities of coming out as transgender, in addition to his desire to begin hormone treatment, and the subsequent conflict that this ignited with his parents.

When I put this theory to him and named what I viewed as my empathic failure, his face completely opened up and his body tensions softened a bit, although not entirely; he was still guarded with me, and understandably so. From the outside, however, it was as if a light had been switched on inside of him, and there was a brief connectedness between the two of us, one where we shared a moment of holding on to the same tapestry and gazing at it together in relationship. I believe that in this moment Dunne felt truly seen by me. He said that he agreed with my theory and immediately followed up that it didn't change his decision to end treatment with me. It did, however, open up a real connection and dialogue between us in those final weeks of therapy when we were working on termination.

During this time, he talked about how he needed more time and space to talk about being transgender and what that meant for him in the world. In retrospect, I know that I, as the therapist and the person in the position of authority, needed to bring these matters up more consistently than I did. So why didn't I? I genuinely believe that it came from a place of blindness, of ignorance, and from a place where my own lens and lived experience as a cisgender, heterosexual, white female converged with some unexamined countertransference, and so I was blind to what I didn't know (Dillon, 2017), but it was my responsibility to seek out more knowledge so that I would and could know more. I didn't go deep enough in asking myself to try to wrap my consciousness around what it means to be a transgender teen and to imagine what the interiority of that emotional experience was like for Dunne. In so doing, I failed certain aspects of the relationship with Dunne empathically and left him alone in the therapeutic relationship to fend for himself in much the same way as his family had.

My lived experience had not pressed me to consider what it means to come out to peers and adults in my life, or to consider all of the attendant projections that are placed upon you by others, because of their own unexplored feelings and biases. I had not done anywhere near enough research (articles, films, plays, novels, memoirs) on the transgender experience, so that I might have had a clearer sense of the themes, feelings, and lived experiences of transgender youth, in the way that I do when working with other kinds of difference, whether it be racial, cultural, ethnic, or economic, among others. I felt, unconsciously at first, but now quite consciously, that having come of age in New York City during the 1990s, at a time when gender and sexual orientation were very much part of the cultural lexicon, that I had enough knowledge. In reality, I did not fully grasp the implications and feeling experiences Dunne was going through. I explored this material with Dunne, but only ever at the surface; we never stayed with it consistently enough for it to develop more fully and deeply, and that was my responsibility as his therapist.

Moreover, I was almost immediately drawn into the intensity and difficulty of the family dynamics, and should have more thoroughly examined what the function of this was in the relationship between Dunne and me. Professionally and personally, I understand the impact family can have on one's growth and development, and so I quite blindly and unconsciously focused on this material with Dunne. This was of the utmost importance for a time. However, in Dunne's case, once the family dynamic had stabilized, he needed for the focus to switch back to his identity as a transgender teenager and the ensuing conflicts and emotions that accompanied that. By the time I became aware of this, I think Dunne felt that the trust we had built had been damaged and he felt it necessary to move on. I don't blame him.

While I attempted to repair our connection, it seemed most important that Dunne have agency, within the container of our relationship, to terminate with me and to choose another therapist. He needed to be fully supported by me in his decision. It's hard to admit, but it seemed as though we had done all the work we could do at that time. This experience has left me with a great deal to consider and explore, so that in the future I might be a better therapist.

References

Bartenieff, I. & Lewis, D. (2002) *Body Movement: Coping with the Environment.* New York, NY: Routledge.

Bonomi, C. (2006) 'Review of Haydée Faimberg, *The Telescoping of Generations: Listening to the Narcissistic Links between Generations,* London and New York, Routledge, 2005.' *International Forum of Psychoanalysis 15,* 1, 62–64.

Danoff, A., Daskalakis, D., & Aberg, J.A. (2013) 'Care for transgender persons.' *JAMA 309,* 20, 2092.

Dillon, A.K. (Guest) (June 4, 2017) '*You've Told Me This Before*' [Audio Podcast]. *Nancy.* Accessed on 12/10/2018 at www.wnycstudios.org/story/nancy-podcast-asia-kate-dillon.

Frankel, R. (1998) *The Adolescent Psyche: Jungian and Winnicottian Perspectives.* London & New York, NY: Routledge.

Fraser, L. (2009) 'Depth psychotherapy with transgender people.' *Sexual and Relationship Therapy 24,* 2, 126–142.

Grossman, A.H. & D'Augelli, A.R. (2006) 'Transgender youth: Invisible and vulnerable.' *Journal of Homosexuality 51,* 1, 111–128.

Jaques, J. (2015) *Trans: A Memoir.* London & New York, NY: Verso.

Levitt, H.M. & Ippolito, M.R. (2014) 'Being transgender: The experience of transgender identity development.' *Journal of Homosexuality 61,* 12, 1727–1758.

Mizock, L. & Lundquist, C. (2016) 'Missteps in psychotherapy with transgender clients: Promoting gender sensitivity in counseling and psychological practice.' *Psychology of Sexual Orientation and Gender Diversity 3,* 2, 148–155.

Russo, F. (2015) 'Transgender kids.' *Scientific American Mind 27,* 1, 26–35.

Siegel, D. (2013) *Brainstorm: The Power and Purpose of the Teenage Brain.* New York, NY: Tarcher/Penguin.

Urban Dictionary (2018) 'Homie hopper.' Accessed on 14/11/2018 at www.urbandictionary.com/define.php?term=homie%20hopper.

7

Identity, Awareness, and Disclosure of Sexual Orientation in Creative Arts Therapy

BRIAN T. HARRIS

Therapists' self-awareness of their sexual orientation has broad implications for our work. It requires placing sexual orientation in the context of other identity components that may be present in the therapeutic setting and critically analyzing our decisions on when and how to make such identity components known. The three case examples used in this chapter outline how I, as a gay man and a music psychotherapist, negotiated my awareness and subsequent choice of disclosure of my sexual orientation to clients. All names and identifying details have been changed to help ensure anonymity. These case illustrations are not presented as how-to guides, but rather to provide insights into the journey of increasing awareness and the complex questions that can emerge around disclosure.

Disclosure

Self-disclosure describes the process wherein the creative arts therapist shares personal information with the client through deliberate, inadvertent, or unavoidable means (Barnett, 2011). Therapists share aspects of personal information to greater or lesser degrees, often on an unconscious level (e.g. clothing and hair choices). In the case of sexual orientation, this sharing may involve placing pictures of family in the work environment or casually mentioning a "wife" or "boyfriend." These kinds of disclosures tend to be more conscious when the therapist experiences the information as sensitive or charged, often the case with information relating to nonvisible identity factors such as minority sexual orientations.

For clients with minority sexual orientation identities, questions of self-disclosure may be complex. Carroll *et al.* (2011) found that participants viewed lesbian and gay therapists who disclose their orientations as being more trustworthy than those who choose not to disclose. However, such disclosures may be evocative for therapists. Moore and Jenkins (2012) looked at how gay and lesbian therapists view disclosure of their orientations to assumed heterosexual clients. Regarding the decision to disclose, they found that therapists experienced "fears of client judgement; increased levels of anxiety; self-awareness of the potential impact of their own fears and prejudices on the therapeutic relationship; and the potential relevance of internalised homophobia" (p.314). These findings speak to the vulnerability therapists with minority sexual orientations may experience when approaching decisions of disclosure.

It is common for new professionals to experience challenges in navigating how much personal information to impart. Oversharing on the part of the therapist can result in boundary infringements, ethical violations, and loss of trust on the part of the client (Audet & Everall, 2010, p.328). However, overly rigid boundaries around the sharing of personal information may accentuate the power imbalances inherent in the therapist–client relationship. To this end, we may view disclosure through the lens of queer and feminist theories on therapy, both of which advocate reducing the traditional power imbalances that can take place in a client–therapist dyad. Through this lens, disclosure is seen as a form of shared vulnerability which, when used appropriately, can allow the therapist to "share power" with the client (Tabol & Walker, 2008, p.93).

When done with careful consideration, self-disclosures can be a useful therapeutic tool. A recent study found that clients experienced therapist self-disclosure as "attentiveness and understanding" when the therapist's disclosure mirrored the client's needs and expectations. However, if the therapist's disclosure was incongruent with the client's state, the therapist was seen as having "an egregious lack of understanding and responsivity" (Audet & Everall, 2010, p.339). This finding indicates that the therapist's awareness of the client's needs is a key determinant in negotiating self-disclosure. Therefore, a thoughtful examination of when and why therapists choose to disclose personal material can help ensure a safer, more effective therapy environment.

Music Therapy and LGBTQ Literature

Music therapy literature discussing LGBTQ-related topics only emerged in the last decade with articles such as Colin Lee's (2008) "Reflections on being a music therapist and a gay man." Lee made the brave choice to come out as a gay man and discuss the impact his orientation may have had on his work. He noted:

> My identification as a gay man and a music therapist has always been apparent in my work. It has been an unconscious, silent guide and protector. It has colored my responses to clients verbally, musically, and relationally at a deep and detailed level. The question then becomes "why have I never formally acknowledged and embraced being gay as part of my counter-transference responses in the therapeutic relationship?" (Lee, 2008, para. 6)

Lee's article opened the (closet) door for further public discourse around awareness of minority sexual orientations and decisions around disclosure.

In the time since Lee's (2008) article, music therapy literature discussing LGBTQ concerns has expanded in the realms of both theory and research. In 2013, Whitehead-Pleaux *et al.* surveyed music therapists in the United States and established best practices in music therapy related to LGBTQ clients, coworkers, and students. The study found that although the music therapy community has increased its awareness of LGBTQ people, more than half of those surveyed had no targeted training to understand concerns related to LGBTQ individuals. These results were similar to a global study conducted among music therapy programs and associations which found only 41% of music therapy program directors surveyed addressed LGBTQ concerns as part of the training (Ahessy, 2011). Both Ahessy's and Whitehead-Pleaux *et al.*'s studies helped illuminate the need for training and education components focused on considerations when working with and alongside those in the LGBTQ community.

Bain, Grzanka, and Crowe (2016) brought the framework of queer theory into the discussion, highlighting music therapy work with LGBTQ youth. The authors posited that music therapists can use queer theory frameworks to help deconstruct power systems inherent in therapeutic relationships. They noted: "Queer theorists assert that power exists everywhere, and critically examining how these systems exist within the safety of a music therapy session imparts youth with the ability to resist and overcome discrimination" (p.29). In 2017, this framework was then qualitatively studied to critically evaluate the model (Boggan, Grzanka, & Bain, 2017). Of note in the findings was that this model could benefit from "more substantively integrat[ing] intersectionality theory" to meet the needs of the broader LGBTQ population (p.402).

Identity

Public discussions around LGBTQ oppression in the United States largely began with the Stonewall riots in 1969 which were primarily led by gay and transgender people of color. Because of this, the imbalances of power at play at the time can be best viewed through a lens of intersectionality, which views identity aspects such as race, sexual orientation, and gender expression/identity as being interconnected. In focusing on the imbalances of power, it was necessary to highlight the minority identity components of the protestors. Because of these imbalances, I, as a gay man, may have felt more compelled to think about the impact of sexual orientation than would my straight-identified counterparts. Like many in the LGBTQ community, I had struggled to come to terms with my own identity. I grew up in a conservative, rural area where being gay-identified did not feel a safe or viable option. I feared for my psychological and physical safety. This internalized fear led to complicated feelings about my own sexual orientation, which have taken years to process and attempt to understand. Although I now have primarily positive feelings about my identity as a gay man, my journey into self-acceptance was long and, at times, painful. Moving through the process made me more keenly aware of the presence of my sexual orientation and its potential impact on those I encounter as a music therapist. However, my awareness does not mean only therapists who struggled en route to understanding their sexual orientations benefit from increased awareness. Indeed, if creative arts therapists want a fruitful discussion about sexual orientation, then we must open up the dialogue to and about all orientations. We all possess sexual orientations at all times. Increased self-awareness of our sexual orientations can help us understand how this identity aspect may be present in and influence our work.

Sexual orientation is situated among a larger context of identity aspects that we, as therapists, bring to our work. Certain facets of our identities enter into sessions more visibly than do others. For example, therapist identity aspects that tend to be visible include race, gender expression, physical ability, ethnic origins, age, height, and weight. These features may be difficult to disguise from a client and are, therefore, likely to enter into the clinical realm as known material. The client's conscious and unconscious responses can be assumed and addressed as needed. Among less visible identity aspects are religious beliefs, cultural background, intellectual (dis)ability, political affiliation, mental health status, and sexual orientation. Because these identities are less noticeable, clients may unconsciously assume or project aspects of the identities on to us. In such cases, therapists decide with greater or lesser degrees of consciousness whether to disclose and allow the identity aspect to be acknowledged for its presence in the therapeutic relationship.

I have learned that people sometimes assume that I am straight. I have complicated feelings about this. As a teenager, I wished to be perceived as straight in order to "pass" in a homophobic environment. *Passing* can be seen as "a cultural performance whereby one member of a defined social group masquerades as another in order to enjoy the privileges afforded to the dominant group" (Leary, 1999, p.85). However, passing is not always intentional and can be inadvertent, based on fear and internalized shame. In my teenage years, I made semiconscious shifts in my voice, carriage, gait, and presentation, in attempts to have not only greater access but also a greater sense of safety through assuming a straight identity.

After years of immersion in queer and feminist theory highlighting identity and oppression, as well as in-depth personal therapy, I developed a much more positive relationship with the conventionally "gay-acting" parts of myself. Some examples of these parts for me include fluidity of movement, range of vocal expression, and even chosen conversation topics. In fact, I have worked hard to reclaim some areas of expression I effortlessly accessed as a young child, as described in the lyrics of a song I wrote when I began to explore the impact of "straightening out" on my psyche:

HOW TO BE

The other day I saw an old home video
Of my family in the Rockies
I was nine years old
And I was skipping down the mountainside
My arms were flailing

My butt was swaying side to side
I hadn't learned yet how to be a boy
To straighten my walk
Find the right kind of toy
No one had told me
The rules of how to be

Later on in the tape I was an awkward 17
With my dad and uncle Paul
At the rock quarry
And we were shooting guns at old tin cans
But I was walking straight
The right toy in hand
And they were teaching me
The rules of how to be
How to be

And now I'm trying to go back to nine years old
Before I learned to act
How I was told
I am trying to go back to the way
I just walked to walk
I just played to play
A move for movement's sake
And fuck the rules I break
No one can tell me
How to be

Because I know that sometimes I am presumed straight until "proven" otherwise, it is safe to guess that some of my clients will assume this as well. In those instances, it is not the case that my orientation is absent from the therapy room. Rather, I may be choosing to allow my clients to project a sexual orientation on to me. It then becomes important for me to analyze why I am allowing it and when it may be therapeutically beneficial to challenge those projections. Clients may unconsciously project many personality traits and identity aspects on to therapists in order to examine their own relationships with those features. How we respond to these projections is a critical negotiation in therapy (Searles, 2017, p.194). Due to my own complicated relationship with some of the projected identity aspects, self-awareness is a key factor in negotiating when to self-disclose. When done effectively, co-examining the projections and transferences with a client can be a transformative component to the work.

Some self-referring clients will choose therapists based on known identity aspects (Cabral & Smith, 2011). For example, clients may seek to work with a female therapist based on qualities they believe she will hold as a woman. Unless explicitly stated, sexual orientation is often unknown to our clients. Similarly, a client's sexual orientation may be unknown or misperceived by therapists unless openly explored. This was the case with Gretchen.

GRETCHEN

When I first began working as a music therapist, there was a spirited woman named Gretchen in a group I ran for people with Alzheimer's and dementia. Gretchen was witty, sarcastic, warm, and full of life in my groups. She brought vibrant energy to the music making and the social environment. I felt a strong connection with Gretchen. When she died suddenly, I began processing her death with the program director and learned more about Gretchen's life. She informed me that Gretchen had identified as a lesbian. I had not been open to the group about my sexual orientation; it had not occurred to me to do so. I assumed being open about being gay to a group of older women in the Midwest United States would have been countertherapeutic, and I may have been correct in that assumption. But learning of Gretchen's orientation raised new questions for me. Why had I assumed all of my older clients were straight? Had I robbed Gretchen of an opportunity to feel she could be out to me or other group members? Might I have had a deeper therapeutic relationship with Gretchen if she had known I am gay? Or would my being out, when Gretchen wasn't out to her peers, have made her feel more vulnerable and exposed in the group? Acceptance of minority sexual orientation identity has changed significantly in the past 50 years. Gretchen primarily lived in a time when homosexuiality was still viewed as a mental illness, and this may have played into my assumptions. Still, this was the first time I began to question the role sexual orientation identity played in music therapy, as well as my assumption that my sexual orientation should be withheld categorically from my music therapy clients.

JOSH

When Josh began therapy, he was experiencing shame and confusion after having recently come out as bisexual. When our work began, I was unsure if he knew I am gay. I chose not to come out to Josh, in part because I felt it might be useful for him to be able to project his self-judgments and questions around sexual orientation on to me. In other words, if he believed I was straight, he might view me as judging him in the same way he judged himself. Not being out to Josh initially allowed me to represent the (presumed) heterosexual community and allowed us to examine more vividly the perceived judgments he had internalized from them.

During one session, Josh's internalized shame related to attraction to men seemed particularly strong. I felt it might enrich our work to disclose to Josh that I am gay. After I disclosed, Josh confirmed he had assumed I was straight. He felt my voice and appearance did not match his perceptions of a gay man. Through processing over time, Josh reflected that learning I am gay challenged his assumptions about himself. Josh began to speak more openly about his attraction to men, noting he no longer worried that I was judging him. Our music-based explorations shifted noticeably following my coming out to him. Josh allowed himself to explore greater vocal range and identify the power that he felt in the upper part of his register but had rarely accessed. At times, the music Josh created held elements of passion and desire that reflected an examination of his own sexuality and sexual orientation.

Although those aspects felt productive, Josh also faced challenges because of my coming out to him. He mentally revisited statements he had made in sessions prior to learning that I am gay. He worried he had said homophobic things that may have hurt or offended me. Ultimately, we processed this in relation to his internalized homonegativity and self-criticism.

It is worth noting that Josh felt our work together could have been productive had I been straight-identified. He had first come to me both because I am a music therapist and because I had stated experience working with LGBTQ clients. When he began his search for a therapist, finding someone with whom he felt comfortable talking about sexuality mattered to him, but the therapist's sexual orientation did not consciously matter. My coming out to Josh in our work together catalyzed some fruitful explorations. However, I believe my *awareness* of my own sexual orientation in relation to Josh, and not simply my disclosure thereof, helped to hold this work. Had I been a different gender or of a different orientation, I suspect the work could have been similarly effective, although the content would have differed—provided I remained aware of how my identity might relate to Josh's identity.

In my work with Josh, I intentionally chose not to come out initially in an effort to further the clinical process. In the following case example, I was out to my client from the beginning. Although this was not my decision, it is one I likely would have made if given the choice.

VICTORIA

Victoria was a young artist with a history of severe abuse and torture. Her abuser had been a man. Although she had worked with therapists before, she had never had a close working relationship with a male therapist. A female psychologist referred Victoria to me with the hope we could provide co-treatment. When Victoria was initially hesitant to work with a man, the referring psychologist disclosed that I am gay, which seemed to help Victoria feel comfortable enough to come for a consultation.

Due to her trauma history, Victoria experienced frequent and often severe dissociated states in which she would lose conscious connection with her surroundings. During those states, I often sang to Victoria and encouraged her to try to sing with me. The containment of the songs was one of the few ways I found to help her gently emerge from dissociated states. The music's rhythmic structure assisted her to regulate her breathing, while the melody seemed to help her find her literal voice and begin to return to the world of my office. The music we created together held a kind of intimacy, and this intimacy allowed for the trust and sense of safety necessary to move through her frozen trauma states.

In the music, I felt I played many roles for Victoria. Sometimes, this dynamic felt parental; sometimes I was a savior. Still other times, the dynamic felt romantic. The roles I held for her seemed crucial to help heal multiple fractures in Victoria's relationships away from the therapeutic setting, allowing Victoria a rehearsal for how she could experience these types of relationships in a healthy way outside of the sessions.

Our work together ended when Victoria moved out of state. In preparation for her departure, we used songs to help explore closure. Among other songs, Victoria requested I sing "Hidden Away" by Josh Groban for her to record and take with her in her transition. The song contains lyrics that describe the physiological changes Victoria experienced in relation to the music, as well as some transferences she experienced in our therapeutic relationship. Inherent in the lyrics is a subtext of a romantic transference that Victoria and I openly discussed. Shortly after our work ended, Victoria became romantically involved with a man for the first time. I feel her ability to "test out" romantic feelings in a safe therapeutic relationship helped her prepare to enter into a romantic relationship. I believe my being out to Victoria was a key component in our work to help her feel safe enough to explore these transferences. Had she not known I am gay, I do not know that she could have felt safe experiencing the same intensity of transferences, particularly the romantic elements. In this instance, that Victoria knew I am gay may have created for her a "safe enough" psychological barrier against the possibility I would "become" her abuser.

However, although I believe my being out to Victoria aided the therapeutic process, in many instances a female client with a history of sexual abuse from a male perpetrator may work successfully with a straight-identified male therapist. Even in Victoria's case, if a straight male therapist had approached the clinical work thoughtfully and sensitively, he may well have been able to establish successful trust and help support transformation. It also cannot be assumed that disclosing my orientation alone was sufficient to ensure a sense of safety. In either case, the key component is the ability to analyze the potential impact of the therapist's sexual orientation (or perceived sexual orientation) on the dynamics of the session.

Discussion

The preceding case examples are specific to my clinical work and, therefore, not meant to be used as generalizable guidelines. My intention in presenting them is to highlight the process of increasing awareness of one's sexual orientation and making decisions around disclosure more consciously.

Notably, in many cases, these decisions were not made in a vacuum. I used peer consultation, clinical supervision, and personal therapy to increase my own understanding of these complicated choices. In addition, I maintained personal creative processes such as dance and music making to reflect on emerging parallels.

Decisions around therapist self-disclosure should be based on an evaluation of the client's needs. Self-directed questions may be useful in this assessment process: What impact might this disclosure have on my client? Might my disclosure aid in the therapeutic journey by increasing trust or decreasing a client's sense of vulnerability? Could it lead to a fruitful new line of self-exploration for my client? Or would my client's cultural background or religious belief system mean my disclosure may provoke unnecessary anxiety? In educational and supervisory roles, what impact might my disclosure have on the individual or the group dynamic? These kinds of questions help therapists be more mindful and make decisions around disclosure more thoughtfully.

Exploration of sexual orientation may feel more acute for me as a music therapist with a minority sexual orientation identity. Surely, I have thought about this topic extensively due to the impact it has had on my life. However, in each case example above, I believe the primary importance was not the nature of my sexual orientation but my attempt to understand how this identity aspect impacted my work.

References

Ahessy, B.T. (2011) 'Lesbian, gay and bisexual issues in music therapy training and education: The love that dares not sing its name/Problèmes des lesbiennes, gays et bisexuels dans la formation et l'éducation en musicothérapie: l'amour qui n'est pas mentionné dans les chansons.' *Canadian Journal of Music Therapy 17*, 1, 11–33.

Audet, C.T. & Everall, R.D. (2010) 'Therapist self-disclosure and the therapeutic relationship: A phenomenological study from the client perspective.' *British Journal of Guidance and Counselling 38*, 3, 327–342.

Bain, C.L., Grzanka, P.R., & Crowe, B.J. (2016) 'Toward a queer music therapy: The implications of queer theory for radically inclusive music therapy.' *Arts in Psychotherapy 50*, 22–33.

Barnett, J.E. (2011) 'Psychotherapist self-disclosure: Ethical and clinical considerations.' *Psychotherapy 48*, 4, 315–321.

Boggan, C.E., Grzanka, P.R., & Bain, C.L. (2017) 'Perspectives on queer music therapy: Analysis of music therapists' reactions to radically inclusive practice.' *Journal of Music Therapy 54*, 4, 374–404.

Cabral, R.R. & Smith, T.B. (2011) 'Racial/ethnic matching of clients and therapists in mental health services: A meta-analytic review of preferences, perceptions, and outcomes.' *Journal of Counseling Psychology 58*, 4, 537–554.

Carroll, L., Gauler, A.A., Relph, J., & Hutchinson, K.S. (2011) 'Counselor self-disclosure: Does sexual orientation matter to straight clients?' *International Journal for the Advancement of Counselling 33*, 2, 139–148.

Leary, K. (1999) 'Passing, posing, and "keeping it real."' *Constellations 6*, 1, 85–96.

Lee, C. (2008) 'Reflections on being a music therapist and a gay man.' *Voices: A World Forum for Music Therapy 8*, 3. Accessed on 11/14/2018 at https://voices.no/index.php/voices/article/view/1767/1527.

Moore, J. & Jenkins, P. (2012) '"Coming out" in therapy? Perceived risks and benefits of self-disclosure of sexual orientation by gay and lesbian therapists to straight clients.' *Counselling and Psychotherapy Research 12*, 4, 308–315.

Searles, H.F. (2017) 'Concerning transference and countertransference.' *Psychoanalytic Dialogues 27*, 2, 192–210.

Tabol, C. & Walker, G. (2008) 'The Practice of Psychotherapy: Application.' In M. Ballou, M. Hill, & C. West (eds) *Feminist Therapy Theory and Practice: A Contemporary Perspective*. New York, NY: Springer.

Whitehead-Pleaux, A., Donnenwerth, A., Robinson, B., Hardy, S. *et al.* (2013) 'Lesbian, gay, bisexual, transgender, and questioning: Best practices in music therapy.' *Music Therapy Perspectives 30*, 2, 158–166.

8

Seeking the Uncensored Self

Music Therapy with Transgender Clients

JULIE LIPSON

In 2009, I was asked to join the founding team of a summer camp for transgender[1] youth. I was enthusiastic about building a camp, as I had been a lifelong camper, counselor, and camp songleader. The work also interested me as a genderqueer person. My own childhood camp memories include many uncomfortable experiences—in the midst of a place I so loved, the gender binary seemed inescapable. Bunks, activities, and camp traditions were often laid upon deeply ingrained gendered foundations. The defining characteristic of our new camp would be that it was "just camp." In other words, children who are genderqueer, gender-fluid, transgender, or between the binary are constantly placed in therapy—either because they are pathologized or simply because insurance requires gatekeeping in order to attain medical interventions—and so our mission was to provide a place for them to simply be children. I would later find that this fundamental mission of providing non-therapeutic space was the thing for which we were most thanked by parents and guardians of campers.

In quintessential summer camp fashion, we ended our week with a talent show. It was here that I began to see the huge power that creativity held in allowing expression of the authentic self. Campers who appeared shy or reserved throughout camp were surprisingly grounded and confident when singing a song on stage. Sometimes campers would bring clothes that matched who they were on the inside, but which they were unable to wear at home or school. Campers' duffle bags often contained the frilly dresses, collared shirts, ties, and baseball caps that were secret belongings, or were only allowed around the house and not to be worn in public. The talent show became a place where these clothes came out of the suitcase, brightening campers' faces and fueling their self-confidence. When meeting parents on pick-up day, I say something like "Your child was amazing last night at the talent show," and inevitably the parents double-check to make sure I'm talking about the right kid: "*My* child danced in front of the whole camp?!"

In 2011, I attended Drexel University to earn my master's in music therapy. As I worked with people of all ages in various settings (inpatient psychiatric hospital, outpatient mental health clinic, therapeutic school), I found that I was most drawn to the work in which music was used to help people relax into their bodies, and I found voice work especially powerful.[2] I wrote my graduate thesis about the ways that transgender people experience their voice as related to their gender and identity (Lipson, 2013). From this research, I learned more about the voice as a part of the body, a place of pain and healing during gender dysphoria and transition, and generally as a reflection of the self.

Each of the three participants in my thesis spoke about the voice as something they had to censor at times because of their gender. One participant said she used to raise her hand often to speak in class, but after beginning her transition, she felt less confident about speaking up in a room of people, and worried her voice would draw attention to her changing gender presentation. The participants also spoke about the voice as a part of the self, and something that reflected their identity. One participant found that after starting on testosterone, his lower voice made him appear less friendly, so he had to "make social compensations" such as smiling more. Another participant was a singer and had strong feelings about his voice and the role it played in his life. He told me that the experience of participating in my research had brought up complex feelings, and therefore he stopped taking testosterone, at least for the time being. The most common and poignant theme from this research was the amount of energy that it takes to think about, change, and get used to one's voice. In addition to considering which words they chose to communicate, they were now also planning, adjusting, and learning how they sounded in terms of intonation, volume, and range. It was a difficult experience to be surprised by one's own voice (Lipson, 2013).

I ran my first transgender music therapy group in 2014 with five members. Prior to the start date, I conducted intakes to discuss if the prospective client would be a good fit for the group and to learn what they were hoping to get from the experience. Throughout these intakes, I found several similarities:

- Many clients described feeling censored from a very young age. They received negative feedback about gender presentation and creative expression.

- Clients often felt isolated and were eager to meet other people going through a similar journey.

- Although most people had prior experience with therapy, music therapy seemed to present new hope for healing. Even those who were not musicians often felt that music enabled them to more easily access emotions. Several people described music as their primary coping skill when feeling depressed or anxious.

- Most clients had a history of depression and/or anxiety. I am often asked, "What do I need to know to work with trans clients?" My answer is always "What are the presenting symptoms?" Therapists should assume that the only skill they are missing is cultural competency. We are never treating someone *because* they are trans—they are coming to therapy for the same reasons as everyone else.

- At each intake, clients described a need for mind–body connection. Some reported the inability to verbally describe their emotions, while others reported a sense of ever-present or frequent numbness.

My groups consist of many different planned interventions, as well as spaciousness for improvised moments. For the purposes of this chapter, I have categorized my interventions into three overarching goals: (1) practicing being uncensored, (2) practicing feeling support from others, and (3) using music as a coping skill.

1. Practicing Being Uncensored

The most important thing that I took away was that I found I was able to relax and have fun, which is something I have not been able to do in a very long time.

Group member

Groups typically run for an hour and a half, once a week for six to eight weeks. I have made it a practice during the first group to discuss how as small children we are uncensored and pleasure-seeking. Then we quickly get messages from society about what forms of expression are acceptable. People who do not fit into neatly organized gender boxes get these messages as very young children and therefore experience negative feedback about their expression, including their clothing, chosen activities, friends, toys, and mannerisms. I offer the invitation that, in this group, we can practice going back to our authentic pleasure-seeking selves. As we return to a childlike preverbal state, we explore sound and movement, we can be free from the need to think before we act, and we can unlearn the censoring that has been instilled in us. In that vein, I introduce interventions which sometimes feel like icebreakers or look like theater warm-ups. My goal here is to practice dropping out of the mind and into the body. We begin group by nonverbally creating an environment of support, with the intention that this space will be a safe place in which to express based on instinct rather than thought.

Syllable Circle

We stand in a circle, and I introduce the syllable "mm" by standing in the middle, rubbing my stomach, and making an "mmmm" sound, as if I am eating something delicious. Together, the group members repeat my "mm" sound and rub their stomachs. I step out of the circle and invite the group to try another version of the sound. Someone else steps in the middle and thinks of a new example—for instance, they might moan "mmmm" while becoming curled and sad. The group repeats the sound, and we continue like this for a few more rounds. Then I change the syllable by stepping in the middle and thinking of something new, such as exclaiming "oh!" and pointing my finger in the air as if I just had an epiphany. The group continues with this new syllable, improvising ways that "oh" can look and sound. I eventually ask the group members to introduce a new syllable.

I learned this game and many others from Theater of the Oppressed, an extensive methodology that uses games and play to explore societal rules, freedoms, and the power of creative problem-solving.[3] I find games like this work well in my groups because they employ playful actions to explore deep content. For instance, Syllable Circle always breaks the ice and we end up laughing at our silly sounds. The deeper meaning emerges as we reflect on how difficult it was for people to step into the circle without a plan, and to be seen, heard, and uncensored in front of relative strangers. As group members challenge themselves to step outside of their comfort zone and use their voice, they see that this group can be a safe testing ground for how they would like to be outside of group.

Embodied Intentions

Another way I like to start groups is to invite each member to think of an intention for the next several weeks we are together. This intervention works well after something like Syllable Circle because it builds upon the concept of creating sounds and movements as expression. I guide everyone in closing their eyes (or simply softening their gaze) and taking some centering breaths. I invite everyone to "think about what brought you to this group" and give them a minute to think. I say, "Now think about what you want to get from this group over the next several weeks" and I leave space for them to think. Then I say, "Now I'll invite you to distill that thought down to a few words." For example, "grow" or "be myself" or "I'm confused why I'm here." I remind the group there is no right answer and to try to go with their instinct—do not think too hard. Then I say, "Now we'll represent those words with a movement." I model an example by making a movement without saying anything. The group repeats. We go around the circle, and each person shares their movement and the group repeats. Finally, I say, "Now I'll invite everyone to add a sound to your movement." We complete a few cycles of going around the circle, learning and repeating each sound and movement phrase, and then removing the repeat-after-me's and just doing the sequence all together. From here, the group could turn down many different paths or a combination of any of the following:

- Verbally debrief what it felt like to create your intention.

- Walk around the room trying on any sound and movement from the original intention circle.

- Ask each other questions about the sound and movement phrases.

- Choose someone's movement and replace the sound with words.

Each of these options is vulnerable in its own way, and can be rewarding to the individual who sees their expression mirrored, as well as for the group members who may see or feel something familiar or comforting in the others' expression.

I love this nonverbal way of sharing intentions because it provides a channel for embodying and sharing experiences, but does not ask people to share too much too quickly. Once the group loosens a little, creating sounds and movements becomes fun, which is a surprisingly important part of group. Group members often comment on the connection between being relaxed enough to have fun and being their authentic self. A client who experiences fun is more able to say what they think without passing their thoughts through a series of filters, wondering if they will be judged, or doubting the value of their contribution. After a sound and movement intervention, one client told me that they now felt more comfortable with the group because they were able to "be ridiculous."

I find that interventions requiring the most creativity and imagination are also the ones that seem most difficult. Many transgender clients struggle with presenting their authentic selves in various settings (work, home, social events, etc.). This inauthenticity can manifest as withholding thoughts and feelings, behaving only to please others without considering the self, or feeling like one is performing instead of simply being oneself. The practice of releasing these roles, which hold tension and anxiety, and instead relaxing into a fun, creative atmosphere can be both daunting and very rewarding.

Each client has their own story about needing to be seen. In the interventions I describe above, the repeat-after-me sounds and movements and trying on each other's words and experiences are all forms of mirroring. Even in the most accepting households, it is difficult for trans children to experience enough mirroring.[4] Most of us grow up with images of who we may become, whether it is celebrities we admire or older relatives we envision looking like. For trans and genderqueer people, these images are lacking, and therefore mirroring experiences are all the more powerful. All therapeutic content aside, just meeting five other people who have varied experiences of gender can be a strong mirror and lead to feelings of empowerment and hope. One client described a sound-mirroring activity as helpful because it enabled him to "envision my own strength and be around others." This client found it particularly meaningful to create nonverbal representations of "how others react to my gender" and "my response to their reactions."

Figure 3.1 The Obstacle

Figure 3.2 The Guide

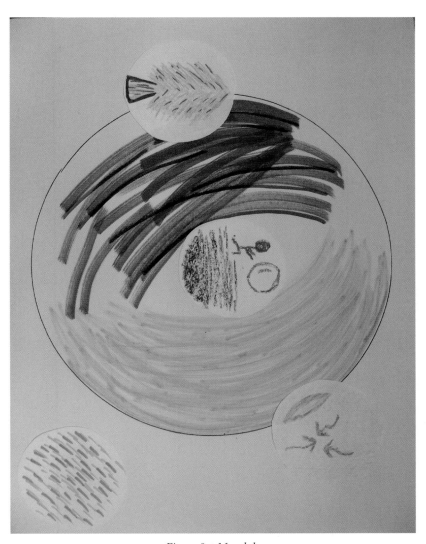

Figure 8.1 Mandala

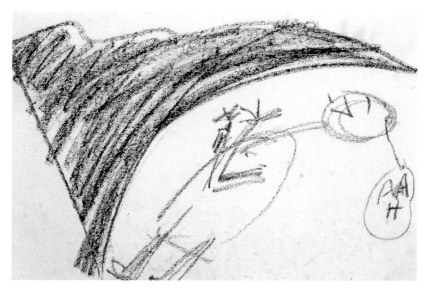

Figure 9.1 Overwhelmed

Figure 9.2 Thinking of My Family

Figure 9.3 Talking to Robert

Figure 9.4 How My Family Makes Me Feel

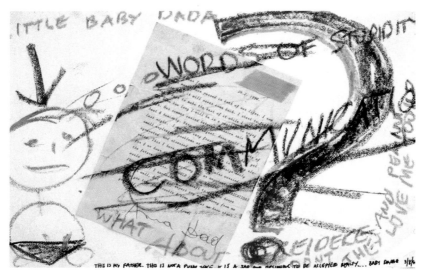

Figure 9.5 Little Baby DaDa

Figure 9.6 Time

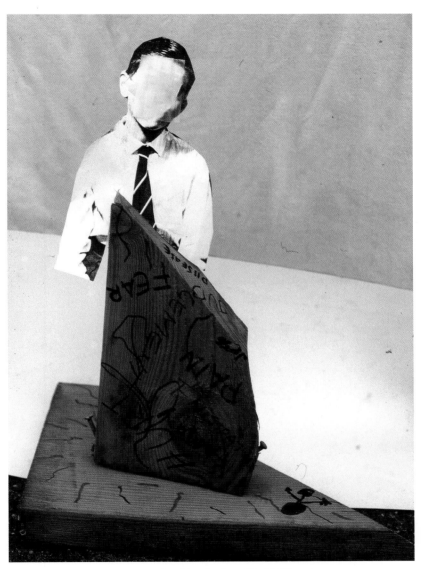

Figure 9.7 Looking Back at His Childhood

Figure 9.8 Crash Test Dummy

Figure 9.9 Welcoming Life Cautiously

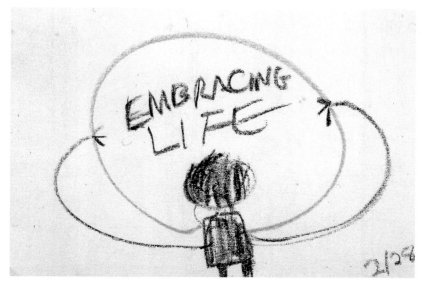

Figure 9.10 Embracing Life

Figure 10.1 Pool

Figure 10.2 Leg

Figure 10.3 Bed

Figure 10.4 Hands

Figure 11.1 Charles's Depiction of the Split in His Mind

Figure 11.2 Elle's Oil Painting

Figure 12.1 LGBT and Allies Group Shared Values Collage

Figure 12.2 Rats

TIFFANY ADAIR
University of Alberta
Faculty Sponsor: Royden Mills

Many people harbor shame and self-hate toward
themselves, caged by their own minds and beliefs
rather than anything around them. I crave a life
of greater meaning. There is nothing to be found
in riches, good looks, or competitive success.
I seek something innately meaningful, maybe more
spiritual—something that brings significance
to small, daily occurrences. My artistic practice,
related to the Surrealist search for the marvelous
and my own pursuit of an expanded awareness,
is a search for hope.

Figure 12.3 Words
Close up of words selected for the shared values collage by the residents. Residents discussed
and connected to themes within the text of hiding, shame, and finding meaning in creativity.

2. Practicing Feeling Support from Others

Thanks to this group I will remind myself to make spaces…
where I feel wholly comfortable being myself.

Group member

Most trans clients I see are seeking to feel supported. They may have never met another trans person, or they may hold deeply instilled transphobic messages rooted in childhood. Their parents and caretakers may not have accepted them, or perhaps the adults in their life were accepting but lacked the information needed to provide a supportive atmosphere. Without that feeling of external support, these clients have had trouble speaking up, feeling heard by others, and meeting others with similar stories.

With Conviction

I give everyone three strips of paper and ask them to write the following: something you know is true, something you are not sure of, and something you would like to be sure of. Each person takes turns standing in the center of the circle and states their first phrase (something you know is true) with conviction, confidence, and strength. The group is instructed to respond using supportive sounds and phrases—"yes!" "mm-hmm!" etc. After everyone says their phrases, we do the same thing with the next two rounds (something you are not sure of and something you would like to be sure of). The group is supportive through each round, as these phrases guide each member through certainty, uncertainty, and hope. Any phrase works, and the collection often ranges from factual statements such as "The Eiffel Tower is tall" to emotional information such as "I feel scared at work." We debrief about the voice as a point of confidence, power, and support for ourselves and others.

A variation on this intervention could go as follows. After each person has written three phrases on strips of paper, put all papers in a hat so they become anonymous. Each person takes turns standing in the center of the circle, reading one paper during each turn. This intervention points to the power of the voice. Anything can sound true if said with conviction, even those phrases written about "something you are not sure of." Then debrief about where the voice helps and hinders us in presenting authentically.

As part of my graduate research, I guided each participant to explore their voice within several contexts, such as talking to a stranger on the phone or approaching a group of new people. This yielded a variety of reactions, including strong feelings about where they felt their voices failed them in social situations. One of the most salient themes throughout this research was that trans people often have to relearn to use their voice (Lipson, 2013). I consider this an act of building a new relationship with a part of the body. Both my research and music therapy groups have taught me that this consistent low-level focus on how one sounds to oneself and others takes an immense amount of mental energy, which at best is distracting, and at worst is frustrating and anxiety-provoking. Interventions like "With Conviction" serve as safe spaces to try out the voice, renewing one's relationship with the body, and experiencing support while practicing confidence and resilience.

Song Sensitation

I learned this basic structure from music therapist, Dr. Joanne Loewy, who created this method as a merging of "sensation and citation" (Loewy, 2002). One person brings a meaningful song to the group. I invite everyone to find a space in the room where they can be comfortable and present (sitting, lying down, etc.). We listen to the song once through, and then we hear from the presenter about the song and why it is meaningful to them. I then hand out lyric sheets, pens, crayons, and markers. As we listen to the song a second time, the group is invited to mark lyrics they relate to or have questions about, draw as they listen, or engage with the song in any other way. We then share thoughts and reactions about the song, and perhaps about the presenter. It feels intimate, as if the presenter is sharing part of themselves.

Dr. Loewy's structure ends with the group playing their own live version of the song (Loewy, 2002). I created an alternative ending which guides the group into another mode of expression. I give everyone a small circle of paper to draw on during the second listening. The instructions are loose—something like "Now we've heard what this song means to Alex. As we listen to the song again, keep Alex's experience in mind, and use any color or images you'd like." The presenter gets a larger paper with a mandala and draws inside the mandala during the song. After the song, each person gives their smaller circle to the presenter and the presenter uses glue to arrange the group's circles on the mandala page. The result is a visual representation of the group's creative reactions to the song (see Figure 8.1).

Figure 8.1 Mandala (see color plate in the center of the book)

During one group, a client shared a song that reminded him of a best friend who had died when they were teenagers. After sharing his song, the group began discussing how passionate he was. The group agreed that his vibrant excitement (this client often spoke enthusiastically about music and animals) felt hopeful and "contagious." In a beautiful moment of really being seen by others, he responded, "No one's ever told me that." This client experienced severe isolation and depression, and he therefore considered it huge progress that he was able to make it to group each week. Although the content of this exercise was not related to the client's trans identity, his vulnerability and expression were fueled by the room full of people who shared his gender experience and understood him.

This kind of intervention opens up the room. The song holds the space for clients to share intimate details of their lives without having to express too much verbally, which can be difficult and intimidating. After this sharing process, the group feels closer and safer.

3. Using Music as a Coping Skill

*On a weekly basis this group gave me the opportunity to pause,
ground myself, reset—whatever I needed for that week. I imagine
that other ways it has affected me are just starting to unfold.*

Group member

It is common for queer and trans people to feel isolated, especially those who lack the resources to connect with others like them. Children, for instance, have less control over their community and, therefore, may not meet another trans person until adulthood. Trans people who live in more rural areas may have a similar experience. Some choose to live as "stealth," which means they are trans but do not share this information with others. This kind of isolation often leads to creative coping skills. For instance, it is common for trans youth to have an extensive online community with relationships that are just as deep as in-person connections. Many queer and trans people grow up feeling acceptance from animals, who are non-judgmental, and finding comfort in music or art. These coping skills are important for building connection, confidence, and resilience, but they can also be maladaptive when relied upon so heavily that the person is unable to connect with others. Because of their history, many trans people have learned to expect that others will not accept them—a protective measure which takes hard work to unlearn.

Although many clients come to group having already experienced music as a coping skill, the idea of playing musical instruments can be daunting. I am careful to ease into using instruments, and only when it feels that the group is ready for a challenge in vulnerability do I ask them to sing.

Song Comparison

On the continuum of passive to active music experiences, listening to recorded music tends to be more passive, and therefore can provide a less intimidating entry point for clients to access. In this intervention, I bring in two songs that have opposing themes—for instance, "The Great Pretender" by the Platters and "True Colors" recorded by Cyndi Lauper. I hand out lyric sheets and pens, markers, crayons, or colored pencils. As I play guitar and sing both songs (or have the group listen to recordings), the group can mark lyrics or draw as they take in the songs.

I leave silence between the songs so the group can react, write, draw, or just have an aural palate cleanse before the second song. After hearing both songs, we discuss: What lyrics stood out to you? Which song do you relate to more? Comparing these two particular songs elicits discussion about authenticity and the energy it takes to censor or filter your true self. Group members discuss the shared experience of "pretending" to be a certain gender, and where in their lives they feel they can show their "true colors."

Group Song

During one group, we read "Andrew," a poem by spoken word artist Andrea Gibson (2007) about growing up with a non-binary gender identity. After reading together, I invited each person to write their own verse, starting with the poem's first line "When I was a kid…" This evolved into a group song, where each person spoke or sang their verse, and the chorus was written as a group: "No matter what others think, flying free, living my true identity, I gotta be me."

During this powerful group, each person had the chance to see part of their own story in "Andrew" and in the other stories in the room. Those who were reserved or scared to speak up in a group challenged themselves to sing! One person chose to have her verse read by another person, which showed strong self-awareness and the ability to share her expression in her own way and at her own pace. I felt that the group was mirroring each other, singing to their past selves, and creating a mantra for their future selves all at once.

Knowing you are one gender but being told that you are another can lead to second-guessing or ignoring instincts. Having feelings consistently invalidated by those around you engenders a lack of trust in your own perceptions and a resulting lack of practice in verbally expressing those feelings. It is no wonder, then, that many trans people have learned to disconnect their minds from their bodies from a very young age.

Referential Improvisation

I introduce instruments as a form of expression that is connected to the body and less reliant on the process of translating thought into words. Instead, the instruments have a direct line to the body's instinctive reactions, like an expanded version of the sound and movement interventions mentioned earlier in this chapter. I employ referential improvisation (Bruscia, 1987) in order to give the group a reference point from which to begin, such as a feeling or image, but no obligation to follow any musical rules. For example, I lay out a collection of small percussion instruments in the middle of the circle. I ask the group to close their eyes (if comfortable) and picture a place where they feel calm. Then I ask the group to choose an instrument and "play that feeling" together. The resulting improvisation is their collective sense of "calm." I repeat these directions using the feeling "anxious." I begin the debriefing by asking questions related to the body: What did each of those improvisations feel like? Where in your body did you feel calm and where did you feel anxious? What was it like to express these emotions nonverbally?

During his intake, one client reported that he has trouble expressing feelings to his partner. After five weeks of group, he reflected on his experience, noting that he felt a connection to the drum. When I asked him to expand upon this thought, he changed the subject and began recounting an inconsequential memory from earlier that day. I perceived his tangent as resistance to sharing a vulnerable moment, and I challenged him to stay with his previous thought. I requested that although it may be difficult, would he try to describe more about the feeling of connection to the drum? He looked at the bongos he was holding and expressed that drumming felt like an important tactile experience. He concluded that touch was a kind of love language for him. The group commended him on sticking with the arduous process of translating an embodied feeling to verbal expression, and he agreed that this was an important realization he wanted to share with his partner.

Quantifying Change

In an attempt to quantify some results from these groups, I used a pre-post questionnaire with one six-week group. I asked the five participants to anonymously rate the following statements on a scale of one to five:

- I feel comfortable with my speaking voice.

- I feel comfortable with my singing voice.

- I feel safe talking about my gender.

- I usually feel comfortable in a group.

- I usually feel in touch with my body.

- When I think about my gender, I feel alone.

- When I think about my gender, I feel hopeful.

- I feel comfortable exploring my gender.

- I am usually aware of sensations in my body.

- In general I am a confident person.

Before the first session, the group's responses ranged from 21 to 35. After six weeks, the group's range increased to 25.5 to 38. For all statements except 2, 6, and 8, the group average increased. Four clients' total scores increased and one stayed the same.

Although this sample only consisted of a five-member group, it was a helpful addition to more frequently seen qualitative results. It is heartening that so much can change in a short time. After only about a month and a half, deeply ingrained characteristics such as confidence and mind–body connection can be influenced and improved. It is inspiring to see this kind of change occur in music therapy groups, and yet I realize I already saw this back in 2010 at our inaugural camp summer. Our program was only a week long back then, and yet campers returned home changed, with new confidence and connections. Seeing campers and clients embrace creativity as a means to uncensored, authentic expression has led me to believe that in an accepting and playful context the mind, body, and voice can weave together to do powerful work.

References

Austin, D. (2008) *The Theory and Practice of Vocal Psychotherapy: Songs of the Self.* London: Jessica Kingsley Publishers.

Bruscia, K. (1987) *Improvisational Models of Music Therapy.* Springfield, IL: Charles C. Thomas.

Gibson, A. (2007) 'Andrew.' In A. Olson (ed.) *Word Warriors: 35 Women Leaders in the Spoken Word Revolution.* Emeryville, CA: Seal Press.

Langer, S.J. (2016) 'Trans bodies and the failure of mirrors.' *Studies in Gender and Sexuality 17*, 306–316.

Lipson, J.B. (2013) *The Lived Experience of Vocal Expression for Three Transgender People.* Master's Thesis, Drexel University, Philadelphia, PA.

Loewy, J.V. (2002) 'Song Sensitation: How Fragile We Are.' In J.V. Loewy & A. Frisch-Hara (eds) *Caring for the Caregiver: The Use of Music and Music Therapy in Grief and Trauma*. Silver Spring, MD: AMTA.

Winnicott, D.W. (1971) *Playing and Reality*. New York: Basic Books.

Endnotes

1. Throughout this article, I use "transgender" and "trans" interchangeably. My intention is to include all gender expressions under the "trans" umbrella (genderqueer, gender-fluid, gender-nonconforming, non-binary, etc.), while also acknowledging that each of these identities has its own nuanced experience.

2. Dr. Diane Austin's work on vocal psychotherapy was particularly inspiring during my graduate studies. I recommend her book *The Theory and Practice of Vocal Psychotherapy: Songs of the Self* (2008).

3. Theater of the Oppressed (TO) was developed by Augusto Boal in the 1950s, and is an excellent way to experience the power of connecting the mind and body. The lines between actor and audience are intentionally blurred as participants explore sound, movement, theater, and improvisation as tools for personal and societal change. If there is a local TO chapter in your area, I highly recommend attending one of their events.

4. For more background, Winnicott (1971) provides theory on the importance of mirroring and creative play, and Langer (2016) offers an exploration of how mirroring often fails trans people.

9

An Artist Affected by AIDS

Putting Treatment Issues into Historical Context

BETH GONZALEZ-DOLGINKO

In the 1980s and 1990s, my art therapy private practice office was in the West Village of Manhattan, New York. The predominant demographic there, at that time, was gay men. Consequently, when the AIDS crisis hit, and gay men were one of two major groups that contracted AIDS, that community was a triage zone. I had many patients and supervisees who were gay and lesbian, many of whom resided in the area. One day, one of my supervisees just put her head in her hands when she came in and said, "I am so tired of going to funerals."

It was a sad and trying time. In 1992, through community action, the Gay Men's Health Crisis (GMHC) opened its doors on 22nd Street as a neighborhood organization offering medical, psychological, vocational, and housing services, among others, to anyone affected by AIDS (GMHC, n.d.). Those of us working as therapists in the area received regular referrals.

As an art therapist who identifies as straight, I realized that it was important for me in treating people with AIDS to better understand gay culture. Facing this crisis with my colleagues, we all used as much support from each other as we could muster. We were working in a war zone. I studied everything I could find about AIDS because there were so many misperceptions and fears. Early on, AIDS was identified as being transmitted by blood, through sexual contact and the use of contaminated hypodermic needles. This information allayed fears that a practitioner would be in danger from airborne pathogens or by contact with other bodily fluids, such as saliva or perspiration, and enabled us to be able to offer psychotherapeutic treatment knowing there was very little risk of being contaminated.

It was a true health crisis and, until AZT came on the market in 1987, it was a death sentence. Even then, there were many years of trial and error, and great cost to patients, and many people were already too sick for it to help.

> AZT, the first drug approved to fight HIV is marketed; the cost of a year's supply is $10,000, making it one of the most expensive drugs ever sold. The recommended dose is one capsule every four hours around the clock—a regimen later shown to be extremely toxic. (GMHC, n.d.)

On top of dealing with a terminal illness, many gay men were also dealing with social injustice. It took six years for President Ronald Reagan to break the public silence and use the term "AIDS" in public for the first time, and he established the Watkins Commission, the Presidential Commission on HIV (GMHC, n.d.). During this time of societal denial, many conservative and fundamentalist people expressed their belief that AIDS was a scourge on gay people because being homosexual is against God's law. However, people who were heterosexual IV drug users were also becoming infected, and, for the most part, lesbians, who are homosexual by definition, were not contracting it. This fundamentalist thinking led to further alienation of the gay community from mainstream society.

What became clear was that society was facing trauma—individual and collective—and end-of-life issues. This informed treatment. Referring to art therapy literature in the areas of trauma, death and dying, and loss and grief was invaluable. The medical art therapy literature and practice had not caught up to this idea of a community epidemic and crisis. Art therapists were going to have to build it.

In this chapter, I tell the story of a gay man who contracted AIDS and used his art to understand his terminal illness and his family's and society's reactions to it. Why am I telling this story so many years later? Context and humanity. It is important to understand the historic context of the gay community in society to best understand how and what interventions to implement in art therapy treatment and how. The AIDS crisis was a significant, while devastating, event that brought the culture of the gay community into the spotlight and more into the mainstream (Talwar, 2015). But AIDS jettisoned gay men into the public eye as diseased outcasts, adding further stigma to an already disenfranchised group. Awareness of this context of shared history cannot be forgotten and informs best practices, and as we can see from current studies, there is still homonegativity in the treatment of patients who are not heterosexual (Gandy, McCarter, & Portwood, 2013).

The stories of gay men who lived and died with AIDS are woven into our society's fabric. These stories must be told so that we remember them and their journeys. A storyteller must touch the audience so that they will listen, learn, and feel the story's lesson or message on a visceral level, and each time the story is told, it brings more meaning to the experience of the teller (Schneider, 2008). Telling and hearing these stories can bring the grace and suffering of these men into our work on a daily basis and enable us to have empathy for any patient who sits before us.

LGBTQ Community and the Cross-Cultural Therapeutic Consciousness

In the 1980s, multiculturalism became a buzzword in public awareness and public education. It was only a matter of time before creative arts therapists paid attention to multiculturalism and its impact on treatment and professional education. By the 1990s, the American Art Therapy Association began publishing articles and developing policy statements concerning the inclusion of cultural issues in professional education.

In New York City, creative arts therapy graduate programs had had curricula in place addressing cultural issues since the 1970s. Pratt Institute in Brooklyn, New York, offered a required course in the Graduate Art Therapy Program called *Race Relations*. It was taught by a social worker and focused predominantly on treatment issues related to African American or Hispanic/Latino families. Recognizing that the world was becoming more diverse, Arthur Robbins, who was the director of the program at the time, asked me to develop a curriculum that was more inclusive of issues related to culture and diversity. I developed a course called *Intergroup Relations*. The focus was on cultural diversity, and on the interaction and intersection of diverse groups both within the therapeutic relationship and within the institutions where they received treatment. If we think of the treatment session as a holding environment for the patient, then imagine that the institution is the holding environment for the treatment session, the therapist, and the patient(s) (Gonzalez-Dolginko, 1987).

Diversity can be defined as understanding that each individual is unique and recognizing our individual differences. These can be along the dimensions of race, ethnicity, gender, sexual orientation, socioeconomic status, age, physical abilities, religious beliefs, political beliefs, or other ideologies. And when unique individuals come together in groups based on shared race, ethnicity, gender, sexual orientation, socioeconomic status, age, physical abilities, religious beliefs, political beliefs, or other ideologies, that group creates a shared culture. Over the years, the LGBTQ community has identified a shared culture.

Identity becomes important to any group and is especially significant for those identifying with a marginalized group. Wagaman (2016) addressed questions raised by professionals regarding the relevance of existing identity categories and labels for lesbian, gay, bisexual, transgender, and queer youth and emerging adults. The author qualitatively explored descriptions and depictions of identities and aspects of self among a group of LGBTQ-identified in an effort to understand how they perceive their own identities and self-define the aspects of themselves that are most relevant to who they are. Findings suggest that this group's uses of socially constructed identities are contextually specific and intersectional, and make use of agency. Participants identified aspects of themselves that they saw as emerging from and existing in relation to their LGBTQ-specific identities, which they use to resist the social stigma and limitations placed on them as a result of this identification, and which may serve as sources of resilience. This information can support practitioners in developing culturally competent treatment. At the time that I was engaged in treatment with people infected with HIV, the men who were gay identified as gay—the LGBTQ identity was yet to come. However, while some terminology in the LGBTQ community has changed, the attempts to resist social stigma and limitations placed on them as a result of non-heterosexual identification was likely also present in the 1980s.

When it came to treatment possibilities for gay people with HIV/AIDS in the 1980s and 1990s, there was massive homonegativity, and GMHC was a tremendous advocate in acquiring medical, dental, and psychotherapeutic services for people affected by HIV/AIDS. Sadly, people who identify as LGBTQ in current times are also subject to homonegativity. We need only look around and see that there is actually a psychotherapeutic treatment called conversion therapy (American Psychological Association, 2000)— the purpose of which is to "cure" patients of being gay, repair them, and make them heterosexual. Shockingly, this practice is currently banned in only four states and a smattering of counties throughout the USA (American Psychological Association, 2000). There are therapists who feel that if a human identifies as being LGBTQ, this is pathology. There is no doubt that this attitude affects treatment for this community. A current study (Gandy *et al.*, 2013) examines mental health service providers' attitudes toward patients who identify as LGBTQ in an agency setting and indicated that job category is associated with mental health agency employees' attitudes toward LGBTQ youth, in that respondents from the Management/Supervisory category reported less homonegative attitudes toward these youth than respondents from the Administrative/Clerical/Support job category. Yet there is still homonegativity, even as there was at the height of the AIDS crisis.

Those of us treating people with AIDS recognized that they were ostracized and scourged by society. Part of our work was to treat them fairly, pay attention to our professional ethics, and recognize their needs, both as individuals and as members of an identified group. Recognizing values and aesthetics when addressing cultural issues is essential in the practice of art therapy (Cattaneo, 1994). Values and social justice surely enter the equation when considering therapists' attitudes towards the LGBTQ community.

Talwar (2015) identified the growth of a social justice framework for culturally competent therapy as a result of the four major human rights movements of the latter 20th century: civil rights, the women's movement, gay rights, and the Americans with Disabilities Act. She identifies the AIDS crisis as the main catalyst for increased visibility of the gay community—their culture and their issues. Invisibility had long been an issue for gay and lesbian communities. Art therapy gave patients with AIDS a chance to externalize what they were feeling and represent this to the world—to become more visible. Brody (1996) described a process of becoming more visible that occurred during an art therapy support group for isolated low-income lesbians. Brody stressed the special strength of art therapy in that it encourages us to envision, on our own terms, our definitions of self and reality, since it provides an opportunity to make oneself seen. Art therapy has a special resonance for the LGBTQ community because of their historical invisibility and isolation.

As a responsible practitioner, I recognized the need to develop competence regarding gay culture, although, in the 1980s, cultural competence was not yet something that was encouraged in education and supervision. Talwar (2015) stated that all too often the cultural competency framework only replicates the power arrangements that it purports to dismantle, thereby perpetuating political correctness and the illusion that our practices address the oppressions of marginalized people. She urges the need to move people "from margins to center" not only by advocating for increasing awareness, but by building a collective vision that is both transformational and grounded in equity and social justice (Talwar, 2015). Shin (2015) envisions new paradigms of care in which practitioners develop critical consciousness—that is, an increased awareness with enhanced agency and empowerment of underrepresented minority groups—and urges us to critically examine the pervasive and insidious damages caused by the existing order of patriarchy, heteronormativity, and class oppression.

Over the years, I have seen the pendulum swing often regarding problems inherent in the cross-cultural interpretation of art and identifying aspects of art therapy and assessment that may be assimilationist or ethnocentric. Hocoy (2002) discussed these issues and brought attention to cross-cultural issues in art therapy by examining the conditions under which art therapy might be a culturally appropriate intervention, ultimately concluding that "[a]rt therapy can serve as a departure from many other Western therapeutic traditions in its critical self-examination and conscientious attempts to be a progressive and ethical enterprise" (Hocoy, 2002, p.141). Calish (2003) considered the prevalent worldview in our country as a significant influence on the ability of art therapists to develop ethno-relativistic thinking and interventions with diverse populations. And the prevalent worldview in our country changes so that, as therapists, we must work hard to support the understanding of diversity in our learning and in our treatment.

Understanding Trauma and Loss in the Art Therapy Treatment of People Affected by AIDS

As already mentioned, referring to art therapy literature in the areas of trauma, death and dying, and loss and grief was invaluable as well as informed practice during the AIDS crisis. One theme in the literature is loud and clear: when dealing with trauma and loss, nonverbal communication, which art therapy offers, provides a tool in treatment that can often say more than words. Art expression in treatment can often support reviewing one's life to prepare for death.

During the first several years of the epidemic, hearing that you had the diagnosis of HIV was receiving a death sentence. A person with HIV or AIDS had to deal with dying and all that brings with it, such as accepting the illness, getting or not getting treatment, providing for loved ones, getting one's affairs in order, or making peace with the universe. Added to this is the shame of having this disease and the perceptions of their being gay related to the rest of the world. Some of the patients whom I treated had to first tell their families that they were gay, and then that they had AIDS.

As an art therapist, I find it particularly satisfying to have patients who are also artists. Some artists may present stylized art in treatment, which can be a resistance because these stylized images may be like a false front disabling genuine contact with the therapist. But many artists engage freely and actively in the interventions. I also feel a kinship with them as artists. During this time, I had a patient who was a graphic artist, and our journey was recorded through his art. Thomas was a 37-year-old gay man who had his own advertising company and was diagnosed with AIDS.

Thomas was referred to me by a colleague with whom he was in psychoanalysis. Together, they felt he had reached an impasse in his treatment. Because he was a graphic artist, she suggested he work with an art therapist, in addition to their work together, in the hope that imagery and symbolism might emerge that would allow them to go deeper into issues and use his art and imagery to make sense of everything that was just too overwhelming for him to deal with through a verbal approach. Thomas was willing to try art therapy and used our time together to explore visual expression to look at his life in review and prepare for the end of life.

When diagnosed with a terminal illness, one is faced with mortality and begins to grieve. Kübler-Ross (1969) outlined five stages of loss and grief as denial, anger, bargaining, depression, and acceptance. In a later work, Kübler-Ross and Kessler (2005) clarified that these classically adopted stages are not necessarily sequential or all universally experienced. These stages are a commonality to people who are grieving.

When reviewing the art therapy work that Thomas did with me in session, I saw these themes ebbing and flowing. His stage of denial led to his inability to tell his family he had AIDS. Perhaps Thomas could hold on to denial in verbal therapy but was able to accept his diagnosis when facing his own imagery.

Thomas chose to work with oil pastels in much of his art—a medium with which you can blur the image and edges, sometimes creating muddiness. This is clear in the first image he made in art therapy. Although he did not mention that he had AIDS when offering a presenting problem to me, an image of himself being bent backwards by a black-and-blue wave told me that he was dealing with something overwhelming (Figure 9.1).

Figure 9.1 Overwhelmed (see color plate in the center of the book)

We discussed the smile on his face in this picture and the different ways he could be saying "AAH," which is in the caption. His denial was clear and subsided a bit as we continued the discussion of this image. Thomas was even able to express that the black-and-blue wave symbolized how "bruised" he was feeling with all that life was presenting him with.

Certainly, Thomas had anger at his disease, but most of the anger he presented and processed in art therapy was his anger at rejection by his family. Thomas's father had a family business in which his brother worked. Although Thomas had a successful design firm, his family thought he was crazy for not just settling into the family business and showed no respect for his creativity and ambition. No one ever discussed that he was gay. Thomas assumed they knew because he was unmarried and only socialized with men, but it was never discussed, and at that time Thomas communicated minimally with them.

Figure 9.2 Thinking of My Family (see color plate in the center of the book)

When Thomas was telling me about his family, I asked him to draw what thinking of his family was like for him (Figure 9.2). It was no surprise that another huge wave, of sorts, is crashing down on him. Again, he is saying "AAH!" This time it is punctuated with an exclamation point, which may be a scream, but it is timidly coming out of a thought bubble and not being said out loud. The Thomas figure here is diminutive, looks frightened, and is running away, as opposed to the first image in which Thomas is facing the crushing force. It occurred to me that Thomas was more frightened of his family than of his disease at this point in our work. It seemed as if we needed to get through some of this anger so that Thomas could give up his denial and deal with the realities of his diagnosis. The fact that he was running away from his family is a good sign, and an image that helped me point out to him that by not joining the family business and limiting contact, he was putting healthy distance between him and his family.

Thomas was visibly shaken when he came in one day and told me of a conversation he had just had with his brother. I asked him to draw it as he was telling me (Figure 9.3).

Figure 9.3 Talking to Robert (see color plate in the center of the book)

His brother is on the left, and Thomas described him as lazy and uncaring. Because he "fell into the family business," he does not work very hard, drives expensive cars, and has a "trophy wife" and a lovely home. His brother is shown here smiling while talking about himself and smoking a joint, which is burning the phone wire—the line of communication. Thomas, on the right, is suffering in silence, feeling unseen and unheard. He is filled with bad energy and disease, and can express neither. Thomas drew a black line through the two brothers' necks, indicating that there's no connection for either of them to their feelings or their emotions in each other's presence. The sun is often symbolic of the paternal authority figure (Hammer, 1980). In Thomas's art, the sun shines down on his brother and an errant ray looks as if it is heading for Thomas's head.

Figure 9.4 How My Family Makes Me Feel (see color plate in the center of the book)

Figure 9.4 is Thomas's image related to how his family makes him feel. At this point in treatment, Thomas was tearing pieces of images that he created and was collaging them on to other images that he was making. I pointed this out as a possible way of his having more control over issues in his life by taking things apart and reassembling them to express a point. Thomas agreed and made the following observations. His eyes are angry, and the back of his head is missing so that "all my thoughts and feelings are falling out." Thomas has a Manhattan in his hand despite the fact that he does not drink alcohol and knows he should not because of his suppressed immune system, but he stated that contact with his family always makes him feel that he needs a drink. He is inside, alone, looking out at a stormy sky. Thomas then noticed the red scribble on his face and became obviously upset. "It's a Kaposi's sarcoma," he remarked quietly. These are lesions that appear on the skin of people who have AIDS as the disease progresses. We sat silently, but it was clear to both of us that Thomas was beginning to accept that he had a terminal illness.

In one of our last sessions, Thomas dealt with his anger at his father. He came in waving a letter he had received from his father. The content was self-referential, whiny, and asking for sympathy. The only part that concerned Thomas was a scolding that if he did not have a communication from Thomas, he would cut him off financially. Thomas immediately glued the letter to paper and began drawing over it (Figure 9.5).

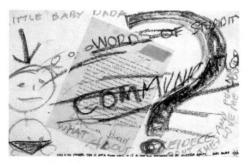

Figure 9.5 Little Baby DaDa (see color plate in the center of the book)

He represented his father as "Little Baby DaDa," whose love was conditional and based on money. Thomas felt angry because he really did not need his father's money; he was well able to support himself through his successful business. But that was his father's conditions of the relationship. Thomas's images and words concretized these feelings graphically, and he was able to process them. When Thomas realized that his father really does not love him, he was briefly subdued, but then shrugged and said, "He never did." He was able to let go of some anger when he realized that love was never there and never would be. This is what his father was like—a narcissistic baby. In many ways, Thomas felt vindicated because he realized that his father could not love, and it was not because there was something wrong with Thomas.

With some of his anger at his family out of the way, Thomas focused more on the present. Figure 9.6 represents Thomas moving through the bargaining phase of the dying process.

Figure 9.6 Time (see color plate in the center of the book)

He was hopeful because of some medical treatments that were slowing down his loss of T cells, but his count was so low at that point that he would not see a reversal of his disease. In this image, Thomas creates a timeline and surmises how long he will be around. His mood is whimsical, and the Thomas figure is smiling and sitting on an arrow going in the same direction as his timeline. Again, he is diminutive but not frightened and is looking towards the inevitable heavens, but it looks as if he is saying, "Not so fast." There is a line over his head that very much resembles the line he previously identified as a Kaposi's sarcoma. It seems to be protecting him or maybe slowing down his journey.

Thomas's stage of depression wove in and out of our work together. Early on, I showed him that I was keeping his art supplies and artwork separate from other patients'. Thomas became very sad, and I asked him why. "It saddens me that you think I could contaminate your other patients." I immediately explained that my intention was to keep his supplies from being exposed to anyone else's contact or germs to protect his compromised immune system. Thomas was relieved and was able to then discuss his depression and the terrible shame he felt because he had such a frightening disease.

Thomas wanted to look at his childhood as he focused on his life review, even though he knew it would be very depressing for him. I suggested working in wood, explaining that carving the wood could be symbolic for him of peeling away layers. Thomas was excited at the thought of working with wood, but rather than carve, he wanted to use a hammer and nails. His wanting to construct something seemed symbolic of his family because their business was construction. After vigorously using a hammer and nails, Thomas used a black Sharpie and drew words, symbols, and designs all over the wood—many angry, some spiritual, some random, per his description (Figure 9.7).

Figure 9.7 Looking Back at His Childhood (see color plate in the center of the book)

The next time Thomas came for a session, he brought a photo of himself that he wanted to incorporate into the sculpture. After many attempts, he decided to affix it to the back and on top of the wooden base, similar to the Thomas figure sitting atop the arrow in the timeline. This was 12-year-old Thomas at boarding school. His sweet face is smiling, but there is sadness in his eyes, even then. He has no arms to hug, and the spike of wood below him would discourage others from hugging him. Thomas was painfully, yet gracefully, coming to the conclusion that he was never loved.

As our work progressed, Thomas was depressed more often. He spoke of feeling like a leper because of his illness and like a crash test dummy because he was accepting any experimental treatments that were coming his way (Figure 9.8).

Figure 9.8 Crash Test Dummy (see color plate in the center of the book)

His use of collage seemed to symbolize trying to repair his damages. Thomas's nature was generous and sincere. I helped him realize that while the experimental treatments and medications most likely would not cure him, he was providing data that would ultimately help others. This thought brought a tremendous sense of peace to Thomas.

Near the end of our work together, Thomas reached a state of acceptance: his acceptance of death and some peace with all that was unknown. He depicted himself in a non-human way, yet solid and grounded (Figure 9.9).

Figure 9.9 Welcoming Life Cautiously (see color plate in the center of the book)

Thomas is touching, maybe even dueling with, the wave of "Life." In this image, the wave is in the future section of the page (Hammer, 1980), and he seems to have some control over it but truly realizes that he does not know what each day will bring, hence the name "Welcoming Life Cautiously." This is one of the only times that Thomas used markers, a medium that is easy to control and makes a definitive statement on the paper.

In one of the last pieces that Thomas did in art therapy (Figure 9.10), he again used oil pastels. Thomas had learned much from the imagery created in art therapy. He was both more aware of and more resolved with his life and what he wanted to focus on in his psychoanalysis. In this image, Thomas is facing away from the viewer. Perhaps it is hard for him to look; perhaps he is saying goodbye and walking into the sunset. However, he represents himself in human form again, which seems like he, Thomas, is "Embracing Life" and ready to move forward, accepting what lies ahead.

Figure 9.10 Embracing Life (see color plate in the center of the book)

Throughout his art therapy treatment, Thomas brought the insights gleaned from his imagery to his psychoanalysis. We decided together when we had got to the point, using art therapy, of breaking through the block he was facing in his psychoanalysis and terminated his art therapy treatment. He was able to go deeply into his process of dying. His imagery allowed him to review and resolve issues with his family that frightened him more than his death, so that he could face his terminal illness. Exploring the visual images and art expression helped Thomas process these issues and supported how Thomas was thinking and relating at that point in time. He was able to understand who he was, as separate from a family that never truly loved him. And he was able to see that it was not because there was something wrong with him. This growth and understanding helped Thomas face his death peacefully about two years later.

Conclusion

The AIDS epidemic in the 1980s and 1990s was a significant time in the history of the gay community. It brought them and their plight into the public eye and issued a challenge to the helping professions to offer care that was both culturally and humanly sensitive. The story of art therapy treatment of an artist who was gay and affected by AIDS offers insight into these times and the clinical issues that emerged. Through art therapy and engaging with his visual images, Thomas was able to acknowledge, reflect upon, and, in some cases, resolve issues of shame, alienation, political strife, family disconnection, grief, and facing death. These issues haunted his own psyche as a gay man infected with AIDS, as well as an entire community of gay men infected with AIDS. As an art therapy practitioner, I was humbled by the dignity and grace shown by Thomas as he courageously faced his destiny, and grateful that he allowed me to be a witness to his painful journey.

References

American Psychological Association (May 2000) *Position Statement on Therapies Focused on Attempts to Change Sexual Orientation (Reparative or Conversion Therapies)*. Washington, DC: American Psychological Association.

Brody, R. (1996) 'Becoming visible: An art therapy support group for isolated low-income lesbians.' *Art Therapy: Journal of the American Art Therapy Association* 13, 1, 20–30.

Calish, A. (2003) 'Multicultural training in art therapy: Past, present, and future.' *Art Therapy: Journal of the American Art Therapy Association 20*, 1, 11–15.

Cattaneo, M. (1994) 'Addressing culture and values in the training of art therapists.' *Art Therapy: Journal of the American Art Therapy Association 11*, 3, 184–186.

Gandy, M.E., McCarter, S.A., & Portwood, S.G. (2013) 'Service providers' attitudes toward LGBTQ youth.' *Residential Treatment for Children and Youth 30*, 3, 168–186.

Gay Men's Health Crisis (GMHC) (n.d.) 'About.' Acccessed on 6/15/2017 at www.gmhc.org.

Gonzalez-Dolginko, B. (1987) 'Institution as Holding Environment.' In A. Robbins (ed.) *The Artist as Therapist*. New York, NY: Human Sciences Press.

Hammer, E. (1980) *The Clinical Application of Projective Drawings* (6th edn). Springfield, IL: Charles C. Thomas Publishers.

Hocoy, D. (2002) 'Cross-cultural issues in art therapy.' *Art Therapy: Journal of the American Art Therapy Association 19*, 4, 141–145.

Kübler-Ross, E. (1969) *On Death and Dying*. New York, NY: Simon & Schuster/Touchstone.

Kübler-Ross, E. & Kessler, D. (2005) *On Grief and Grieving: Finding the Meaning of Grief through the Five Stages of Loss*. New York, NY: Scribner.

Schneider, W. (ed.) (2008) *Living with Stories: Telling, Re-Telling and Remembering*. Logan, UT: Utah State University Press.

Shin, R.Q. (2015) 'The Application of Critical Consciousness and Intersectionality as Tools for Decolonizing Racial/Ethnic Identity Development Models in the Fields of Counseling and Psychology.' In R.D. Goodman & P.C. Gorski (eds) *Decolonizing "Multicultural" Counseling through Social Justice*. New York, NY: Springer.

Talwar, S. (2015) 'Culture, diversity, and identity: From margins to center.' *Art Therapy: Journal of the American Art Therapy Association 32*, 3, 100–103.

Wagaman, M.A. (2016) 'Self-definition as resistance: Understanding identities among LGBTQ emerging adults.' *Journal of LGBT Youth 13*, 3, 207–230.

10

Exploring Gender Identity and Sexuality through Portraiture and Mixed Media

MIKELLA MILLEN

Sexuality and Gender Expression: Separate but Interrelated Dimensions

Although gender and sexuality exist on separate continuums, there can be multiple points of intersection; inevitably, the two are intertwined because sexual orientation is largely defined by attraction to same or different gender identity. This is the limitation of a categorical perspective on gender. When considering fluid identities, both gender and sexual, it is necessary to expand beyond this construct. For the purposes of this chapter, I will be outlining common stereotypes and biases, in order to deconstruct these presumptions. The reader may examine and challenge their own beliefs about gender, sexuality, and sexual orientation identity, which may be different from the views presented here, but the goal is to use the fully deconstructed foundation as the starting place in clinical work. For the purposes of this chapter, sexuality refers to what one desires to experience in sexual encounters, the "how and what," and sexual orientation identity is how one labels oneself in regard to what gender or gender expression one is attracted to (Piphus, 2017). It is worth noting that the term "sexual preference," though generally considered pejorative and related to "lifestyle choice," may have different application and relevance to a bisexual, fluid, or otherwise sexually non-binary individual who experiences attraction of varying degrees or has preferences in regard to romantic attraction/compatibility.

To some extent, the idea of gender having concrete and explicit components is a concept that fails to hold its shape upon deeper examination.

The biological factors of gender and sex differences, often taken for granted as a scientific fact, hold ambiguities. The existence of intersex individuals directly contradicts the concept of a two-gender system. The concept of hormone-based behavioral and social differences emerged concurrently with increased societal pressure to emphasize the empirical basis for prescribed gender roles, beginning with early medical practices to correct intersex individuals' sexual anatomy shortly after birth or in early childhood (Fausto-Sterling, 2000). To critically examine what it means to label something as masculine or feminine requires parsing out the intersections of gender expression, sexual orientation identity, and sexuality. Is being male or female about your genitals, social behavior, sexual practices, leisure activity choices, physical appearance, or some other externally visible/objective criterion? Who determines the hierarchy?

A predominant social bias is the equating of gender non-conforming behavior/appearance and non-straight sexual orientation identity, namely that gay men are more "feminine" (less male) and lesbians are more "masculine" (more male). This bias can apply to inherent physical characteristics such as voice pitch, physical stature and height, face shape, and muscular strength; and chosen aesthetics such as hair length/cut, clothing choices, use of makeup, hair removal, jewelry, nail hygiene, etc. Studies exploring the gender non-conforming childhood behaviors of gay men and lesbians have suggested that there may be some statistical merit to the stereotype that, for example, boys who play with dolls may later identify as gay (Li, Kung, & Hines, 2017). But there are important caveats: while there are some predictive relationships between early gender-stereotyped behaviors and adolescent and adult sexual identity, this is not as strong among those who identify outside of a sexual binary, such as bisexual or sexually fluid individuals. This becomes further complicated when considering individuals who engage in non-heterosexual sexual behaviors but do not identify as LGB (again, sexual orientation identity and sexuality may be different).

Similarly, hierarchy and categorization within the LGBQ population emerges with aesthetic descriptors *femme* (including "high femme" or very feminine-presenting and "soft" or somewhat feminine-presenting), *butch* (including "stone" or very masculine-presenting and "soft" or somewhat masculine-presenting), and *hyper masculine*; and behavioral descriptors in reference to roles during sex such as *top* (more assertive, sexually initiating), *bottom* (more passive, sexually receiving), *switch* (interested in both topping and bottoming), and others (Green &

Peterson, 2003–2004). Both aesthetic and behavioral attributes contribute to heteronormative presumptive pairings of "masculine" and "feminine" roles within two-person relationships. Additionally, it prescribes sexual roles with gender labels, allowing for presumptions of "feminine" or "masculine" sexual behaviors and desires. An example of a common presumptive stereotyped pairing would be an aesthetically feminine-presenting individual who prefers to be penetrated during sex and an aesthetically masculine-presenting individual who prefers to penetrate during sex; additionally there may be stereotyped gender roles ascribed as well, regarding money, passivity/dominance, household responsibilities, etc. This is evidenced by a social question that may be familiar to many LGBQ individuals: "So who's the man?"

Concepts of primary and secondary identities can offer needed structure and narrative context when attempting to self-identify outside a binary (Galupo, Mitchell, & Davis, 2015). One can accommodate gender, sexual orientation identity, sexuality, and relationship styles within this broader system, and including monosexual (attracted to one gender) and plurisexual (attracted to more than one gender) definitions creates the necessary distinctions to articulate queer identities. Galupo, Mitchell and Davis highlight the relationship between minority stress and plurisexual identities, concluding that due to the difficulty articulating experience using the primary labels of gay, lesbian, bisexual, and queer, plurisexuals struggle to communicate their experience and have higher levels of minority stress and rumination in relation to their identity than monosexual peers. The researchers sought to address the "Queer catchall" category with the expansion on sexual identities shown in Table 10.1.

Table 10.1 Sexual Identities

Monosexual	Plurisexual	Asexual	Romantic	Alternative
Gay	Bisexual	Asexual	Aromantic	Kinky
Lesbian	Pansexual	Demisexual	Homoromantic	Polyamorous
Homosexual	Queer	Greysexual	Biromantic	Sapiosexual
Heterosexual	Fluid		Panromantic	Homoflexible
Androsexual	Omnisexual			Questioning
Gynephilic	Tri-Sexual			
	Multisexual			
	Spectrasexual			

Source: Adapted from Galupo et al., 2015

When addressing minority stress, the ability of a clinician to have both a nuanced understanding of gender and sexuality and the ability to help individuals articulate and find language to describe their experience becomes imperative for improving mental health and developing cohesive identity. This necessitates a broadly deconstructed approach to gender and sexuality that allows clients to determine their own descriptors and select them freely over time. A clinician's ability to remain aware of biases and assumptions directly determines that freedom of expression.

A Cultural Approach to Gender and Sexual Orientation

When working with diverse populations in the realm of ethnicity and race, particularly outside of one's culture of origin, there are varying levels of awareness impacting the ability to be culturally competent. The developmental model of intercultural sensitivity attempts to define six stages of cultural awareness, beginning with an ethnocentric perspective and moving towards an ethnorelativist perspective: denial, defense, minimization, acceptance, adaptation, and integration (Bennett, 1993). If gender can be viewed as a cultural construct, then one's relationship to gender can be viewed through an intercultural lens with similar stages.

In this perspective, gender awareness and competence could be seen in the following internalized statements:

Denial: There are two genders, determined at birth based on sex organs present in the body. It cannot and should not be changed. There is a biological basis for "gendered" behaviors.

Defense: Some people think you can be born into the wrong body, but this is wrong because distinctions in gender are important for a healthy society. Hormones determine your behaviors and sexual development, so it can't be "wrong."

Minimization: Gender dysphoria exists, and is real, but if gender is a social construct, then it shouldn't really matter how your body is in alignment with internal identity. We all have masculine and feminine qualities so, in a sense, we are all gender non-conforming. Gender-affirming treatments don't necessarily improve mental health.

Acceptance: Trans individuals need access to services that allow them to be themselves fully. They should not be discriminated against. Trans individuals require access to medical treatments that confirm gender identity.

Adaptation: There are multiple genders, and individuals can self-identify for a variety of reasons. Sexuality and gender may interrelate in myriad ways. It's important to know how people identify, and even children can make these declarations.

Integration: There is a lot we don't know about gender and we must remain teachable. It's important to validate individuals' identities, but not necessary to categorize them unless that is their choice. Gender and sexual identity can change for some, and others experience it as constant. It is important to validate the individual's perspective because it belongs to them. Cis individuals cannot dominate this narrative.

Understanding one's place on this continuum, and embarking on the challenging task of moving towards the above-stated "integration" phase, provides the scaffold for joining clients in the path of self-understanding. The more that gender and sexuality is deconstructed, the greater flexibility in meeting individuals where they are, and allowing freedom of expression. Similar to the concept of owning white privilege, cis individuals and therapists must be aware of limitations in understanding gender outside of a binary.

Clinical Applications and Bias

Challenging internal bias can be initiated through approaching gender and sexuality from a place of curiosity and openness in every encounter, whether it appears relevant at first glance or not. Some examples include:

- avoiding assumptions about sexual orientation based on the physical appearance or gender association by name or label of significant others

- conducting a more expansive sexual and relationship history with new clients

- considering aesthetic presentation as a factor not immediately contributing to a client's sexual or gender identity

- exploring sexual development and puberty in the course of gathering past history.

A Self-Study to Explore Gender and Sexuality

The primary goal of developing a protocol exploring gender identity and sexual orientation is to help the participant develop a more cohesive sense of their own identity and increase one's awareness of the intersections between developmental, social, sexual, environmental, aesthetic, behavioral, and internal dimensions. One's own gender identity and sexual orientation inevitably influences views of self and other. Undoubtedly, my own experiences influence the development of this protocol; however, the intention is to be as expansive, inclusive, and open as possible. I consider myself fluid in the dimension of gender identity and sexual orientation; however, based on a chosen aesthetic that is widely considered feminine, I am most often perceived as a heterosexual woman. As a result, my perspective has been shaped by exposure to subtle homophobia, lack of understanding regarding the difference between gender identity, sexual orientation, and aesthetic choices, and the need to "come out" frequently in social interactions.

Even within the field of mental health, I have observed microaggressions, perhaps most clearly in the issue of whether or not to be "out" with patients. To ask a person most often perceived as heterosexual whether they are out at work, regardless of field, implies that given the choice of being perceived as heterosexual by default or actively correcting that assumption, it might be desirable to pass as straight. Early on this was a great source of internal struggle, as many training programs encourage the therapist to maintain a level of neutrality with patients. However, to apply this to sexual orientation is to suggest that it is a lifestyle and not a part of who you are. My eventual conclusion was that deliberately concealing my sexual orientation or gender identity was not simply an act of neutrality, but a denial of self.

Being perceived so differently from my internal sense of identity remains a vital source of empathy, compassion, and desire to explore a multitude of pathways to understanding not only who an individual is internally but how they wish to be seen and perhaps who they wish to become. As a person who consistently passes as straight, I feel it important to use that assumption to challenge perceptions in daily life.

The perspective I have now did not take shape until my 30s, and like many I struggled for many years to communicate how I felt about myself and what I wanted in a partnership. At any age, a person's sense of gender and sexuality may be clearly understood, or may have layers of ambiguity. The development of this protocol mapped aspects of my own journey, while drawing upon the observed experience of my patients over the years. Through engagement in this series of artworks, the participant can explore more deeply their sense of self through concepts of identity, external perception, attraction and comfort, aesthetic preferences, and gender roles.

Participants of this protocol are challenged to:

- develop greater understanding of how they feel internally about themselves

- consider how the perceptions of others impact sense of self

- explore feelings and attitudes of connection, comfort, and attraction to multiple/one/no genders

- reflect on how experiences in culture, family of origin, and social systems influence the expression of self both aesthetically and behaviorally.

The materials may include paper, drawing materials, painting materials, collage materials, old photos, or any desired media. Some sessions may include considerable verbal components, and although this series is designed in eight parts, each part may take any number of sessions. For the purposes of this chapter, I will refer to each part as a "session."

This series could be approached in a literal way, utilizing self-portraits, old photos, and the human figure; can be abstract with focus on line, shape, tone, color, texture, diptychs or triptychs; may be symbolized through anthropomorphism; or any combination of the above. It is not trauma-focused, but can be appropriately used with individuals with trauma histories and/or relational challenges. Similarly, it can be utilized by both individuals with a clear sense of identity and those with ambiguity; in this context it is intended for an LGBTQ population, but may be equally applicable to anyone who seeks a greater understanding of themselves.

Any number of artworks can be used, including one artwork per session, one ongoing piece, multiple works per session, or a combination.

The flexibility in interpretation and prompts is intended to allow a spectrum of approaches, mirroring the spectrum of identities that may be relevant for the participant. Each session begins with a series of questions. It is not necessary to answer every question exactly as written; rather, the aim is to encourage the participant to think about their experiences from a variety of dimensions. The progression of sessions begins with concrete and historical knowledge and becomes increasingly abstract.

My experience developing this protocol was that these topics naturally unfolded, and anecdotal experience repeating this in clinical practice appears to support an intuitive progression. The following is a personal narrative of that process.

Session 1: How Was I Perceived, and How Do I Remember Myself as a Child?

Consider how you may have been perceived and influenced as a child. What were the behavioral expectations? How did you prefer to express yourself in outward appearance and behaviors? Were these expressions impacted by prescribed gender roles, and how? Who did you seek out for friendship and closeness?

Figure 10.1 Pool (see color plate in the center of the book)

Beginning in early childhood, I developed interests that were both stereotypically for girls and for boys. I had close friends that were both boys and girls. My mother dressed me in very feminine clothes, often adorned with accessories and with attention to detail. I loved to play with Barbies and dolls, to play house, watch Disney Princess movies, and other widely accepted "young girls' activities." I also had an interest in playing outside, running through the woods getting dirty, experimenting in different sports, and I was always tall and strong for my age. Perhaps for this reason I often perceived messages, both explicit and implicit, that if I was to have masculine characteristics, it was very necessary to balance them with feminine characteristics.

Looking back, I realize that most of my friends had a similar ambiguity and interest in activities that were gender conforming and non-conforming. At the age of five, my best friend and I decided to get married in his basement. He insisted on wearing the wedding dress and I wore a long T-shirt with a printed tuxedo pattern down the front. However, I remember being upset that he had wanted to wear my mom's red high heels that I brought for this occasion, and so we compromised and I was able to wear those.

Session 2: Development of Sexual Identity

At what point did you become aware of yourself as a sexual being, or become aware of attraction to others as shown through affection and desired closeness? How has this changed over time?

Figure 10.2 Leg (see color plate in the center of the book)

In elementary school, I had both boyfriends and girlfriends, but in middle school I started to have a creeping awareness that I was different from many of my straight female peers. I knew that it was expected that I should want to have a boyfriend and kiss boys, and I wanted so much to be like my friends. Although I had previously preferred, and perhaps still prefer, friendships with boys, I began to physically develop at the age of ten and began to experience being sexualized and teased by the boys in my class. My previously androgynous child's body starting to become curvy and feminine, I could no longer fit in children's clothes. By the age of 12 I was five foot six, appeared much older, and was treated as such.

When I came out as "gay" at 16, I was lucky to be widely accepted by my peers. However, I found myself attracted to multiple genders, and my relationships reflected this. In my mid-20s, after a long-term relationship with a cis man, I was surprised to find myself coming out again as queer. Many friends had not known, or viewed me as queer, and I did not experience the acceptance of my teenage years. This did not take the form of outright rejection, but the subtle suggestion that it was a "reaction" to the breakup.

Session 3: Development of Gender Identity

How do you identify now? How have you identified in the past? How has this changed or not changed over time? What does "female-ness" or "male-ness" mean to you?

From childhood, I always considered myself to have a wide variety of personality and behavioral characteristics both "masculine" and "feminine," and I struggle to define myself in a categorical system. In my upbringing, masculinity was associated with power, intelligence, assertiveness, speaking loudly, physical strength, and a reliance on self; femininity was associated with softness, naiveté, caring, expression of emotion, weakness, sexuality, and, perhaps most importantly, *beauty*. My physical appearance was of great value; in my family environment, this was the closest a woman came to being powerful. It was also a liability, because it was a power given by men. In hindsight, it seems obvious how this dichotomy would create great conflict in my own sense of identity.

Session 4: Influential Experiences

Are there any experiences that affected your sexual or gender identity/affiliation, or relationship to your body? How much do you think your environment has impacted your expression of self? If relevant, this may also include exploration of trauma.

Figure 10.3 Bed (see color plate in the center of the book)

Because of my early physical development and unwanted attention from boys and men at a young age, I came to view certain visual indicators such as a curvy shape, breasts, and softness as being directly connected to not having agency over my own body. In addition to other experiences throughout my upbringing, this contributed to a very poor sense of body image and overall esteem. I felt this was best expressed in an image, which depicts a memory that shaped my self-conception (Figure 10.3). My choice of art media (collage, paint, and ink) attempted to express multiple images and memories within a single frame. The process of making the image required accessing feelings that required containment. Both the symbolism and the process itself provided a space to explore these elements in a manner that allowed me to choose the level of privacy or openness I wished to express, depending on the audience. The potential value of using an art process in doing therapeutic work can be demonstrated in the ability to express something through an image in this book that I would not explicitly describe in words to an open audience. It may appear vague to the reader or viewer, but I know what it means, and sharing it in this form allows me to feel a sense of power and agency, but also safety.

Session 5: Perceptions of Others, Social/ Cultural Messages, and Heteronormism

How did the perceptions of others influence, shape, alter, or confirm your inward sense of who you are, and who you are attracted to?

When I first came out in my adolescence, I made an effort to look and act in the way that I had seen lesbians portrayed in the media and my very limited experiences in person. I cut my hair short, wore more loose-fitting and masculine clothes, and tried to imagine living in a place where there were more than a couple of people like myself.

This was somewhat effective at communicating to others how I saw myself; however, I came to understand that, overall, I was still most often perceived as straight. Over time, I accepted that I liked more stereotypically feminine clothing and began to dress as I wanted. Throughout my life, numerous individuals have expressed their confusion and sometimes disbelief that I was not straight. Although I was not always aware of this, for many years it created a deep sense of alienation from my peers, even within the LGBT community. Further, it created confusion within me about how it was that I could have relationships with both men and women, that I could dress in feminine clothes but feel more "male" in some ways, and that these relationships would somehow feel similar to me, regardless of what gender my partner was. Perhaps the most damaging outward response of my peers was the suggestion that my identity and orientation changed concurrently with the beginning and end of a relationship, while internally I was (of course) the same person.

Session 6: How Am I?

How do you act? What are the behaviors and outward expressions of who you are? If salient, you may also include how you appear/look/dress.

My interpretation and understanding of feminism allows me to integrate what may be considered more masculine characteristics into my identity as a woman; more importantly, it doesn't concern me to categorize or justify these characteristics. I am outspoken, opinionated, chatty, and likely to express my thoughts if I feel I am being mistreated. I am partnered with a woman, passionate about social justice, and spiritual. My appearance changes based on my current aesthetic interests and is unrelated to my sense of gender and sexuality.

Session 7: Where Am I?

How do you see yourself in the greater landscape of gender, sexuality, and affiliation?

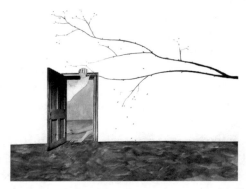

Figure 10.4 Hands (see color plate in the center of the book)

I identify as sexually and gender-fluid and use the word "queer," and primarily maintain social relationships with women and non-straight men. Although internally I see myself as very androgynous, I identify deeply with the experience of being a woman. From this perspective I identify deeply as a female from a social construct, use she/her/hers pronouns, and do not have conflict about the discrepancy between my very female appearance and life experience and a strong internal sense of "maleness."

Session 8: Who Am I? What Makes Me, Me?

Having explored the previous seven sets of concepts, attempt to represent or symbolize your sense of who you are from any/some/all/none of the previous dimensions. What is most important to know about you? What has changed?

This question is not possible to answer in a single session, a single image, or even an idea. This last prompt is an ongoing question that I cannot answer in this chapter. A participant can answer through their continued participation in therapy, through their interaction in the world at large; ideally, this question is explored over the long term. I feel I would have answered many of the previous questions differently at different points in my life, and I suspect at a later point in my life some of these answers may change. Some topics felt too personal to explore in this narrative, and similarly, in work with patients, there may be questions too personal to be explored or maybe even expressed.

However, in spite of a considerable amount of time thinking about my own sense of gender and sexuality, both from a personal and academic standpoint, I learned a great deal about myself by attempting to express these ideas. In some of the questions, I'm not yet satisfied by my understanding. I learned that there are aspects of my own identity that are not so clear to me, and through this process I understood other aspects on a far deeper level, allowing me to share new parts of myself with those closest to me.

By using a combination of personal narrative, mixed media, collage, and drawing, I was able to express my responses to these questions in multiple ways. I could move between intuitive and affective response, and direct and concrete answers. Looking at myself through different lenses allowed for exploration of self-concept on a time continuum and highlighted the interplay between the external and internal factors impacting identity development.

Anyone seeking to repeat this protocol in their clinical work or setting would be well served by first completing this as a self-study. Much as it is necessary to explore one's own cultural background and beliefs in order to do meaningful work with diverse populations, in order to do meaningful work with those who are gender non-conforming, LGBTQ, or otherwise consider themselves outside of the straight world, it is necessary to understand how personal identity may impact the dialogue. By breaking down the barriers between masculine and feminine, social and behavioral, gender and sexuality, we can attempt to build new definitions and ideas with each individual patient.

References

Bennett, M.J. (1993) 'Towards a Developmental Model of Intercultural Sensitivity.' In R.M. Paige (ed.) *Education for the Intercultural Experience*. Yarmouth, ME: Intercultural Press.

Fausto-Sterling, A. (2000) *Sexing the Body: Gender Politics and the Construction of Sexuality*. New York, NY: Basic Books.

Galupo, M.P., Mitchell, R.C., & Davis, K.S. (2015) 'Sexual minority self-identification: Multiple identities and complexity.' *Psychology of Sexual Orientation and Gender Diversity 2*, 4, 355–364.

Green, E.R. & Peterson, E.R. (2003–2004) 'LGBT Terminology.' Accessed on 11/16/2018 at https://lgbtrc.usc.edu/education/terminology.

Klein, F. (1990) 'The Need to View Sexual Orientation as a Multivariable Dynamic Process: A Theoretical Perspective.' In D.P. McWhirter, S.A. Sanders, & J.M. Reinisch (eds) *Homosexuality/Heterosexuality: Concepts of Sexual Orientation.* New York, NY: Oxford University Press.

Li, G., Kung, T.F., & Hines, M. (2017) 'Childhood gender-typed behavior and adolescent sexual orientation: A longitudinal population-based study.' *Developmental Psychology* 53, 4, 764–777.

Piphus, L. (2017) 'Sexual Orientation vs. Sexuality.' Acccessed on 11/16/2018 at https://campusconnect.uwp.edu/news/3419.

Riggle, E.D.B., Rostosky, S.S., Black, W.W., & Rosenkrantz, D.E. (2016) 'Outness, concealment, and authenticity: Associations with LGB individuals' psychological distress and well-being.' *Psychology of Sexual Orientation and Gender Diversity* 4, 1, 54–62.

Zaylía, J.L. (2009) 'Toward a newer theory of sexuality: Terms, titles, and the bitter taste of bisexuality.' *Journal of Bisexuality* 9, 2, 109–123.

11

There Is no Black or White in the Rainbow

Expressive Art Therapy for LGBT Individuals in Religion-Based Conflict

SARA GLUCK AND MICHAEL KARIYEV

Introduction

Organized religion may provide a sense of spiritual meaning and structure to its practitioners. In fact, some research has shown that religion and spirituality can be a predictor of effective coping with life stressors (Pargament, Koenig, & Perez, 2000). However, for individuals who identify as LGBT, religious constructs and communities may become sources of stress. The individuals who do not fit the norms of their religious environments may struggle to reconcile their own identities with the desire to maintain a connection to their faith-based cultures. Those struggles may result in cognitive dissonance, in feeling torn, alone, or even abandoned. The conflict may make it difficult for individuals to acknowledge their gender or sexual orientations to those around them, or even to themselves.

The conflict between religion and identity may be explored in the context of expressive arts therapy, within which participants are offered a non-judgmental space for self-exploration. The primary tenets of expressive arts therapy include allowing clients to reach inner healing through self-exploration (Malchiodi, 2005). For some, that exploration may lead to a decision to continue to belong in a religious community. Others may discover a desire to advocate for acceptance of their individual selves and for societal change. The process of creative expression may guide some to the decision to distance themselves from their culture of origin. Religion and spirituality are complex factors that are often intertwined with politics, families of origin, and core values (Rodriguez & Oullette, 2000). Because these topics are sensitive in nature, they require careful, non-directive intervention. Therefore, creative arts therapies are particularly useful tools that may assist psychotherapists in maintaining ethical objectivity while performing effective clinical treatment.

The Conflict

Elle sits before me as her eyes well with unshed tears. She describes a relationship with a significant other to whom she refers as "they." I know this look, this fear, this doubt. The trademark hesitation in her voice and the pain in her words are dynamics I have seen before, among clients who are afraid that I will judge them. I gently say, "By the way, I haven't gotten to this question yet: How do you identify in terms of your own gender and sexual orientation?" She looks up, making direct eye contact. "I identify my gender as female, but as far as my sexual orientation goes, I don't know. I have dated men and women, and I'm so torn about it, but you are the first therapist who actually asked me that question." She breathes a sigh of relief and begins to talk openly about the struggle she has been experiencing: the dissonance between her faith and her feelings.

This conflict is one that is rooted in thousands of years of religious tradition. Hers, like most monotheistic religions, condemns homosexuality as a sin. Religions such as Mormonism, Islam, Christianity, and Judaism have scriptures that detail the punishments to be meted out for homosexual behavior, ranging from excommunication to execution (Heermann, Wiggins, & Rutter, 2007). Religious leaders, especially those in fundamentalist congregations, often speak out against homosexuality, calling it an "abomination" or "disgusting." At the same time, religious congregations often impose cisnormative roles on their members. Religious educators may assume that girls will become homemakers and that boys should be trained toward becoming strong leaders. This sort of preassigned destiny leaves no space for individuals to decide on their own gender identities and roles (Sumerau, Cragun, & Mathers, 2015). Those individuals who were raised attending churches, temples, or mosques may have heard the scriptures cited over the course of their entire lives. When being anything other than cisgender and heterosexual is considered akin to murder and robbery, what are the options for LGBT individuals in faith-based cultures?

We (Michael and Sara) collaborate in treating a diverse population of individuals and families. We have found that those who enter our offices often feel stuck, trapped. They often feel that coming out of the closet would mean losing their faith, their families, and their communities in one fell swoop. At our practice, we have seen individuals and couples at many stages of conflict. We've listened to parents debate whether they would still love and accept their child if she or he turned out to identify as LGBT. We've supported young adolescents who express fear of "being gay." We have felt the pain of young adults who emerge from conversion therapy experiences. We have treated depression and anxiety among those who have chosen to enter heterosexual marriages solely in order to stay in their communities of origin. We have validated the fear of our clients who struggle to fulfill the religious commandments associated with the genders they have been assigned at birth. In the face of societies and therapies that attempt to dictate sexual orientation and gender identity, we have strived to provide a therapeutic environment where no judgments are made, and internal conflict is welcomed and honored.

Spirituality and Religion

There are several reasons for the intense conflict often experienced by LGBT individuals who associate with religious beliefs and communities. There are often many positive aspects to the same religions that condemn non-cisgender and non-heterosexual identities. In addition, at times, family and community support is dependent on conformity, making the choice to "come out" extraordinarily difficult.

First, spiritual beliefs may provide a sense of coping, support, and meaning (Fallon et al., 2013; Halkitis et al., 2009; Shilo, Yossef, & Savaya, 2016). In a recent study of men who self-identified as both religious Jews and gay, researchers found that practicing religious coping skills such as talking with a rabbi and performing mitzvoth (Jewish commandments that are seen as the law of God) was correlated with improved mental health. In a study of urban LGBT adults, researchers found that 75% of participants were raised religious, and only 25% identified themselves as currently religious. However, many still chose to engage in private spiritual practices such as prayer (Halkitis et al., 2009). The benefits of having a spiritual connection may be especially relevant for those who feel lost and alone.

A second factor that may keep people tied to religion is the related support system of family and community. For many, choosing to come out as LGBT may result in losing the emotional, physical, and even financial support of their loved ones (Rodriguez & Oullette, 2000). Although that support may seem conditional or shallow to an outside observer, it may be too painful or pragmatically difficult to lose. It is a determination that can only be made by the individual who will have to live with the consequences. The decision to lose one's entire support system is very, very personal.

Third, individuals who were raised in monotheistic religious traditions may have learned to hide their sexual inclinations or diverse gender identities not only from the public but also from themselves. When faced with the evidence that they would be rejected for feeling attraction toward or for identifying as the "wrong" gender, it is logical to repress those feelings and attempt to maintain a safe status quo. This denial of self may create a deep sense of dissonance, a core split self. Individuals may deal with that by living a double life, in which LGBT identities are kept hidden from the outside religious community. Others may cope by undergoing conversion therapy, ignoring their "sinful" thoughts, or even getting married to a socially accepted spouse (Pietkiewicz & Koodziejczyk-Skrzypek, 2016; Rodriguez & Oullette, 2000).

Religious individuals, or those who were raised religious, may face many very real and tangible barriers to coming out of the closet. These are not barriers that can or should be easily dismissed, for the implications of crossing them are often irreversible and life-altering.

Barriers to Traditional Psychotherapy

LGBT individuals who struggle with religious conflicts may experience barriers to traditional psychotherapy approaches. First, they may have experienced some level of trauma and dissociation, which may make talk therapy challenging. Second, past experience may make it difficult to trust people who claim to be healers or helping professionals. Third, they may be engaging in current sexual behavior that contributes to increasing levels of dissonance.

Trauma

Trauma has been defined as feeling fear and immobilization at the same time (Levine, 1986). This can occur when a child sits in the pews of their church, knowing they (which is intended as a singular, gender-neutral pronoun) feel gender or sexuality conflicts, while hearing that those feelings are cause for intense punishment. This can be a terrifying reality. It can create a sense of internal collapse, as the child's brain struggles to cope with the dissonance between parts of self. Trauma can cause real, neurobiological changes to the brain, such as shrinking of the hippocampal region responsible for verbal expression (Van der Kolk, 2014). In the treatment room, this may present as apparent resistance to engaging in talk therapy.

Trust

Many religious cultures encourage their congregants to bring challenges and conflicts to their spiritual leaders (Heermann *et al.*, 2007). As a result, by the time individuals present for treatment, they have often already approached those within their faith in an attempt to get help. While some religious leaders and guides are able to accept LGBT individuals, others may be less capable of doing so. At our practice, we have heard clients report the things they have been told:

- "Do you want this up your behind? How is that normal? What is wrong with you?" Religious mentor holding up a stick and chastising an 18-year-old male reporting attraction to other men.

- "It is your sacred duty to be a good wife and mother. Deciding you just want to 'cop out' of that is the definition of disgusting." Religious parent to 15-year-old child begging for permission to undergo gender confirmation surgery.

- "You can feel these feelings, but you can never act on them." Religious mentor to 15-year-old female who confided her feelings for her female friend.

- "This is an abomination. It is against the Bible. It's just your evil inclination trying to get you to sin. But you can be stronger than that, you can overcome this." Religious leader to 40-year-old woman debating leaving her marriage.

Statements like these can create deep mistrust of helping professionals. When congregants approach their religious leaders with a spiritual struggle, and are met with judgment, this can lead to internal hesitation regarding further self-disclosure (Hill & Pargament, 2003).

Shame

"Love the sinner, hate the sin" is a belief system that is often adopted by faith-based cultures that value loving kindness while condemning diverse gender identity and homosexuality. This sort of attitude may result in intense feelings of shame and guilt related to identity and sexuality. Therefore, when LGBT individuals who have participated in organized religion venture toward exploration of themselves, they may face extreme internalized shame, homonegativity, and/or transphobia (Lease, Horne, & Noffsinger-Frazier, 2005). We have seen this present in our treatment rooms as habitual covering up and denial regarding any behavior that deviates from cis- or heteronormative. Our clients often report feeling intense guilt and shame related to sexual exploration, which they have been taught to view as "immoral" or "acting out."

In addition, we have seen individuals who have committed to heterosexual marriages in an attempt to suppress their identities and follow the script laid out by their religious cultures. This often leads to another layer of self-flagellation, as individuals reach a point where they feel or act on desires outside of their marriages. That is a conflict that may be too painful to bring into the open space of talk therapy, as those individuals may deny the reality of their split lives, even to themselves. However, in the context of expressive arts therapy sessions, they can process the conflict, shame, fear, and pain without being limited by words alone.

Treatment

Charles, 22, fidgets with his electronic cigarette as he fills me in on what brought him to my office. He was born as Charlotte, the sweet little girl his parents dressed in bows and ruffles. He remembers being five years old, trying to figure out why the pink tulle didn't feel right on his little body, why he cringed at the cherubic face he saw in the mirror, framed by long ringlets. He had been hoping and praying that he would learn to fit in, to do and feel what was expected of him. Eventually, the counselor at his religious, all-girls summer camp noticed that Charles wore board shorts instead of bikinis. The counselor also perceived that Charles "looked at the other girls in a way that seemed more than just friendly." During our session, Charles reports that the counselor was right. He had been developing feelings for one of the other campers, and had been sneaking glances her way despite his best attempts to repress those feelings. He takes a deep drag of his e-cigarette and looks at me sheepishly. "I was just a teenage boy, a straight one, trapped in a girl's body. They made me feel like that was evil. Like I was a freak." Thus began years of family conflict and conversion therapy. Charles's shame is palpable. His previous therapist attempted to assist Charles in naming his non-conformist gender identity and sexual orientation as "optional." Several rounds of therapy left Charles feeling suicidal, wanting to end the pain of his inner conflict.

When treating individuals who struggle to reconcile religiosity with gender identity or sexual orientation, the single most critical task of the therapist is to be aware of his or her own prejudices (Fallon *et al.*, 2013). The first step to recognizing those prejudices is being aware of the gender identity and sexual orientation conflicts with which clients may present. The APA Office on Sexual Orientation and Gender Diversity (American Psychological Association, 2011) offers support and guidance for clinicians who seek to improve on their competency and knowledge in treating individuals who identify as lesbian, gay, bisexual, and/or transgender. In Charles's case, his journey toward self-acceptance was complicated by his conversion therapist's lack of insight and education. "When I told my therapist I felt like my female anatomy didn't match how I felt, he just told me that was a sin. When I told the therapist I might be attracted to girls, he said that was a sin too. It was all a sin. None of the feelings were supposed to exist. How could I even figure out what any of it meant if it was all the same: sinful?"

Clinicians who believe that homosexuality, bisexuality, or diverse gender identity is sinful may find that it is difficult for them to endorse true exploration of self within their clients. Clinicians who have been through a coming-out process of their own may feel hesitant to create space for the possibility that their clients may choose to stay closeted or to live double lives. And those therapists with minimal exposure to LGBT struggles may be afraid to have open dialogues with their clients. Those are just a few examples of biases and attitudes that may inhibit effective treatment.

According to the APA code of ethical treatment (American Psychological Association, 2012), psychologists are urged to remain non-judgmental of LGBT individuals, to avoid trying to change the sexual orientation or gender identity of their clients, and to do whatever they can to increase their clients' sense of safety both within and outside of the therapeutic environment.

Play and Art Therapy

The effectiveness of play and art therapy lies in the belief that clients are the experts on their own selves; clients already have the information they need in order to resolve their struggles. The information was initially processed and stored, and thereby only accessible in full at a multi-sensory, multidimensional level. Play and art reach beyond the verbal, cognitive, and conscious into the vastness of human experience. The clinician observes, amplifies, and reflects what clients have presented through play and art, thereby elucidating clients' knowledge and experience of self (Lusebrink, 2010; Malchiodi, 2005; Slayton, D'Archer, & Kaplan, 2010).

Play and art therapy can provide a forum within which the complex components of a client's life can be accessed and addressed. Verbalization is not necessary, as a whole world can be built, drawn, or painted in a tactile manner. Sensory expression is inherently more primary to humans than speech. Babies' interaction with their environment is through their senses. As children grow older, they are taught to talk, but this speech is censored; there are certain things that may not be said. Additionally, there are often no words applied to threatening realities. Play and art reach for the preverbal and nonverbal, and through the socially imposed barriers, therefore accessing the undefended unconscious truth in its most basic form (Malchiodi, 2005; Slayton *et al.*, 2010).

As Charles began to explore his identity in session, he often seemed to choke on his words. The external stigma imposed by his previous therapists and his pastor became evident as he censored his speech, even in the safe space of the therapy room. He would grow frustrated with himself: "I know I can talk here…but I can't. I just can't." This makes perfect sense given the ways in which his language development was impacted at a young age, as his prefrontal cortex was developing the ability to formulate thoughts (van der Kolk, 2014). As per Goodman (2017), transgender individuals are often silenced within extremist religious cultures. They may internalize the pressure to hide their questions, concerns, and lived realities. They may find themselves at a loss for words with which to express their experiences. Creative therapies such as art, storytelling, and writing can bypass those inner barriers and allow for free expression of self.

Within the context of our sessions, Charles chose art as his form of therapeutic expression. The expressive therapies continuum provides a model for understanding the use of various art mediums in the context of art therapy. As per Lusebrink (2010), when clients use art to create visual representations of their internal experiences, they may be depicting their brain processes. The use of paint, as a fluid medium, may enhance the processing of sensory, affective, and symbolic functioning (Lusebrink, 2010). There are times when it may be appropriate to guide clients toward the use of one medium over another. However, during our second session, Charles walked over to the art therapy shelves on his own and seemed to gravitate toward the paints. I supported his choice because he was new to art therapy and I sensed that he needed to use the medium with which he felt comfortable. After overcoming his resistance to painting (he had self-judged "that's so gay"), he produced the art in Figure 11.1.

Through painting, Charles was able to depict the split in his mind. He spent many moments emphasizing the barrier between the two distinct sections of his work. As he painted, the tension in his shoulders seemed to decrease, and the e-cigarette he had been clutching was forgotten on the side of the table. Charles focused on his work and accepted my assistance in finding the right colors and brushes. The first thing he painted was the red barrier across the page. On one side of the barrier, two males stand close, but not touching. Of the smaller figure, Charles said, "He's so, so sad, and his friend is there but can't take away the sadness." Charles appeared to breathe a sigh of relief while painting the rainbow section. "This is full of color, and life, and joy, but I don't know how to get there." Once the painting was complete, Charles smiled and expressed the inner peace he felt at putting the conflict out there so that we could examine and hold it together.

While Charles chose not to have a detailed conversation about his artwork, I noted the red barrier as a possible representation of internal splitting or compartmentalizing. He may have isolated his feelings and affect from his actions because that is what was required of him in the past. This would be explored in later sessions as Charles would begin to integrate his experiences of self.

Figure 11.1 Charles's Depiction of the Split in His Mind
(see color plate in the center of the book)

Another client, Elle, related to using art as a form of expression as well, in her own way. She struggled with being vulnerable in session, and chose to paint at home and then bring her canvases in for discussion. I understood that Elle had been faced with judgment and criticism in the past, when she had confided in religious mentors. I was honored that she felt comfortable sharing her completed work in session, and viewed it as a sign of the trust that was building in our therapeutic alliance. Elle had been to art lessons as a child, and she drew upon her experience with oil paint in her work. She also expressed that she preferred oil paints because they allowed for smooth mixing of colors. Elle liked to create her own colors when she worked, and I hypothesized that may be a representation of how she defied the prearranged norms of her external community. At the same time, Elle's confidence in forming unique colors and images may have been a glimpse of her inner strength and empowerment.

She described spending days on the oil painting in Figure 11.2. The similarity between her works and Charles's was astounding. Each depicted a sense of dissociation, of split self, of walls and barriers. Each used the rainbow as a symbol of feeling at peace in their respective gender identities and sexual orientations.

Elle said that the wall between her worlds was beginning to crumble. There were two distinct parts of her life. In one she was a dutiful religious daughter who told her parents she would eventually marry a man with whom she would have children. At the same time, she had already been in a significant relationship with another woman, and had acknowledged that she felt more whole with women than she had ever felt with her boyfriends. She was still afraid to face the full impact of that, but was beginning to discover a sense of internal truth. She said, "I can't come out to my family or community; they would cut me off and never speak with me again. Because I'm an evil sinner. I shouldn't be attracted to women; there's something wrong with me."

In Figure 11.2, the dark waves streaked with blood and bones represented the pain of trying to fit the mold that was imposed upon Elle by her family and religious community. Her girlfriend became a beacon of light, the lighthouse, that allowed her to see just how dead inside she had been feeling. Elle was both the skull, haunted by the years spent hiding, and the brilliant bird, beginning to spread its wings and fly into a golden rainbow.

Figure 11.2 Elle's Oil Painting (see color plate in the center of the book)

Expressive Writing

Much research has shown that expressive writing can help people process traumatic or stressful life events in ways that are adaptive (Cook *et al.*, 2014). LGBT individuals who have experienced religious conflict may often feel that their voices are silenced. They may be afraid to articulate the nature of their struggles to the people whom they love most. In some cases, the conflict between identity and religion may result in feelings of fear, trauma, and dissociation (Rodriguez & Oullete, 2000). According to Steven Porges (2009), when people feel threatened, there are actual neurobiological changes that occur in their minds and bodies. For instance, the dorsal vagal complex may shut down non-essential functions, such as speech, in order to conserve energy toward survival.

Expressive writing can be a powerful tool for bypassing the inner barriers toward having a voice. Through writing, individuals can express the real struggles and pain without having to cope with anyone else's facial expressions or reactions to those truths. Pachankis and Goldfried (2010) performed a research study of gay men who participated in writing about the stressors related to their sexuality. They found that writing was correlated with higher levels of openness about sexuality and overall improvements in psychosocial functioning (such as self-esteem, positive affect, and physical health) in the months following the study. These benefits were especially significant for individuals with lower levels of social support in their environments. Similar results have been found in studies of lesbian women, where expressive writing was correlated with decreased stress, especially for those who reported being closeted (Lewis *et al.*, 2005).

POETRY: CASE EXCERPT

Natasha, a 17-year-old who presented with depression and low self-esteem, was most comfortable using writing to express her conflict. Natasha's parents had brought her in for treatment because she was failing some of her classes at school. At first, they had believed that Natasha had some learning disabilities, but when she achieved the highest SAT score in her school, her parents knew that something was not adding up. Natasha revealed that she wanted to explore her sexual orientation; she thought she might be bisexual but was afraid to tell her father, who was a prominent supporter of the local church. Natasha tended to withdraw into her bedroom and into herself, in an effort to hide her pain.

After two months of avoiding eye contact in session and talking about anything but herself, Natasha finally said, "I write more freely than I think." I encouraged her to bring some of her work into session, and when she saw that I could be trusted to be supportive, she began to ask for a notepad during sessions. At first, she would write short stanzas and ask me to turn my chair around so I would not watch her work. Then she would pass the notebook to me, and her face would seem to light up when I asked questions. Eventually, we created a system of sorts, where the writing component of the session would segue into verbal processing. One day, she wrote the poem below, and I could hear her writing and erasing until she got the words right. This became the start of us discussing her inner battles about exploring and discovering her sexual orientation.

TASTE THE RAINBOW

The little bird flew low
Skimming the ocean and the trees
"The world is black and white" they said
The larger and older leaders of the pack
The bird saw the sharpness of the charcoal waves
The stillness of the white meadows
And stayed in the safe formation
Guided by the rigid flight of those sharp-eyed hawks

One day a daring shade of red reflected
Off the little bird's wings
She flew over the hillside to see if it was real
A brilliant rainbow bathed in golden tones
Illuminated the sky above
Phoenixes and eagles and doves all dancing in the light
The bird flexed her wings
Spread them wide
Basked in the glow
She felt the blood rush through her body
The hope run through her soul
She felt alive

"That was sin" they chastised
They pulled her beneath the mountainside
Into the cave of darkness
She fasted
She prayed
She bowed her head
And vowed to stay in the world of black and white
She hid the memory of vibrant sin
And pulled her wings
Modestly backwards
Into submission

For what was the rainbow but evil temptation
That would singe the wings
Of all those headed along its gentle curve
And fly them straight into the bowels of hell

The little bird repented deeply
And buried the small still voice within
The one that wept as she gave her mind
Her body
Her love
To the world of black and white
"The rainbow is a mirage" they said
And so she believed
That she'd seen a wish
A dream
And she clipped her wings
Tied them back
And stayed on her side of the mountain
Flying in straight lines
Holding her heart down
And willing it to stop straining
Toward the hues bursting through the clouds
Taunting her with the vision
Of what could have been

Natasha, 17

FREE WRITING: CASE EXCERPT

Donovan presented for treatment following his release from an inpatient psychiatric hospital. He had swallowed a handful of pills after his girlfriend found gay porn on his browser history. Donovan wrote a detailed narrative during his hospital stay, and he brought a copy of it into his first session. He seemed ready to face the layers and years of repressed struggle. Donovan said that the suicide attempt was a "wake-up call," and a sign that he needed to be honest with himself and those who love him.

> This is my story. Everyday, I wake up and it all comes down on me like a bolt of lightening…the misery of having to hide and conceal and never be who I really am. I'm 13 years old and my adrenaline is kicking. I start noticing my draw towards men. I look a little stranger, skinnier perhaps. My peers call me faggot, pussy boy.
>
> I'm 16 years old, working my way through high school. My peers all have girlfriends and talk about how they made out for the first time. I keep

thinking of the jock after last week's football game in the boy's locker room. I force myself "to get over this shit" and start dating girls. I feel wrong, my body is yelling at me...but this is "normal" I say. This is the way it should be.

I'm 18 years old, excited for life and college. I want to date a man. I feel religious guilt as I confide in my priest and he tells me how this is forbidden. Under no circumstances can I date a man and be considered religious or accepted "in the fold." I try to express my feelings...but the same reoccurs. "The Bible says otherwise." "You have the ability to overcome your desires if you so choose." "You can just get married and things will sort themselves out." "God wouldn't just make you gay...you must be bisexual or something." "You'll be rewarded in heaven for living a straight life."

I'm 22 and my parents start telling me that they met this pretty, nice girl. I finally break it to them after years of being in the closet. "Mom, Dad, I'm gay." For those lucky enough to have supportive families...God bless their souls. For me, that wasn't the case. "listen here mister you better get your act together and not ruin the family name" says my mom. My dad shakes his head and starts yelling "this is all the liberal media's fault, that fucking rainbow parade is messing with you." Slowly but surely reality kicks in. Resentment starts to build and avoidance occurs. The worst. It's one thing to express your feelings around homosexuality but to feel a slow and painful disconnect...as if they "lost their son to the devil."

I'm 25 years old and I meet this wonderful man. He is struggling with his own identity given he is a member of a fundamentalist religion. He expresses his concerns; anxiety but we start acting out. The relationship grows but remains a secret. The guilt is intense. The feelings are suppressed. The split self starts to emerge. Guilt mixed with pleasure. The minister finds out. Parents find out. And the relationship is split. Alone again.

I'm 28 years old. I am referred to the top therapist specializing in "homosexuality." That therapist convinces me that I can "experience opposite sex attraction" if I "just work hard enough at my childhood wounds." I am told that my early childhood issues have "created this orientation" and that it can be reversed. I get excited...finally the solution to my problem!

I'm 42 years old. After years of therapy with no success in changing my orientation, I "give up." I have made a choice. I either lose my faith, friends, community and family or I continue to be what society wants me to be and be miserable inside.

Finally, my narrative…all I want is to love and be with a man. I've been told I can be "cured" and "treated." I feel like fucking shit. No matter where I go and where I turn, everyone wants me to fit into their society. I can never just be me. I feel like I'm bombarded with what God's plan is, what He wants for me. Does God see me? Does He notice my thoughts? Where is He in my struggle? The Bible tells me I can't act on my struggles. There's a part of me that is damned to misery. People look at me weird. They call me queer. I need to stop being me. My pastor tells me I need to change. I need to go to conversion therapy. I go. It's soul crushing. I'm miserable. I want to die. I'm a fucking mess, day after day. I can't please myself, I can't please anyone else. All I want is to love and be loved. My body is exploding with sexual feelings that I cannot and should not acknowledge. It's a yearning, a desire for deep, deep connection. Not because I want to go against the Bible. Just this is what I feel in my heart and soul. This hurts. It hurts so much I can't speak. The lump in my throat…it kills. All I want is support but everywhere I turn there's judgment.

Donovan, 42

Conclusion

As mental health practitioners, we often see and feel psychic pain along with our clients. If we are brave, we face that pain without rationalizing it or utilizing defense mechanisms to block it out. The challenges faced by our LGBT clients can be immense. The fight to be who they are, to simply exist as a real version of themselves, that fight can build or break one's spirit. When that struggle is compounded by religious conflict, it may involve choices between self and community, between honesty and denial, between acceptance and excommunication. In those cases, our roles become even more crucial.

LGBT individuals may have already been told what to feel, who to be, and how to act by the competing voices in their lives. It is our task to provide a space for acceptance of all sides of the conflict, of all parts of self. As stated in the APA practice guidelines (American Psychological

Association, 2012), it is not our job to judge or to make decisions for our clients. Rather, we can allow our clients to come to their own truths, of their own volition.

Expressive arts therapies are ideal modalities for allowing clients to explore their own inner psyches without imposing any external expectations or beliefs. Clients may use art, play, and writing to put their intense feelings and thoughts out into the world. And we can simply be there. That may turn out to be the most powerful intervention of all.

References

American Psychological Association (2012) 'Guidelines for psychological practice with lesbian, gay, and bisexual clients.' *American Psychologist 67*, 1, 10–42.

American Psychological Association (2011) 'Transgender People, Gender Identity and Gender Expression.' Accessed on 3/25/2018 at www.apa.org/topics/lgbt/transgender.aspx.

Cook, J.E., Purdie-Vaughns, V., Meyer, I.H., & Busch, J.T. (2014) 'Intervening within and across levels: A multilevel approach to stigma and public health.' *Social Science and Medicine 103*, 101–109.

Fallon, K.M., Dobmeier, R.A., Reiner, S.M., Casquarelli, E.J., Giglia, L.A., & Goodwin, E. (2013) 'Reconciling spiritual values conflicts for counselors and lesbian and gay clients.' *Adultspan Journal 12*, 1, 38–53.

Goodman, S.V. (2017) 'Spirituality, healing and the whole person: Reconciling faith in the transgender community.' *Journal of Family Strengths 17*, 2, 4.

Halkitis, P.N., Mattis, J.S., Sahadath, J.K., Massie, D. *et al.* (2009) 'The meanings and manifestations of religion and spirituality among lesbian, gay, bisexual, and transgender adults.' *Journal of Adult Development 16*, 4, 250–262.

Heermann, M., Wiggins, M.I., & Rutter, P.A. (2007) 'Creating a space for spiritual practice: Pastoral possibilities with sexual minorities.' *Pastoral Psychology 55*, 6, 711–721.

Hill, P.C. & Pargament, K.I. (2003) 'Advances in the conceptualization and measurement of religion and spirituality.' *American Psychologist 58*, 1, 64–74.

Lease, S.H., Horne, S.G., & Noffsinger-Frazier, N. (2005) 'Affirming faith experiences and psychological health for Caucasian lesbian, gay, and bisexual individuals.' *Journal of Counseling Psychology 52*, 3, 378.

Levine, P.A. (1986) 'Stress.' In M.G.H. Coles, E. Donchin, & S.W. Porges (eds) *Psychophysiology: Systems, Processes, and Applications.* New York, NY: The Guilford Press.

Lewis, R.J., Derlega, V.J., Clarke, E.G., Kuang, J.C., Jacobs, A.M., & McElligott, M.D. (2005) 'An expressive writing intervention to cope with lesbian-related stress: The moderating effects of openness about sexual orientation.' *Psychology of Women Quarterly 29*, 2, 149–157.

Lusebrink, V.B. (2010) 'Assessment and therapeutic application of the expressive therapies continuum: Implications for brain structures and functions.' *Art Therapy 27*, 4, 168–177.

Malchiodi, C.A. (ed.) (2005) *Expressive Therapies*. New York, NY: The Guilford Press.

Pachankis, J.E. & Goldfried, M.R. (2010) 'Expressive writing for gay-related stress: Psychosocial benefits and mechanisms underlying improvement.' *Journal of Consulting and Clinical Psychology 78*, 1, 98.

Pargament, K.I., Koenig, H.G., & Perez, L.M. (2000) 'The many methods of religious coping: Development and initial validation of the RCOPE.' *Journal of Clinical Psychology 56*, 4, 519–543.

Pietkiewicz, I.J. & Koodziejczyk-Skrzypek, M. (2016) 'Living in sin? How gay Catholics manage their conflicting sexual and religious identities.' *Archives of Sexual Behavior 45*, 6, 1573–1585.

Porges, S.W. (2009) 'The polyvagal theory: New insights into adaptive reactions of the autonomic nervous system.' *Cleveland Clinic Journal of Medicine 76*, Suppl. 2, S86.

Rodriguez, E. & Oullette, S. (2000) 'Gay and lesbian Christians: Homosexual and religious identity integration in the members and participants of a gay positive church.' *Journal for the Scientific Study of Religion 39*, 333–347.

Shilo, G., Yossef, I., & Savaya, R. (2016) 'Religious coping strategies and mental health among religious jewish gay and bisexual men.' *Archives of Sexual Behavior 45*, 6, 1551–1561.

Slayton, S.C., D'Archer, J., & Kaplan, F. (2010) 'Outcome studies on the efficacy of art therapy: A review of findings.' *Art Therapy 27*, 3, 108–118.

Sumerau, J.E., Cragun, R.T., & Mathers, L.A. (2015) 'Contemporary religion and the cisgendering of reality.' *Social Currents 3*, 3, 293–311.

Van der Kolk, B.A. (2014) *The Body Keeps the Score: Brain, Mind, and Body in the Healing of Trauma*. New York, NY: Penguin Books.

12

Finding New Communities in Long-Term Care

Creating an LGBT and Allies Group for Older Adults

LIISA MURRAY AND OLIVIA COHEN

Douglas shuffles to open the door after a knock. He has a "do not disturb" sign on the door, unlike the other rooms. As he opens the door, the social worker peers into a small room, with a twin bed, and memorabilia covering the walls. A desktop computer is in the room and a walker, as well as several books and newspapers on tables and the bed. Douglas is an 85-year-old resident at a nursing home and a gay cisgender man, though many more people know the first part than the second. She has taken to coming to visit him often, as he spends much of his time in his room apart from the other residents. As they talk, he hits upon a point he's discussed with her before. "I feel like a petunia in an onion patch," he laments. "Do you think there are any other gay residents here?" The social worker can only nod with uncertainty. He continues, "I mean, there have to be, right? But I haven't met any."

Introduction

Moving to a long-term care facility can be a challenge. It can be especially challenging for an LGBT older adult, as they face specific issues adjusting to their new home. This chapter aims to give background on LGBT older adults in long-term care and the bias they face, and discuss the creation and implementation of an LGBT and allies group in a long-term care community. We will discuss some of the experiences in the group, the importance of this group, and some of the outcomes from participants.

Older Adults in Long-Term Care

In the United States, the population of adults 65 years or older was recorded at 47.8 million in 2015, representing 14.9%, or about 1 in 7 Americans. These numbers are expected to more than double to over 98 million by the year 2060 (Administration on Aging, 2016). This is a significant and important part of the population of the United States, and it is a group that is often neglected or overlooked. Of the current number of older adults, 1.5 million (3.1%) were in institutionalized living, the percentage increasing as their age increased, from 1% for persons 65–74 years to 3% for persons 75–84 years and 9% for persons over 85 (Administration on Aging, 2016). Older adults face many issues with their increasing age, and for those with significant health issues, moving to long-term care may be an important choice. While it may be helpful for their health concerns, it often presents its own host of challenges.

Older adults who move to a long-term care facility may experience a range of losses: their home, their freedom, their pets, friends, family, their predictable lifestyle (Nay, 1995). These are huge losses individually, and the stress of each combined can be at times overwhelming during this adjustment. This can also change people's perceived identities. Where they may have once seen themselves as an independent person, they may now see themselves as someone dependent on others for care, and may feel degraded by this change (Nay, 1995; Riedl, Mantovan, & Them, 2013). Our popular culture in the United States has few images of how a person living in a nursing home can be a vibrant contributor to society; individuals entering nursing homes may see them, as many do, as places where sick people go to die. The role of nursing home resident is not one that is culturally valued. This can both be a damaging blow to a person's sense of positive identity and bring up issues of facing their own mortality (Nay, 1995).

LGBT Older Adults in Long-Term Care

There is a lack of accurate data on the actual population of LGBT older adults in the United States. One study estimates that there are more than 2.4 million LGBT adults over 50 in the United States, and it is expected that this number will double to more than 5 million by 2030 (Choi & Meyer, 2016). Due to current homophobic and transphobic attitudes of society, it is assumed that LGBT older adults feel discouraged to come out, which results in under-reporting. It is anticipated that by 2050, however, more accurate numbers will be available as societal views continue to affirmatively shift and LGBT minorities become more visible and have their needs and concerns addressed (Orel & Fruhauf, 2015). However, during the latest draft of the National Survey of Older Americans Act Participants, questions related to sexual orientation were removed, critically altering the data collection practices that allow for many researchers, service providers, and advocates to address the unique needs of the LGBT older adult population (Loewy, 2017).

As a group, LGBT older adults may be disproportionately affected by poverty and mental and physical health conditions because of minority stress, a lifetime of victimization, and internalized stigma (Fredriksen-Goldsen *et al.*, 2015). They may be affected not only by ageism, but also by discrimination based on their minority gender identity or sexual orientation. They have higher rates of social isolation, are more likely to be living alone, as they are less likely to have children or be married, and more likely to be estranged from their family of origin. They often look to support from their peers, and that support may become unstable as their peers experience their own challenges or pass away (Choi & Meyer, 2016). These challenges are compounded when LGBT older adults enter a long-term care facility.

There is some emerging data on the experiences of LGBT older adults in long-term care facilities and the challenges they may face. In a survey of LGBT older adult residents in long-term care and their family members, 89% believed that residents would be discriminated against by staff, 81% thought they would be discriminated against by other residents, 77% expected isolation, and 53% expected abuse (Justice in Aging, 2010). These numbers represent the many fears LGBT seniors may have in long-term care while in an already vulnerable state, illustrating the compounding nature of the intersections of being older and LGBT.

These fears are not unfounded—the medical and psychiatric communities have often treated LGBT identities as illnesses. Until 1973, homosexuality was listed as a mental illness by the American Psychiatric Association (Orel & Fruhauf, 2015). For a resident at a nursing home, that might have happened when they were in their 30s or 40s, and they might have spent decades either believing or living with others' belief that their sexual orientation was a disease. Gender identity disorder was removed from the same listing only in 2013 (Orel & Fruhauf, 2015). It was replaced by gender dysphoria, and while this change is a move forward, there is also a belief that a diagnosis pathologizes transgender individuals and therefore has no place in the DSM (Lev, 2013). There has also been a resurgence in the use of conversion therapy, despite the APA and many other organizations rejecting the use of it (American Psychological Association, 2015).

Residents' fears of discrimination by other residents are understandable. Unlike staff, who may be trained in cultural competency for working with LGBT patients, residents receive no such training, and may have a wide variety of biases and assumptions about LGBT people. Our residents grew up during an era when, as discussed earlier, homosexuality and transgender identities were pathologized, and these views may be carried into their exchanges with other residents. Compounding their fear of discrimination, LGBT older adults may have been removed from their chosen family to move into an unknown community where, for all the above reasons and more, they may not feel secure or safe. These fears may all cause previously out older adults to feel they need to go back into the closet. For Douglas, who entered the nursing home with some medical and physical challenges, he now had to learn to depend on others for help with medications, getting ready for the day, and maneuvering around safely with his walker, and also found himself questioning who he could share his sexual orientation with in his new community.

Who We Are

We (Liisa and Olivia) are both music therapists who have a passion for working with and advocating for older adults. In the LGBT and allies group, we play the role of allies and model the ally role for the other group members. In our work, we try to be mindful of any bias we may have, by keeping each other in check, which is a benefit of working with another therapist. We are mindful of the difference in generations between us and the residents, as millennials working with much older residents. Our work in the group is guided in part by the guidelines for best practices in music therapy with LGBTQ clients suggested by Whitehead-Pleaux et al. (2012). It is important for us to continually educate ourselves, as well as be aware that we may get things wrong and need to look inward to evaluate our own biases or blind spots in knowledge. We are drawn to this work because of the many ways LGBT issues have touched our lives and the lives of those we love.

Our Nursing Home Community

The nursing home where we work is in a 720-bed organization with a large campus spread over several buildings. The home provides both long-term care and short-term rehabilitation, and neighborhoods for both residents with skilled nursing needs and those living with memory loss. The organization is guided by Jewish values yet is home to a diverse community of residents and staff of all faiths and backgrounds. The nursing home is progressive and prides itself on being open to forward-thinking initiatives to advance elder care in the United States.

The residents of this nursing home have a variety of ways to spend their time. They can spend time in their rooms, watching TV or reading, socializing with peers on their floors or "neighborhoods," or they can engage in group programs, each facilitated by a staff member. Each neighborhood has multiple programs each day in the shared lounge space, including art, music, dance, or drama therapy, games, discussion, or sensory programs.

Additionally, there are community programs that residents from any floor can come to, escorted by transport aides or on their own. Each of these programs is open and continuous, with no formal ending date. The groups take place in the library, a room that is unlocked and which people can enter at any time, although they are encouraged to enter quietly. This creates unique challenges for conducting a group. Members may be hesitant to share, knowing that someone could walk in at any moment. Unlike groups that have the same members returning week after week, this group may have different members each session, making it difficult to build on each week's shared experiences. Group members might not feel the space is private enough because they have not yet built the trust with a visiting resident to share intimate details of their lives. The lack of privacy in the group space is parallel to the lack of privacy that is often experienced living in long-term care, and this could bring up feelings of resentment, or breaches of confidentiality. Group work can provide an opportunity for residents to process any feelings that may arise as a result of the change in their environment.

Beginning an LGBT and Allies Group

This group formed as the result of a conversation with an 85-year-old resident, Douglas. In discussion, Douglas disclosed to us that he identifies as a gay man. Although he shared this with us and a few other staff members and residents, he did not feel comfortable being completely out at the nursing home, as he was concerned about how staff and other residents would treat him. He felt isolated and unsure of his belonging in the nursing home community as he was not aware of any other gay residents. As there was a lack of formalized visible supportive community, we believed that other LGBT residents felt similarly to Douglas in that they were not sure if they could be out and safe. We wanted to start this group to offer a space to residents who identify as LGBT where they could find each other and be themselves. We proposed the group to administration and received support to begin the program.

The addition of allies was crucial to include in the group as well. An ally is someone who supports LGBT people, whether it is a person who is a part of the LGBT community (a bisexual person supporting transgender people, for example) or part of the dominant culture (a heterosexual cisgender person supporting transgender people) (Human Rights Campaign, 2015). Identifying and including allies in the group allowed LGBT participants to rebuild a supportive peer group. It also empowered the allies to advocate for individuals outside of the group, as well. And for many of the allies, this was a role they had played for many years outside the home, an important one they may have felt they lost when they left their communities and entered long-term care.

One of the residents, June, had spent years as an activist for women's rights and gay rights. With a change in her physical mobility, and a loss of independence entering the nursing home, she no longer had opportunities to advocate for others, by participating in marches or other acts. June also lives with memory impairments. Although she may not be able to write a letter to a congressman, she still has the heartfelt desire to support others in the LGBT community directly. Arthur, a member of our group in his 60s and an ally to the LGBT community, found himself compelled to join a meeting after the shooting at a gay nightclub in Orlando, Florida. There was also Shirley, who joined the group in part because of her connection to the AIDS crisis, speaking of the many gay friends she lost during the 1980s. The ally was an essential role, as LGBT residents in the group could know with whom they could feel safe within the larger nursing home community, and the allies could feel empowered to advocate for others outside the group as well.

Conducting the Group

Even though we are music therapists, we often explore the use of different modalities within our practice, and our approach to this group was similar: finding and providing relevant experiences for the residents that allowed them the autonomy to choose the direction of the group while also experiencing something new, regardless of modality. At each meeting the group discussed and explored topics and challenges relating to the LGBT experience. The objectives for the LGBT and allies group were:

- to create a space for those who identified as LGBT to feel supported and safe to share, and for allies to join in supporting their LGBT peers

- to provide group content that allowed for education and connection between group members

- to provide opportunities for older adults to advocate for others

- and to create a forum to discuss both past and present issues, challenges, and strides related to the LGBT community.

We utilized art making, storytelling, singing and analyzing lyrics, multimedia resources (National Geographic, 2017; TrentAndLuke, 2017; Val's LGBTI Ageing & Aged Care, 2016; wickydkewl, 2017), and/or group discussions. While we use many directives in the group, for ease of discussion and for other therapists' replication, in this chapter we will discuss group format, creating a shared values collage, and lyric analysis as tools to use to begin an LGBT and allies group in long-term care.

In the beginning it was challenging for the residents to stay on topic with LGBT issues. Some of the difficulty stemmed from cognitive issues, or some residents' tangential communication or understanding. Other difficulties were a little more vague at first. The residents would often connect to the feeling of a topic—"That person feels so mistreated, it must be so hard"—and then move to a discussion of how hard it can be to depend on others for everything. As group leaders, this could be frustrating for us—we're here to talk about LGBT issues, not the struggles of being at nursing home. As we continued to work with the topics, they were able to stay "on task" more easily. Looking back at this phase in our work, it seems to us that this was actually an important step for them to recognize the similarities between their struggles and feelings, and to empathize in a way that connected to their daily lives.

Another aspect of the group that was important to us as facilitators was that no one is under any obligation to disclose their sexual or gender identity at any time during the group. All disclosure is entirely optional and a personal choice. This is important both so that people don't feel obligated to disclose when first entering what may be a space they are nervous to be in and to allow for people to feel that their identity doesn't have to be one fixed thing throughout the process. Respecting a resident's right to privacy about their sexual orientation or gender identity is also one of the music therapy best practices in working with LGBT clients (Whitehead-Pleaux *et al.*, 2012). Members do not need to identify specifically as an ally to join the group, but all members need to agree to the values we share as a group.

GROUP FORMAT

Group format is consistent. The group is one hour in length and is continuous, with no end date. While we are the facilitators of the group, the members decide what direction to take. Format consistency and group autonomy are essential to empowering the members of our group. Our role as facilitators is sharing information, guiding, and modeling the behavior of our shared values. This is important not only for general group structure, but also to help make the group accessible for our residents with memory impairments, to orient them to what group they are attending and why.

The group begins with reviewing its shared values (to be outlined later in this chapter), which are the rules and guide the group created together at the first meeting. These can be read by a group member or group facilitator. From there, we do a check in, recapping our last group meeting and opening the floor for discussion or presenting the LGBT topic we are focusing on for the day. Some of our topics focused on the letters in LGBT; other topics related to understanding sexual orientation, gender expression, and gender identity, or exploring the life of a historical LGBT figure. Each group ends with the identification of one concept, feeling, or idea they are taking with them or have learned from the day's session. As the group is still continuing at the time of this writing, we will be discussing the process of the group during its first year.

EMBRACING DIFFICULT CONVERSATIONS

Leading this group brings many challenges. This group often revisits the topic of group openness, initiating dialogues and exploring new discussions and ways of thinking for the members. This is challenging for everyone—it's distressing to realize you've been wrong or that you might make or have already unintentionally made a microaggression that hurt someone. One aspect that we model as group leaders is being open and kind to yourself about what you may not know, and being honest about your mistakes when you make them, while working to learn more. We want the group members to be able to be honest with their biases and assumptions so they can move through them. We also want them to be open to uncomfortable feedback from others in the group.

One area where this was especially important was education on the transgender community. During our discussion on the topic of transgender terms and issues, Susan expressed some confusion over her own gender identity, sharing how she always hung out with the boys and never felt "girly." We referred to the concept of the "Genderbread Person" to help discuss the concept of the spectrum of gender expression (Killerman, 2015). The Genderbread Person is a visual aid for helping to understand gender identity, expression, and biological sex as existing along a continuum. As we tried to explain, we realized some of the limitations included the lack of someone with lived experience and a lack of our residents having exposure to transgender representation. We watched a video (Refinery29, 2015), and invited a transgender speaker to the group who specializes in educating others on transgender issues. In an open forum discussion, our guest speaker set the ground rules for what questions she felt comfortable to answer, shared her life experiences, and spoke about her experiences with her grandparents. All of the residents who joined us that meeting stayed after to express their gratitude to the speaker. This moment gave us all a person to connect with and help with understanding more fully the terms we had been learning about in the group.

As group leaders, we are constantly aware not only of the individuals in our group but also how generational culture can shape an individual's experiences. How comfortable does a group with members from the "Silent Generation" feel with openly discussing the topics of gender identity and sexual orientation? The Silent Generation is a cohort of older adults around 70 years or older who lived during a time in history where LGBT people were socially invisible (Fredriksen-Goldsen et al., 2015). As a new generation enters the nursing home, how do some of the Baby Boomers (those aged 50–69) in the group make space with their comfort levels? As group leaders, we acknowledge that we are younger than the group participants and that our experiences and world views also inform the group process. While being conscious of our perspective, we must also honor the foundations for LGBT strides made by the generations before us.

One discussion that touched upon these issues involved the shades in the room. Eight months into our year with the group, the library had newly installed shades on the windows to help the feeling of privacy for the many groups that meet there. As we, the group leaders, began to close the curtains, Douglas asked us, "Why?" We had assumed the residents would want privacy, but as the discussion developed, it became clear that having the shades up and open was a representation of their pride. They did not want to hide the group or, as an extension, who they are. This was notable growth for Douglas and the group.

Sometimes questions may arise regarding how the group feels with new members joining or stopping by. How do we feel about younger generations or students observing or visiting? At times, the group answer is unanimous. Other times, it is a room of differing thoughts and feelings. As group leaders, we make space for all to feel safe to share, often helping to navigate the difficult conversations.

Our first experience of a perceived unity among the group members took place during a difficult conversation, when a new resident, Bob, joined the group. Bob seemed to be looking for something to join that morning to pass the time, and found himself in the library, curious as to what we were discussing. We informed him this was the LGBT and allies group, and he decided to stay, not knowing what LGBT meant, but receptive to learning more. What took place was an overt opportunity to create group cohesion.

Many questions Bob asked rubbed group members the wrong way. He would ask questions using outdated language, or asked the group, "But what about them raising children?" Group members responded with frustration and confusion toward the lack of awareness and tolerance Bob expressed in his questions. They each took turns addressing and educating him on the topics he brought up. It was an opportunity for our LGBT-identified residents to share their experiences, and our allies to support them and advocate on their behalf. The group gave him clear, respectful, and passionate answers. It was also gratifying for us as group leaders to see the group come together as a unit to share what they've learned and advocate for one another so strongly. It gave the group members an opportunity to begin a dialogue, motivated by their desire to educate others and share the values they found so important in this group.

Using the shared values, they were able to communicate in a respectful manner, speaking from their experiences as older adults who grew up during a similar era, in a way that we, as members of a different era, could not speak to. The allies were able take a more prominent role in support of their LGBT peers. As group leaders, it was one of our first moments witnessing members join together without our facilitation to share what they have learned in the group—not only with terminology and history, but in the connections they made with one another, sharing compassion and tolerance for people as individuals and stepping proudly into their identities.

This was a lesson for us as well. It reminded us that although this group of older adults is open-minded and interested in educating themselves on LGBT issues, the reality of older adults lacking knowledge on LGBT facts and issues does exist. This was a very moving interaction to see, especially during a time in the United States when it seems as if these difficult conversations are nearly impossible to have. Even more than that, it was meaningful to see that people, even people in their ninth decade, can learn and grow and have mind-changing conversations. While our visiting resident may have only joined us that one day, he left the group thanking us and expressing how much he just heard in one session that he never knew about before. For the group it was the first exchange in what would become a continuing conversation between them and other residents in the nursing home.

Creating Shared Values

At the very first meeting, we watched a few short videos about LGBT seniors (Los Angeles LGBT Center, 2013; Upworthy Video, 2016), discussed the purpose of the group, and then invited those attending to help create the shared values, which were discussed and solidified at following meetings.

Figure 12.1 LGBT and Allies Group Shared Values Collage
(see color plate in the center of the book)

SHARED VALUES

What's said in the group stays in the group
Stay non-judgmental
Have fun!
Feel comfortable
Learn in the group
Feel able to confide and open up in the group
Having a shared purpose
Respecting one another
Assuming good intentions of others in the group
Treat others as you wish to be treated

These are helpful for several reasons:

- There is something concrete to refer to each session.

- Beginning each session with a ritual focuses the group, bringing us into the room and the group topic.

- It helps with orienting some of our residents who benefit from reminders for memory support.

- They function as the group rules.

These values also helped keep our group within the best practices for music therapists working with LGBT people, some of which are helping to create a safe space for the residents, keeping the group free of hate speech or bullying, and supporting all clients with respect (Whitehead-Pleaux et al., 2012). These best practices are essential for guiding the creation of groups for LGBT clients.

MAKING SPACE FOR ALL IMAGES

In the beginning stages of the group, we worked together on a collage project assembled on a shared board, cutting out pictures they felt related to the group or the shared values, even staying after the group to make sure it was finished. It provided a visual reminder of our shared values and helped those who benefit from added memory support to orient to the group. It is an anchoring object that is meant to cue their memory and cognitions around the group as a construct. June, who was also an artist, took a prominent role in placement of the images. Although she may have some trouble at times remembering the content of the group week to week, she always remembers her contribution to the collage and feels proud. The images chosen for the collage included a man holding a baby with the words "safe and sound" underneath; a group of female soccer players joyfully embracing; two women dressed in professional medical attire to represent the environment the residents live in, and different colorful sculptural images including a rainbow-colored structure with the words "portal" underneath and "up & out" above. Words were also added to the collage such as "reclaim," "creating the conversation," and a short paragraph explaining shame and the expression of art. Although the paragraph was a quotation from an artist describing her process, the residents felt it explained "everything" about our group. After the collage was completed, the written shared values were placed at the center of the collage.

Figure 12.2 Rats (see color plate in the center of the book)

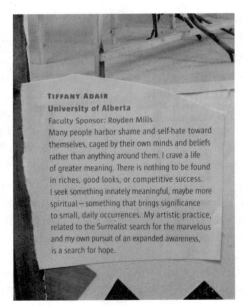

Figure 12.3 Words (see color plate in the center of the book)

Close up of words selected for the shared values collage by the residents. Residents discussed and connected to themes within the text of hiding, shame, and finding meaning in creativity.

As we looked through the images together, Susan found a picture of rats that she wanted to bring into the group. Many residents felt it did not belong on the board. It is interesting to note that Susan, who identifies as bisexual, was the one who championed the unpopular "doesn't belong" rat. Bisexual people often express not finding a space within the LGBT community (Barker & Langdridge, 2008). Had we not been aware of the existence of bisexual erasure and invisibility, we may not have seen the fuller significance of the image's inclusion. Our understanding of this moment speaks to the need of LGBT cultural competency. As therapists, using the distance of metaphor and the image of the rats, we facilitated a dialogue to make space for the image. We encouraged the group to slow down, take a second closer look at the image, and listen to why it felt important to Susan. Susan's voice needed to be heard to fight for the rats, so Susan could assert her place in the group, and assert her place as a bisexual woman within our microcosm of the LGBT community. Once the group was able to hear Susan, they understood that the rats had a place in the values, and this informed us as group leaders how conversations involving bisexuality would need to be explored further.

Song Lyric Analysis

As we continued to facilitate the group, we found it hard at times to keep the residents focused on the subject. We wanted to find directives that would keep the group focused on LGBT issues, both for residents who would float in and out, and for the consistent members as well. Additionally, as the group grew, so did the diversity of our residents' abilities. It was important to use directives that take into consideration our residents with memory impairments, physical impairments, and communication impairments, so that all residents in the group can engage and participate in their own way. This was the impetus for using song lyric analysis. Gadstrom and Hiller (2010) note: "Clients with temporarily or permanently diminished cognitive abilities (as a result of injury, illness, and disability, etc.) may require more concrete textual and musical forms in order to attend to and comprehend what is happening in the song" (p.50). Another factor in the use of lyric analysis is that song lyrics provide a storytelling medium in which an individual can empathize and project their own feelings on to the characters in the music (Jones, 2005). All of these reasons made song lyric analysis a good intervention to use for this particular group.

Choosing a song was challenging in several ways. We wanted a song with concrete and clear lyrics discussing LGBT issues directly, but we also wanted a musical genre that was familiar to our residents. Often in music therapy, we seek to use client-preferred music, and especially in older adult work we look to finding songs from their era, often when they were around 20 years old (American Music Therapy Association, 2013), a time in history when homosexuality was considered a mental illness. While music that deals openly with challenges impacting the LGBT community exists, much of it was created in the second half of the 20th century, and much of it very recently (Hardy & Whitehead-Pleaux, 2017).

Ultimately, we chose a modern pop song as its song structure and lyrics were easy to hear and understand. Although this song was not familiar to the group, listening to a song for the first time places listeners on common ground, without any pre-established associations, and amplifies attention to what may be happening lyrically or musically as no one knows what takes place next (Gadstrom & Hiller, 2010). The lyrics describe the exciting early flirtatious beginnings of a relationship, and have a repeated theme of not changing who they (the romantic partners in the song) are. To support the residents' connection to the lyrics, we used large-print lyric sheets. Gadstrom and Hiller (2010) note: "A lyric sheet also negates the need for the client to remember what he has heard, which may be of comfort to a person who has memory deficits" (p.153). We decided to use the music video as well, in order to have concrete imagery of love between two women. In the video, we watch two women engaging in acts of courtship. There are the simple interactions of a budding romance, small glimpses of two lovers glancing into each other's eyes, hands brushing against one another, conversations over coffee, even a kiss—many moments that may remind the residents of their own interactions when dating during their younger years or even now. We watched the video on a large screen in the library, as the residents held the lyric sheets.

We were nervous to share this video. We had discussed the importance of equality with others, but this was the first time we would view two women kissing as a group. Although the group had been open-minded, were they really as open-minded as we hoped? After viewing, what the residents immediately connected to was the feeling of young love. Instead of what we might have feared and assumed—"Will they judge this? Will they think it's strange?"—their reactions were reminiscing and relating to young love and "What's the big deal of two girls together?" This reminded us of our biases regarding older adults. Our group members showed us a response based on the discussions that challenged old ways of thinking and supported their acceptance and compassion for others. It shows that older adults are able to learn and grow beyond what we, as a culture or as individuals, may think are their limitations.

Conclusion

LGBT older adults face specific challenges and issues when they enter a long-term care facility. The creation of an LGBT and allies group can help to address some of their fears, create a safe space, help build a new community, and encourage them to live more openly, authentically, and healthfully. This group also benefits the allies who join as well, by encouraging them to reclaim former roles and identities, to advocate for others, learn, and engage with a supportive community. Advocacy inside and outside of the group helps create a strong and more accepting nursing home culture. It is important for those working in eldercare to meet the unique needs of LGBT older adults and make the space for those still in the closet to feel safe to come out throughout the lifespan, giving them the opportunity to meet others to stand by their side.

Douglas was able to come out to more residents in his community and find more people he could relate to. He even sat with us at the nursing home's very first pride table, and passed out rainbow stickers to the staff and residents. June was able to show one of her strengths at this table too, with Arthur and Sylvia, calling out to passers-by, beckoning them to learn more about the issues of LGBT older adults. June was able to continue to express the deep caring that motivated her throughout her activist life. Susan learned more about gender expression, and began to explore her own gender identity. And all of them were able to share information with residents, staff, and caregivers about LGBT older adults, spreading awareness and increasing knowledge about caring for this population.

Conversations within the group can be difficult, surprising, and moving, but they are necessary to give voice to a marginalized group. As music therapists, we know the power of the voice both literally and metaphorically. We are always questioning and making sure we are doing the best we can for the residents, both LGBT and ally. Most importantly, as therapists who work in eldercare in a society focused on youth, it is important for us to share the fact that these conversations are happening. This is our own effort to share the resiliency, creativity, and beauty of our elders. Growing older does not mean you stop learning, growing, and transforming. As one of our residents says of himself and his older adult kin "Don't underestimate us!"

> *Douglas walks out of the home's library, taking his time with his walker as he passes by one of the facilitators holding the door open for him. This has been an especially important group for Douglas, as he has realized not only are there are other LGBT residents, but some of them are also members of several support groups he's been a part of. Douglas was enthusiastic and talking throughout the session. As he leaves the group, he grabs the facilitator's arms, looks into her eyes, and says, "I didn't know there were other people here like me. Thank you. I'm home."*

References

Administration on Aging (2016) *A Profile of Older Americans: 2016*. Washington, DC: US Department of Health and Human Services, Administration on Aging.

American Music Therapy Association (2013) *AMTA Professional Competencies*. Silver Spring, MD: American Music Therapy Association.

American Psychological Association (2015) 'American Psychological Association applauds President Obama's call to end use of therapies intended to change sexual orientation' [Press Release, April 9]. Accessed on 11/16/2018 at www.apa.org/news/press/releases/2015/04/therapies-sexual-orientation.aspx.

Barker, M. & Langdridge, D. (2008) 'II. Bisexuality: Working with a silenced sexuality.' *Feminism and Psychology 18*, 3, 389–394.

Choi, S.K. & Meyer, I.H. (2016) *LGBT Aging: A Review of Research Findings, Needs, and Policy Implications*. Los Angeles, CA: The Williams Institute.

Fredriksen-Goldsen, K.I., Hoy-Ellis, C.P., Muraco, A., Goldsen, J., & Kim, H. (2015) 'The Health and Well-Being of LGBT Older Adults: Disparities, Risk, and Resilience across the Life Course.' In N.A. Orel & C.A. Fruhauf (eds) *The Lives of LGBT Older Adults: Understanding Challenges and Resilience*. Washington, DC: American Psychological Association.

Gadstrom, S.C. & Hiller, J. (2010) 'Song discussion as music psychotherapy.' *Music Therapy Perspectives 28*, 2, 147–156.

Hardy, S. & Whitehead-Pleaux, A. (2017) 'The Cultures of the Lesbian, Gay, Bisexual,Transgender, and Questioning Communities.' In A. Whitehead-Pleaux & X. Tan (eds) *Cultural Intersections in Music Therapy: Music, Health, and the Person*. Dallas, TX: Barcelona Publishers.

Human Rights Campaign (2015) 'How to be an LGBT Ally.' Accessed on 11/16/2018 at www.hrc.org/blog/how-to-be-an-lgbt-ally.

Jones, J. (2005) 'A comparison of songwriting and lyric analysis techniques to evoke emotional change in a single session with people who are chemically dependent.' *Journal of Music Therapy 42*, 2, 94–110.

Justice in Aging (2010) *LGBT Older Adults in Long-Term Care Facilities: Stories from the Field*. Washington, DC: Justice in Aging.

Killerman, S. (2015) 'The Genderbread Person v3.' Accessed on 11/16/2018 at http://itspronouncedmetrosexual.com/2015/03/the-genderbread-person-v3.

Lev, A.I. (2013) 'Gender dysphoria: Two steps forward, one step back.' *Clinical Social Work Journal 41*, 3, 288–296.

Loewy, K.L. (2017) 'Erasing LGBT people from federal data collection: A need for vigilance.' *American Journal of Public Health 107*, 8, 1217–1218.

Los Angeles LGBT Center (2013) *LGBT Seniors Tell Their Stories | LA LGBT Center* [Video File]. Accessed on 11/16/2018 at https://youtu.be/JDOdv792rBA.

National Geographic (2017) *The Genderbread Person | Gender Revolution* [Video File]. Accessed on 11/16/2018 at https://youtu.be/89Az3m-qJeU.

Nay, R. (1995) 'Nursing home residents' perceptions of relocation.' *Journal of Clinical Nursing 4*, 5, 319–325.

Orel, N.A. & Fruhauf, C.A. (2015) *The Lives of LGBT Older Adults: Understanding Challenges and Resilience*. Washington, DC: American Psychological Association.

Refinery 29 (2015) *What Being Trans is Really Like | Get Real | Refinery 29* [Video File]. Accessed on 11/16/2018 at https://youtu.be/e5FviqVGtOE.

Riedl, M., Mantovan, F., & Them, C. (2013) 'Being a nursing home resident: A challenge to one's identity.' *Nursing Research and Practice*. doi:10.1155/2013/932381.

TrentAndLuke (2017) *YOUNG, GAY AND ILLEGAL - Then & Now* [Video File]. Accessed on 11/16/2018 at www.youtube.com/watch?v=yOXKf_nPWpk.

Upworthy Video (2016) *After 48 years of being together, this lovely couple is finally celebrating their one-year anniversary thanks to progress* [Video File]. Accessed on 11/18/2018 at www.facebook.com/UpworthyVideo/videos/768096296628253.

Val's LGBTI Ageing & Aged Care (2015) *Then and Now - Older Trans Women Share Their Stories* [Video File]. Accessed on 11/16/2018 at https://youtu.be/92GOtFyFNrs.

Whitehead-Pleaux, A., Donnenwerth, A., Robinson, B., Hardy, S., Oswanski, L., Forinash, M., & York, E. (2012) 'Lesbian, gay, bisexual, transgender, and questioning: Best practices in music therapy.' *Music Therapy Perspectives 30*, 2, 158–166.

wickydkewl (2017) *95 Year Old Comes Out As Gay* [Video File]. Accessed on 11/16/2018 at https://youtu.be/USukifYeFVo.

Glossary of Terms

ASHLEY L. KOENIG

Language is the social and cultural concept with which we, as humans, communicate; it is an ever-changing, expanding system. As discussed in the introduction to this book, the following glossary of terms is simply a collection of socially and culturally time-specific terms and their current, generally accepted definitions. While the social and cultural origins of language are important to consider, historical uses of terminology are not discussed at length in this glossary. This glossary is by no means exhaustive, in part due to the ever-changing and evolving nature of LGBTQ+ terminology and the fact that terms presented here are limited to Western and specifically North American clinical terminology.

Each of these terms and concepts is connected to individualized and nuanced human experiences. Terminology is constantly being created and reclaimed by members of the LGBTQ+ community to better describe the wealth of experiences and identities we hold. The available language around LGBTQ+ identity and experience will continue to expand as we deepen our understanding of intersectionality within our community and embrace the idiosyncratic and vast experiences of our people. That being said, a generalized and consistent understanding of current terminology is invaluable in our work with clients.

The terms in this glossary speak to individual human experience and complex group identity. The definitions of the terms provided will fail to encompass the vast and nuanced idiosyncrasies that come with individual experience and identity. Engaging individuals in the experience of their identity will offer us boundless insight, but we cannot put the onus on our clients to educate us. We must take it upon ourselves to become versed in the available theory and terminology. As a secondary note, due to the individual nature of language, any term presented in this glossary should only be used once a client has self-identified with said term, even as we may hold our own assumptions in the course of our work.

As a final note on the "alphabet soup" that these terms can present, the acronym LGBTQ in itself is a limited portrayal of sexual and gender minority identities. Other common acronyms include LGBTQQIA (lesbian, gay, bisexual, trans, queer, questioning, intersex, and asexual or ally), LGBTQTS (lesbian, gay, bisexual, transgender, queer, and two-spirit), among others. Even these longer acronyms are not exhaustive. In this glossary, LGBTQ+ is used, with the + acting as a place-holder for missing letters.

Glossary of Terms

A

Agender A term used to describe an individual who identifies as not having a particular gender.

Ally An individual who does not personally identify with the LGBTQ+ identity, but who has a concern for the acceptance, equality, and well-being of the sexual and gender minorities within the LGBTQ+ community. This individual may use their privilege to confront instances of prejudice and discrimination that come from homo-, bi-, and transphobias.

Androgynous Appearing, usually physically due to dress or behavior, indistinguishly feminine or masculine and/or identifying as neither male nor female; presenting one's gender as either mixed or neutral.

Asexual Describes the experience of an individual who experiences limited or no sexual desire or who experiences limited or no desire to engage in sexual activities. Asexuality can exist on a spectrum, and can describe individuals who only experience sexual desire under certain circumstances or with certain people. Asexuality is not necessarily an exclusive sexual orientation as asexual individuals may also identify as lesbian, gay, bisexual, etc.

B

Biphobia The fear or hatred of and discrimination against bisexually oriented people, usually in relation to beliefs regarding the normative binary systems of gender and sexuality. As with any phobia and prejudice, biphobia can be present within the general population as well as within the LGBTQ+ community.

Bisexual A sexual orientation characterized by one individual's sexual, physical, romantic, or emotional attraction to people of two genders (i.e. both men and women). Attraction to each of the sexes may not be simultaneous and may vary in intensity. While *bi*, in *bisexual*, grammatically refers to a binary understanding of gender, it is used frequently to describe attraction to more than one gender (see the lesser-known term *pansexual*).

C

Cisgender A term used to describe an individual whose gender identity aligns with the sex they were assigned at birth.

Cisnormativity The assumption, on an individual, institutional, or societal level, that everyone is cisgender; the belief that a cisgender identity is the superior gender/gender identity, over and above all minority gender/gender identities. This assumption and belief leads to the further stigmatization and marginalization of people with minority gender identities. Ideas of cisnormativity can be present within the general population as well as within the LGBTQ+ community.

Cissexism A term used to describe the behaviors that grant preferential treatment to cisgender individuals and groups as well as the discriminatory treatment towards transgender and gender non-binary individuals and groups. Cissexism reinforces the idea that cisgender identities and individuals are superior to transgender and gender non-binary identities and individuals.

Closeted A term used to refer to sexual and gender minority individuals within the LGBTQ+ community who have not disclosed their gender identity or sexual orientation to themselves or others. This term can be used to describe not disclosing identity (being out) in certain environments or group settings and/or with certain people (e.g. closeted at work).

Coming out The process in which an individual comes to acknowledge and accept their gender identity, sexual orientation, and/or status as an intersexed person. This "coming out" to oneself may lead the individual to share their identity with others. This process may be continuous and lifelong, especially as people may choose to come out in new settings or social groups.

Conversion therapy An intervention, often psychological or spiritual, with the goal of changing an individual's sexual orientation from gay, lesbian, bisexual, pansexual, etc. to straight; or with the goal of changing someone from transgender or gender non-conforming to cisgender. Conversion therapies can include violent, intrusive, and traumatizing interventions and are dangerous and discredited; they have been made illegal in many states. The clinicians who have contributed to this text, creative arts therapies, and the American Psychological Association reject the idea and implementation of conversion therapies.

Covering The process by which an individual withholds aspects of their marginalized identity while working to ensure that disclosed aspects of their marginalized identity are not perceived by others as the most emphasized characteristics of the person. This process is most prominent in a minority–majority relationship.

Cross-dresser An individual who wears clothing that has a greater association with the sex/gender opposite to the individual's. Cross-dressing can be a form of gender expression.

D

Dominant group Also known as the majority group, in any given society this is the group with the greatest amount of power, privilege, and social status. In the context of LGBTQ+ identities, cisgender and heterosexual individuals make up the dominant group.

G

Gay A more common term/identifier for homosexual individuals or groups. A term describing the sexual orientation of an individual who is sexually, physically, romantically, and/or emotionally attracted to people of the same gender. The term *gay* most often refers to men who are attracted to men, but it is increasingly used to describe the sexual orientation of any individual who is attracted to people of the same gender.

Gender binary The idea that every individual is either one of two genders based on two biological sexes: male and female.

Gender confirmation surgery One of many possible avenues of *transitioning*, describes medical/surgical procedure to alter the biological sex of an individual. Not every transgender individual chooses to or can access or afford gender confirmation surgery. Avoid outdated terms such as *sex reassignment surgery*, *sex change operation*, and *pre-op/post-op*.

Gender dysphoria A controversial diagnostic term which replaced *gender identity disorder* in the 2013 American Psychological Association's *Diagnostic and Statistical Manual of Mental Disorder*, 5th Edition (DSM-V). While the change in terms and diagnostic criteria was meant to better categorize the psychological distress experienced by individuals whose identity is different from their sex assigned at birth, the fact that it remains in the DSM represents a pathologizing of identity. An additional controversial element of the DSM-V diagnosis is that the manual recommends surgeries and/or hormonal treatment, whereas not all transgender individuals or gender-expansive individuals desire or can access these treatments. Conversely, some transgender advocates believe that the diagnostic terminology aids in advocating for insurance coverage of gender-affirming therapies and surgeries.

Gender-expansive The idea that there is a wider and more flexible spectrum of gender/gender identity and gender expression than is stipulated by the idea of a gender binary; the idea that gender extends beyond binary notions of male and female. Also an identity used by individuals and groups to describe a range of identities including transgender, non-binary, and gender-fluid. Can also be used to describe individuals and groups who test expectations of gender/gender identity and gender expression.

Gender expression Also referred to as *gender presentation*, an individual's external expression of their gender/gender identity; elements of this expression can include clothing, hairstyle, manipulation of voice, name, pronouns, and social behavior, among other elements of individual expression. Gender expression is generally identified on a socially constructed scale of what is usually considered masculine or feminine.

Gender-fluid A gender identity describing an individual who has a dynamic, unfixed, and/or fluid gender identity, not identifying with a single, rigid gender. A gender-fluid individual may fluctuate between femininity and masculinity, or a mix of the two, or may identify completely outside of these notions.

Gender/gender identity The individual and internal understanding a person has of their gender. An individual's gender may align with the sex they were assigned at birth or vary from that assignment and may fall within or outside of the gender binary. Examples of gender identity include woman, man, gender-fluid, genderqueer, and trans. There has been recent push back in the LGBTQ+ community against the term *gender identity* as it can invalidate the reality of a person's gender as differing from their sex aligned at birth, and can serve to reinforce cissexism and further marginalize those whose gender lies outside of the gender binary (e.g. we do not often refer to a cisgender woman's "gender identity"). Since "gender identity" is still widely used colloquially and in the therapeutic community, this glossary uses both terms *gender* and *gender identity*: "gender/gender identity."

Gender identity disorder An outdated clinical term; see *gender dysphoria*.

Gender non-binary, non-binary and/or genderqueer Terms used by some individuals whose gender/gender identities and/or gender expressions fall outside of or expand upon the gender binary. These individuals may identify their gender as existing between femininity/masculinity, as a combination of the two, or as completely separate from and outside the gender binary. Gender non-conforming and gender non-binary identities can fall under this umbrella term.

Gender non-conforming A broad term used to describe individuals whose gender expression or presentation differs from the social/cultural expectations of their gender. Being transgender does not make an individual gender non-conforming. This term has been rejected by some members of the LGBTQ+ community, as it pathologizes the experience of non-binary genders.

Gender normative A term that describes an individual whose gender expression or presentation, whether by nature or by conscious creation, aligns with the expectations of that gender in a particular society or culture.

Gender role expectations Gender roles and gender role expectations are socially and culturally specific expectations of how an individual or group of a certain gender/gender identity will dress, behave, express emotions, etc.

Gender transition See *transition*.

H

Hate crime An intentional crime or unlawful act directed towards an individual or group, typically motivated by an individual's or group's prejudice towards a minority group. Hate crimes can be committed against LGBTQ+ individuals as well as many other marginalized/ minoritized communities.

Heteronormativity The assumption, on an individual, institutional, or societal level, that everyone is heterosexual; the belief that heterosexuality is the superior sexual orientation, over and above all minority sexual orientations. Also, the assumption that masculine-presenting men and feminine-presenting women are straight. This assumption and belief leads to the further stigmatization and marginalization of minority gender and sexual identities. Ideas of heteronormativity can also be found in the LGBTQ+ community.

Heterosexism Describes the behaviors that grant preferential treatment to heterosexual individuals and groups and the discriminatory treatment towards gay, lesbian, bisexual, pansexual, and other individuals and groups with minority sexual identities. Heterosexism reinforces the idea that heterosexual identities are superior to minoritized sexual identities.

Heterosexual A term describing the sexual orientation of an individual who is primarily sexually, physically, romantically, and/or emotionally attracted only to people of the opposite gender (as dictated by the gender binary)—men who are attracted to women and vice versa. Frequently termed *straight*.

Homophobia The fear or hatred of and discrimination against individuals who are attracted to those of the same gender, usually in relation to beliefs regarding the normative binary systems of gender and sexuality. As with any phobia and prejudice, homophobia can be present within the LGBTQ+ community as well as within the general population. This fear is closely related to sexism and heterosexism.

Homosexual A term describing the sexual orientation of an individual who is sexually, physically, romantically, and/or emotionally attracted to people of the same gender (as dictated by the gender binary). Until 1987, the *Diagnostic and Statistical Manual of Mental Disorders* classified homosexuality as a mental illness, and therefore the term remains stigmatizing. See definitions of *gay, lesbian, pansexual,* and *bisexual* for preferred terminology.

I

Intersectional identity A concept deriving from the theory of intersectionality, an analytical structure that seeks to identify how multiple identities relate to and affect each other, especially in the context of minority/marginalized identities. Every individual's identity consists of a variety of factors, including race, class, religious affiliation, gender, and sexual orientation, among others. The idea of an intersectional identity seeks to convey that disadvantages, interpersonal discriminations, and systemic oppressions are compounded in groups or individuals who have multiple minority/marginalized identities.

Intersex A term describing an individual whose sex does not align with the expectations of either male or female embodiment. Intersex classification of an individual is based on the physical appearance of their external sexual anatomy as well as the individual's hormones, chromosomes, external and internal reproductive organs, and other reproductive characteristics. The term *hermaphrodite* was formerly used to describe an intersex individual, but is now considered derogatory and outdated.

L

Lesbian A term describing the sexual orientation of women who are sexually, physically, romantically, and/or emotionally attracted to people of the same gender: women.

LGBTQ+ An acronym that encompasses the following identities: lesbian, gay, bisexual, transgender, and queer/questioning. There are many other acronyms that encompass other identities including intersex, pansexual, asexual, two-spirited, etc. In this glossary, the plus sign acts as a place-holder for missing letters in what could be a much longer acronym.

Living openly A state in which LGBTQ+ individuals are comfortably out in regard to their gender/gender identity and/or sexual orientation. An individual can be "living openly" in all settings or in specific settings, social groups, and/or with certain individuals.

M

Microaggression The verbal comments or statements, nonverbal snubs, and any other action or incident, whether intentional or unintentional, that discriminate against marginalized individuals or groups, solely on account of their membership of the group. These can be negative, hostile, and/or derogatory messages communicated to members within or outside of the LGBTQ+ community.

Minority stress A type of stress experienced by members of minority/ marginalized groups, including, but not limited to, the LGBTQ+ community. The term *minority stress* describes the often chronic stress experienced by members of minority groups related to their marginalization/stigmatization. This stress is often a result of discrimination and prejudice, but can also be related to additional factors such as limited access to social services, low socioeconomic status, and other systems-level inequalities. Such experiences of minority stress increase with the number of minority identities an individual holds— for example, it is generally accepted that a transgender individual of color experiences more chronic stress than does a white transgender individual.

O

Out A state of being in which an LGBTQ+ individual has intentionally or by involuntary exposure shared their gender/gender identity and/or sexual orientation with a person or group of people. An individual can be out in all environments or in specific settings or social groups, and/or with certain individuals. Also see *Living openly*.

Outing The act of exposing an individual's or group's gender/gender identity or sexual orientation to other people, without the express consent of the individual. An individual who is outed may experience serious repercussions to their safety, employment, relationship status, religious involvement, and family relationships. *Outed* is a term used to describe an individual whose minority identity was involuntarily exposed to another group or individual.

P

Pansexual A sexual orientation characterized by one individual's sexual, physical, romantic, or emotional attraction to people of all genders/ gender identities and expressions. Attraction to different genders may not be simultaneous and may vary in intensity.

Passing When an LGBTQ+ individual is perceived, either intentionally or unintentionally, as belonging to the majority group. This could be a trans individual passing for a cisgender member of their gender/gender identity group or an individual with a sexual minority identity passing as straight. Passing can be a contentious concept and is sometimes inaccurately seen as a positive experience by outside observers without consideration for the potential that passing might isolate an individual from their minority community or render their identity invisible.

Pronouns In the English language, a grammatical tool used to stand in place of an individual's name or likeness. While the most widely used pronouns are gender-specific and binary—he/him/his and she/her/hers—gender-neutral pronouns are used with increasing frequency and include they/them/their, ze/zir, co/cos, xe/xem/xyr, hy/hym/hyr. Similar gender-neutral pronouns can also be found in non-English languages, including the pronoun "hen" in Swedish. Since an individual's pronouns are associated with an individual's gender/gender identity, pronouns should be clarified with that individual and not assumed. While the term *preferred gender pronouns* (*PGPs*) is also used in this context, many members of the LGBTQ+ community advocate for simply using the term *pronouns* so as not to inaccurately suggest that correct pronoun use is simply an individual preference rather than an inherent right.

Q

Queer An umbrella term used to describe sexual and gender minority identities. Also used by some as a synonym for "LGBTQ+" in terms such as "queer community." The dictionary definition of queer is something strange or differing from the norm, and the word was used derogatorily against members of the LGBTQ+ community for years. It has been reclaimed, especially by younger members of the community, but still holds negative connotation for many others.

Questioning A term used to describe an individual who is uncertain about or exploring all or parts of their sexual orientation and/or gender identity. Can also describe a time in an individual's life during which this exploration is occurring.

S

Sex A term used to describe the biological/physiological classification of an individual, at birth, as either male or female, in a gender binary society. Male or female assignment for the individual is based on the physical appearance of their external sexual anatomy. Other factors that may go into an individual's sex assignment include the individual's hormones, chromosomes, external and internal reproductive organs, and other reproductive characteristics. A third classification of sex based on biological/physiological features is *intersex*, describing a person with some combination of characteristics from both typical male and female anatomy.

Sex assigned at birth A term used to describe an individual's classification as male or female at the time of their birth in a gender binary society. Based on visible sex characteristics, most specifically the presence of a penis or a vagina.

Sex reassignment surgery (SRS) An outdated clinical term; see *gender confirmation surgery*.

Sexual and gender majority A term used to describe an individual or group whose sexual orientation and gender/gender identity lies within what is considered the norm in a given society: heterosexual and cisgender. While the term *majority* speaks to a greater numerical population compared with the *sexual and gender minority*, it also refers to the socially accepted idea that there are certain "normative" identities and other "inferior" identities.

Sexual and gender minority A term used to describe an individual or group whose sexual orientation and gender/gender identity lies outside of what is considered the norm in a given society: non-heterosexual and non-cisgender. Sexual minority communities include, but are not limited to, homosexual, bisexual, and pansexual individuals. Gender minority communities include, but are not limited to, transgender, agender, and gender non-binary individuals. While the term *minority* speaks to a lesser numerical population compared with the *sexual and gender majority*, it also and more specifically refers to the marginalized nature of these individuals and groups. For this reason, the term *minoritized* is often used to indicate the disenfranchisement of these identities regardless of the realities of numerical majority and minority.

Sexual identity A term used to describe how an individual considers themselves in terms of their *sexual orientation*, as compared with *gender identity*, which is used to describe how an individual considers themselves in terms of their gender.

Sexual orientation An individual's enduring sexual, physical, romantic, or emotional attraction to other people, referring to the relationship between the genders/gender identities of the people involved. Examples of sexual orientation include, but are not limited to, heterosexual/

straight, gay, lesbian, bisexual, pansexual, and asexual. Sexual orientation should not be confused with an individual's *gender identity*, *sexuality*, or *sexual preference*.

Sexuality A term used to describe an individual's sexual drives and interests. Sexuality encompasses an individual's thoughts, feelings, and behaviors around their sexual, physical, romantic, and/or emotional attractions; it can also include elements of an individual's sexual turn-ons and fetishes. The term *sexual preference* can also be used to describe *sexuality*. *Sexuality* and *sexual preference* are not synonymous with sexual orientation.

Social stigma A term used to describe the severe disapproval or disgrace toward an individual or group based on a characteristic or trait (or perceived characteristic/trait) that separates that individual or group from others within a society. Membership in the LGBTQ+ community (or suspected/perceived membership) can be a socially stigmatized characteristic.

Straight A more common term/identifier for heterosexual individuals or groups.

Subordinate group Also known as the minority/minoritized or marginalized group, the group or groups with the least amount of power, privilege, and social status in a given society. Individuals within the LGBTQ+ community (transgender, gender non-binary, gay, lesbian, bisexual, pansexual, etc.) make up the subordinate group.

T

Transgender Generally used as an identity for a person whose gender/ gender identity is other than that associated with their sex assigned at birth. For example, a person who was assigned male at birth but identifies as female/as a woman may use the term transgender (or trans woman) to describe her identity. Transgender can also be an umbrella term describing a variety of identities that go beyond or against social expectations of gender. "Trans*" is often used to encompass the variety of identities that go beyond gender norms. Outdated terms include *transexual* or *transvestite*. These can be extremely derogatory to some, but are also still used by some trans individuals as identifiers. It is important to note that trans* individuals can have any sexual orientation including straight, gay, lesbian, pansexual, and that their sexual orientation is based on their gender/gender identity, not on their sex assigned at birth.

Transition The many processes through which an individual may alter their self-expression or physical appearance in order to more closely align with their gender/gender identity. This can include social transitions such as changing pronouns and social behavior; legal changes to name or legal documents; and physical changes through clothing changes, hormone use, and surgeries. It is important to note that not all trans individuals want or are able to procure medical transitions. Avoid terms such as *sex change* and *pre-op/post-op* as these are outdated and can be offensive.

Transphobia The fear or hatred of and discrimination against transgender individuals, usually in relation to beliefs regarding the normative binary systems of gender and sexuality. As with any phobia and prejudice, transphobia can be present within the LGBTQ+ community as well as within the general population.

Two-spirited A traditionally Native American and First Nations term used to describe an individual who possesses the attributes and/or fills the roles of both genders. These individuals are highly regarded in their culture and take on distinct gender and social roles within their tribes. The two-spirited are thought of as a separate and distinct gender from male and female. Many indigenous cultures around the world have local terms to describe two-spirited individuals, including *Wintke* among some Native American tribes, *Hijra* in India and South East Asia, and *Muxe* in Mexico.

Contributors

Ashley L. Koenig, BFA, MA

Ashley L. Koenig is the school coordinator for Pace University's School of Performing Arts, one of the top performing arts programs in the United States. As school coordinator, she has worked to strengthen partnership between the School of Performing Arts and the PACE LGBTQA Social Justice Center, with the goal of supporting the artistic work of students of all gender identities. Ashley has worked extensively with non-profit organizations, leading the development of LGBTQ-inclusive and affirming services, policies, and public relations campaigns. She has also worked as a production stage manager in theaters across Los Angeles and New York City. Ashley holds a BFA in technical direction from the University of Southern California and an MA in psychology from Pace University, where she was the representative for her graduating cohort. In her master's program, Ashley's academic work focused on the socialization of gender and sexuality norms and the need for improved education on treating these populations. She has also served as a research assistant for writings on drama therapy. Ashley is currently applying for PhD programs where she plans to research the supportive potential of the performing arts within the queer theater community.

Beth Gonzalez-Dolginko, EdD, LCAT, LP, NYATA-HLM

Beth Gonzalez-Dolginko, EdD, LCAT, LP, has worked clinically as an art therapist for 40 years, in academia for 28 years, and in private practice for 36 years. Beth has worked with children and adults in the areas of psychiatry, addictions, aging, PTSD, chronic illness, special education, developmental disabilities, and child development. Beth currently serves on the New York State Office of the Professions for Mental Health Practitioners Board.

Brian T. Harris, PhD, MT-BC, LCAT

Dr. Harris is a music psychotherapist in private practice in New York City. He holds a PhD in expressive therapies and is an adjunct faculty member at New York University and a core faculty member of the Kint Institute's creative arts therapy and trauma training program. Dr. Harris is the past head of the Pavarotti Music Center's music therapy department in Mostar, Bosnia, where his work focused on children with post-war traumas. He has published and presented nationally and internationally and has worked for more than 20 years with a diverse range of clients including LGBT clients and clients in the realms of trauma, psychiatric, autism, and Alzheimer's.

Briana MacWilliam, MPS, ATR-BC, LCAT

Briana MacWilliam is a creative arts therapist and Reiki practitioner, in private practice in New York City. She has more than 12 years of clinical experience and has held two directorial positions in community-based and day-treatment settings. She was also a research and outcomes coordinator for four years, at the Amen Clinics, Inc.—a brain research and diagnostic facility. She specializes in psycho-spiritual approaches to working with attachment wounds in adult relationships, and edited and co-authored the book *Complicated Grief, Attachment, and Art Therapy: Theory, Treatment, and 14 Ready-to-Use Protocols*. Additionally, she is the director for continuing education for Pratt Institute's Creative Arts Therapies Department, and provides online courses for personal development and continuing education through her online school, CreativeArtsTherapiesOnline.com.

Britton Williams MA, RDT, LCAT

Britton Williams, MA, RDT, LCAT, is a registered drama therapist and licensed creative arts therapist. She currently works in private practice in New York City and is an adjunct faculty member at New York University in the Program in Drama Therapy. Britton's work extends to non-clinical settings. In this capacity, she uses drama therapeutic techniques with organizations, companies, schools, and universities to help guide and facilitate discussions and creative processes in support of socially just practices. Britton has published and presented on: the impact of assumptions, biases, and stereotypes on individuals, relationships and communities; creative and embodied approaches to clinicians' self-assessment; and developing a relational-role theory framework and protocol. She is interested in processes that allow students and clinicians to use drama therapeutic and other creative interventions to illuminate and challenge their implicit assumptions in support of just practice. Britton is currently pursuing her doctorate in social welfare at the CUNY Graduate Center.

Cara A. Gallo-Jermyn, MS, BC-DMT/LCAT

Cara Gallo-Jermyn is a board-certified Dance Movement Therapist and LCAT in NYC. She completed post-graduate training in the practice of Authentic Movement and Group Psychotherapy. She has been practicing in NYC for the duration of her career, working in psychiatric hospitals, educational settings and non-profits. Presently, she maintains a private practice in Chelsea, NYC. In addition, she is adjunct faculty at the Pratt Institute Graduate Creative Arts Therapy Program and SUNY Empire State College in the Human Services undergraduate studies program.

Dana George Trottier, MA, LCAT, RDT/BCT

Dana George Trottier is a registered drama therapist and board-certified trainer with the North American Drama Therapy Association and a licensed creative arts therapist. He is an adjunct faculty member at New York University where he provides clinical training in the Drama Therapy graduate program. He is a clinical supervisor for acute inpatient psychiatry at NYC Health + Hospitals/Kings County, where he works with therapists across all modalities. He recently earned a Certificate of Advanced Training in LGBTQ Healthcare through the Fenway Institute/National LGBT Health Education Center. Also in private practice, Dana offers therapeutic services to adults, children, and groups as well as clinical supervision and career consultation for therapists. In addition to his clinical work, Dana is an arts-based researcher, utilizing art modalities to explore the human experience. His research has focused on a variety of topics including the playability of race, the experience of traumatic loss, and the use of embodiment in clinical training and practice.

Judith Luongo, MPS, LCAT, LP

Judith Luongo is a fully licensed creative arts therapist and psychoanalyst. She received her master's degree from the Graduate Creative Arts Therapy Department of Pratt Institute in May 1977, and became a fully credentialed psychoanalyst in May 2003 after completing her course of training at the Institute for Psychoanalytic Training and Research. Ms. Luongo has been in private practice since September 1980 and has been on the faculty of the Pratt Creative Arts Therapy Program since September 1978. She has given numerous workshops and is fully credentialed as an open studio facilitator.

Julie Lipson, MA, MT-BC

Julie Lipson is a board-certified music therapist. They own Inner Rhythms Music and Therapy Center and work with groups and individuals at several Philadelphia locations. Julie provides consultation for individuals and organizations and offers trainings on LGBTQ competency, private practice start-up, and using creativity in therapy. Julie received their master's in music therapy from Drexel University. They are also an assistant director at Camp Aranu'tiq, summer camp for transgender and gender-variant youth. Julie is a dynamic speaker, and focuses on a range of topics related to the voice (literal and metaphorical), creativity, and finding the authentic self. They have presented in a variety of settings, including the Philadelphia Trans Health Conference, the World Professional Association for Transgender Health, and New York City's School of Visual Arts.

Kristin Long, MA, RDT/BCT, LCAT, LP

Kristin Long, drama therapist and psychoanalyst, has a full-time private practice in New York City, working with children, adolescents, families, and adults. As a graduate of the Institute for Expressive Analysis, she currently serves as public relations chair and is faculty member/supervisor at the postgraduate institute where she teaches classes on the therapeutic use of the body. She has taught expressive therapy with children at New York University's Gallatin School of Individualized Study. Kristin has trained as an eye movement desensitization and reprocessing (EMDR) therapist and has a specific interest in the transmission of intergenerational trauma. She's presented nationally and internationally on the importance of attunement within relational dyads.

Liisa Murray, MS, MT-BC, LCAT

Liisa Murray is a music therapist at the Hebrew Home at Riverdale in New York. Currently, Liisa is focusing on empowering marginalized groups within geriatric care in her work pioneering an LGBT and allies group, as well as running a women's group for older adults. She also runs workshops and individual sessions utilizing singing as a form of wellness.

Mark Beauregard, RDT/BCT, LCAT

Mark Beauregard, drama therapist, specializes in gender- and sexuality-affirming therapy, receiving postgraduate certification through the Psychotherapy Center for Gender and Sexuality at the Institute for Contemporary Psychotherapy. Mark has presented frequently on various topics in the private and public sectors, in addition to providing years of direct service to LGBTQ people and their families. Mark is a published author, discussing ways to creatively engage LGBTQ youth, as well as exploring the relationship between clinicians' attitudes and actions toward sexual and gender diverse individuals to create more inclusive and affirming practices. Mark serves as supervisor of LGBTQ Services for NY Creative Arts Therapists, PLLC, in Brooklyn and has a private practice in Manhattan, NYC.

Michael Kariyev, LCSW, PC

Michael Kariyev specializes in trauma treatment with individuals, couples, and families. Michael has received training in multiple therapeutic modalities including cognitive behavioral therapy (CBT), EMDR, emotional freedom techniques (EFT), emotionally focused therapy (marriage and couples work), and art therapy. His primary focus is on working with adults struggling with past trauma in conjunction with family conflict and relationship issues, in his private practice, SoulWellnessNYC.

Mikella Millen, MA, LCAT, ATR-BC

Mikella Millen is a graduate of New York University's master's program in art therapy, and holds a BFA in sculpture from the School of Visual Arts. She has worked in residential, acute care, community-based, outpatient, and private practice settings. With a focus on complex trauma, traumatic grief, and gender-based violence, she has worked with diverse populations across the age spectrum. She lectures at New York University and offers professional training on trauma, bereavement, and working with children. Mikella is a consultant with Sanctuary for Families and, supervisor of the art therapy program at Camp Good Grief with East End Hospice, and has a small private practice in Manhattan.

Olivia Cohen, MS, MT-BC, LCAT

Olivia Cohen is a manager of therapeutic arts and enrichment programs at the Hebrew Home at Riverdale. Olivia's current work in long-term care focuses on music therapy with older adults, individuals with dementia, intergenerational groups, and co-leading an LGBT and allies group.

Sarah Gluck, PhD, LCSW

Sarah Gluck is the clinical director of the Five Towns Wellness Center, where she performs detailed psychological assessment and counseling, and is available to help direct clients to resources. She specializes in trauma treatment that combines evidence-based modalities with a little bit of soul.

Subject Index

Author Index